WICKED UNCLES
& HAUNTED CELLARS

WICKED UNCLES
& HAUNTED CELLARS
What the Gothic Heroine Tells Us Today

MARY PHELAN

Greenwich Exchange
London

'I dedicate this book to my late mother, Maureen, for all her love and encouragement'

Greenwich Exchange, London

First published in Great Britain in 2024
All rights reserved

Wicked Uncles and Haunted Cellars:
What the Gothic Heroine Tell Us Today
© Mary Phelan, 2024

This book is sold subject to the conditions that it shall not, by way of trade or otherwise, be lent, resold, hired out or otherwise circulated without the publisher's prior consent in any form of binding or cover other than that in which it is published and without a similar condition including this condition being imposed on the subsequent purchaser.

Printed and bound by imprintdigital.com
Cover design by December Publications
Tel: 07951511275

Greenwich Exchange website: www.greenex.co.uk

Cataloguing in Publication Data
is available from the British Library

ISBN: 978-1-910996-82-9

CONTENTS

Preface *13*

Introduction *15*

The Gothic Narrative: Fairy Tale, Romance or Novel? *31*

- The History of the gothic novel
- The Novel and the Romance
- Mythos of romance
- Mythos of comedy
- Mythos of irony, tragedy and satire: the rise of the low mimetic
- The rise of the low mimetic
- The significance of the fairy tale
- The Byronic hero

Maid in the Mirror *58*

- Into the past
- Seduction, Beauty and the maiden
- The maid in the mirror
- Curiosity and the maiden
- The ice maiden
- Madness and the maiden
- The adolescent sleep
- Maid of the future

The New Alchemists: Text, Time and Travel *84*

- In the beginning
- The learning enigma
- As dreams are made on

The Allegorical Castle *107*

- What is a castle: past, present and future?
- Establishing Atmosphere
- Movement and stasis
- The Remote Conundrum
- Omnipresent authority and individual consciousness
- Identity: masculine and feminine
- Order and chaos

Danger in the family? *132*

- Why the family?
- The aristocracy fixation
- Orphans and children
- The matriarch and the patriarch
- Siblings: warring and benevolent
- The individual, individualism and Eleanor's rampage

The Lexicon of Haunting *155*

- Why the supernatural?
- The lexicon of haunting
- Haunted people
- The sleep of reason
- Projections and perceptions
- The ghosts of things to come

The Journey *177*

- Stasis and movement
- Moving away from authority
- Bildungsroman: The unfinished journey

Deception, the Doppelganger and the Dark Dis *191*

Deception: Shakespearean, refusal to deceive, self-deception
Deception and *The Turn of the Screw*
The doppelganger: comedy and fantasy
Perception of reality
Mirroring, projecting likenesses and changing places
Dichotomies and duality
Uncovering the truth
Modernity, surreality and the doppelganger today
The nebulous dis
The servant/housekeeper
The governess
The lawyer and the detective

The Power of Nature *227*

The origins of the landscape in literature, the pastoral and the Romantic
The female paradigm
Healing and perverted nature
An expulsion from paradise
The landscape as metaphor: pathetic fallacy, turbulence and calm
Chiaroscuro

The Future of Gothic *254*

Chronology

Bibliography
Glossary

Preface

It is many years since I first read *Northanger Abbey* by Jane Austen and I still remember rolling about with laughter at the sketch of the gothic heroine's adventures, as painted by Henry Tilney. Curiously, I had not read any truly gothic narratives at that hour of my life. But as a creature of the film and television age, I recognised all of the motifs that storytellers and directors use to hook an audience, the uncertain young woman arriving at the unfamiliar house (or mansion or castle) – to work, to live, whatever – who happens upon an unspeakable secret and ends up fighting, possibly for her life and/or those of others.

The publication of this book is timely because the most recent comprehensive study of this subject I can find is *The Madwoman in the Attic* (Sandra Gilbert and Susan Gubar, Yale University Press, 1979) which was published a generation ago. I have chosen fifteen English fictional works to refer to and to explore. My chosen publications span the approximately two hundred years from the apogee of the genre to the strands present in the literature of today. My original intent was to include twenty novels, one from roughly every decade since the 1790s. But I soon removed this crude and artificial stumbling block and, for reasons that will become obvious, reduced my selection of major texts to those listed in the **Introduction**.

Overall, I believe that the popularity of the genre is due to its appeal to the nascent adolescent within every adult: the uncertain young person enduring an alienating journey to an unfamiliar place to live with unknown relatives, the initial unease in the gathering air of mystery, the kindly but limited help of the servant or friend, the constant suggestion that the visible is but illusory and that consciousness survives beyond this world, even following the lifting of the veil of darkness. But the reader is free to disagree. Maybe this work will provide the reader (scholar? writer?) with new insights into the genre?

I arrived at the idea for the book when I was doing my Master's dissertation on the subject of American Gothic literature and I realised that no comprehensive work was available on the genesis of the subject. I stress now that this book is not a 'history' of the gothic novel, but an exploration of the development of themes, symbols and motifs that have driven the genre in Great Britain, from its heyday around 200 years ago to the present day. Furthermore, I have chosen to delineate the chapters along the division of definite symbols. It was my interest in symbols that led to the publication of my book *Dreams: Exploring Uncharted Depths of Consciousness* in 2020.

The symbols that I have identified for this work have threaded their way into other major and minor works of literature, changing in certain ways yet remaining recognisable.

Such is the profundity of the genre that I envisage it lasting as long as the literary form does: whether it remains 'fashionable' indefinitely or not is for the reader to decide.

Introduction

IT IS MORE THAN 250 YEARS since Horace Walpole penned his seminal novel, *The Castle of Otranto*, which ignited an insatiable readership for tales of innocent maidens in peril, of mysterious documents begging to be deciphered, frantic journeys across unfamiliar terrain, coffins in the crypts and bats in the belfries of rambling, ruined castles. Other motifs abounded, for instance, lush descriptions of rising suns and luminous moons, of picturesque lakes and majestic mountains and acres upon acres of forest. In the late 1700s, writers such as Ann Radcliffe and Clara Reeve seized upon the seed sown by Walpole and produced novels that were eagerly bought by a newly-literate readership, the genre honed to its apotheosis in Radcliffe's *Romance of the Forest*. Why did Walpole write his novel and what were the reasons for the proliferation of its successors? Hitherto, the best-selling novels had been tales of male adventurers.

First published in 1719, Daniel Defoe's *Robinson Crusoe* ran into many editions, including over one hundred in America, between 1774 and 1830.[1] Other eighteenth-century writers, such as Henry Fielding (1707-1754), Samuel Richardson (189-1761) and Tobias Smollett (1721-1771) produced narratives of picaresque male characters conquering their worlds, a tradition reaching back to the Greek epics of old and reiterated more recently by Cervantes when he wrote *Don Quixote*, which was published in the sixteenth century.

---

[1]Daniel Defoe, *Robinson Crusoe*, ed. Thomas Keymer (Oxford: Oxford World's Classics, 1983), pviii. Subsequent references will be to this edition and will be inserted parenthetically into the text, for example "(Crusoe, viii)".

What then, heralded the sea-change in literature?

In order to answer the question, I present my outline of a typical gothic heroine. In the earlier gothic works (typically by Walpole, Radcliffe, Reeve), she is presented as a pubescent female with the added value of beauty, sometimes (superficially) her only market worth. Generally, she loves the good things in life: poetry, music and animals. She is almost always dissociated from her family, whether by virtue of being orphaned, having been kidnapped or simply by having left her immediate relatives to work for or to visit hitherto unknown cousins. The earlier part of her narrative almost always necessitates her making a journey to an unknown and extravagant building, a castle or abbey, a mansion or an old house. In this unexplored territory, the heroine stumbles across a repository of secrets, quite often a document or documents that she feels bound to decipher.

The building itself is mysterious, a site of historical events and/or misfortune attached to previous residents. Locked chambers, cries in the night and wooden panels and tapestries that pull back to reveal 'secret' passageways, add to the mystery. Often, the protagonist allies herself to a well-intentioned but undereducated servant, mainly a housekeeper, whose cryptic comments keep the heroine in thrall to the secret at the heart of the house. For this reason or maybe even in spite of it, the gothic protagonist is hyper-aware and endowed with a keen sense of the supernatural, which I define as an 'unknown capacity'. As a foil to this unknown capacity, she has a heightened awareness of the beauty of the natural world and spends much time gazing at sunsets, contemplating moonlight and walking, often alone, in flowered gardens and meadows.

These constant dichotomies of dark and light, day and night, unsettle the reader and make them feel that someone, somewhere is deceiving the protagonist, concealing knowledge that might be to her or someone else's advantage. Whatever, the maiden is sooner or later obliged to escape her situation and flees, often embarking on a perilous journey. This journey is an energetic foil to the more benign journey at the opening of the narrative. Somewhere on the trajectory of the narrative, the heroine meets a handsome youth destined to be her lover and her eventual spouse. At the close of *Romance of the Forest*, we see Adeline happily married to Theodore and bringing up their children.

Daniel Defoe had indeed produced female protagonists such as Moll Flanders, but Moll and her literary sisters were essentially pawns in the society of the alpha male, typically politicians and industrialists, women ensnared by the day-to-day issues of socially prominent people. In contrast to the ebullient Robinson Crusoe who spends nearly thirty years in isolation, yet builds a successful society in the wilderness *and* finds himself a wealthy man when he finally arrives back home, the gothic heroine seeks to escape her social isolation and find peace, prosperity and familial happiness amongst contemporary and conventional society. She fights back against the circumstances in which she finds herself trapped, if indeed she is trapped, and struggles to move from danger and intrigue into the world of domesticity and love, social order and peace.

But even as Defoe wrote his seminal narrative, the winds of change were driving into the political and materialist world of early eighteenth century literature. I stress that paradox, as I do throughout this text, that that great materialist triumph, the Industrial Revolution, heralded the world of the imagination, of Romanticism and spiritualism, of the nineteenth-century mania for ghosts, fairies and communicating, even notionally, with the dead. The birth of psychology and parapsychology was not far away. And Defoe more than hints at this advent. In his Journal, Crusoe tells of a dream in which he sees 'savages' arriving at his island, and he rescues one that they are about to kill, and he, Crusoe, makes the man his servant. Crusoe awakens, filled with 'Impressions of Joy' and parallel disappointment that he has had 'only' a dream (Crusoe, 168). Whether (from the point of view of this argument) the band of savages who delivers him his man Friday ever appeared in the narrative, is moot. What matters is Crusoe's realisation that not every solution to life lies in the material, in reason or in logic, which is a sign of his growing wisdom. And the episode may demonstrate that Defoe, who died in 1731, sensed the emergence of this literary sub-genre, with its focus on foreshadowing and symbols, or something akin to it.

On the same matter, the gothic protagonist is ever prone to dreaming because she or he is *becoming*, that is, moving from the margins of society to material appreciation and success, thus occupying the liminal ground between yearning and realisation. It is, I believe, the evolving situation of the *typical* middle-class woman between c. 1760 and 1810 that made for the success of the genre. Among the reasons for its success is the appeal of the *perception* of the 'long ago and far away'. The mid to late-eighteenth century saw a readership eager for this cocktail of ingredients: the glow of the past, the suggestion of the supernatural, the presence of an authority in a stronghold or castle, which according to Tim Middleton, was the questioning of 'established truths'.[2]

The language of the new gothic literature was never didactic but observed how the protagonists extricated themselves from their dilemmas, rather than morally implying what they *should* have done. Indeed, this renaissance of the self-determining heroine may have had an indirect and beneficial effect upon female authorship.

Again Tim Middleton explains how the sub-genre serves to expose the thin veneer of civilization that was the sophisticated society of the time in which it is written (DJMH, xii). The gothic genre continues to flourish in the fables of psychological isolation rather than physical remoteness. The new gothic writer is dealing with another kind of isolation, a state that is chimeric rather than actual; we can see this happening in the later novels of the nineteenth century. Henry James's Governess could have chosen to leave the haunted Bly with Mrs Grose and Flora, but she did not. Why?

In the chapter **The Lexicon of Haunting**, I argue that the reader may see the Governess as a nineteenth-century proto of the present-day employee so anxious to do the 'right' thing from the point of view of an employee, she or he loses sight of whatever moral right or wrong is involved. So many ways exist for the modern writer to transpose the gothic genre or, at least, elements of it, into contemporary writing. Today, modern living conditions can make the most physically comfortable individual feel isolated and neglected. The perilous journey inherent in so many gothic tales could parallel with the difficult, notional journey from childhood, to adolescence, to adulthood. The castle can be metaphorical or actual, a place that the young person is bound to go to daily, usually for economic necessity. If conditions in this place are less than salubrious, then this castle/office/school whatever, can seem like a prison. Eschewing the traditional family for friendship and other interest groups does not necessarily dispense with 'family' troubles; if the relations between individuals are less than harmonious, then trouble will certainly ensue. Another angle is to regard the individuals that the protagonist encounters as the varying, often contradictory, aspects of the protagonist's personality. The plight of Eleanor in Shirley Jackson's narrative is the finest

---

[2]Robert Louis Stevenson, *Dr Jekyll and Mr Hyde*, ed. Tim Middleton (Hertfordshire: Wordsworth Editions, 1999), p.xi. Subsequent references will be to this edition and will be inserted parenthetically into the text, for example '(DJMH, xi)'.

example of this.

Imagine how the narrative might have progressed if Jackson had written her novel in the smartphone era. Instead of seeing writing on the wall, Eleanor would simply have received the chilling texts to advise her to 'come home' on her phone – and would they have been any less frightening? And would she have been any less likely to blame the other house inmates of trying to terrorise her out of the place?

It is impossible to write about gothic fiction and not address the question of irrationality and of course, I quote from Edmund Burke's eighteenth century dissection of fear and suspense, *A Philosophical Enquiry into the Origin of Our Ideas of the Sublime and Beautiful*, first published 1757: 'Whatever is fitted in any sort to excite the ideas of pain, and danger, that is to say, whatever is in any sort terrible, or is conversant about terrible objects, or operates in a manner analogous to terror, is a source of the *sublime*; that is, it is productive of the strongest emotion which the mind is capable of feeling.'[3]

Much of the text involves juxtaposing the author's presentation of gothic heroine and the later intrusion into the literature by the Byronic hero, the definition of which I lay out in my chapter **The Gothic Narrative: Fairy Tale, Romance or Novel?** Here, I point out to the reader that the qualities that I present as 'male' and 'female' are notional and conventional, rather than actual and, according to Jay Griffiths act as a 'cultural shorthand'.[4] Before I expound my primary texts, I point out that, with the exception of Walpole's text, they all post-date modernity in publishing. A text like this requires succinct classifications, many of which the reader can find in the **Glossary** at the conclusion of the chapters. The majority of these references can be objectively and readily defined. But a minority are not easily definable: witness the conundrum in Chapter 1 over defining a term like 'romance'. Another problematic term is 'modernity'. The reader is bound to ask: just when did modern times begin?

Older readers will think of the twentieth century as modern, as in modern

---

[3] Edmund Burke, ed. Paul Guyer, *A Philosophical Enquiry into the Origin of Our Ideas of the Sublime and Beautiful*, (Oxford: Oxford University Press, 2008), p33-34. Subsequent references will be to this edition and will be inserted parenthetically into the text, for example "(Burke, 33-34)".

[4] Jay Griffiths, *Pip Pip: a Sideways Look at Time* (London: Harper Collins, 1999) p130. Subsequent references will be to this edition and will be inserted parenthetically into the text, for example "(JG, 130)".

art and architecture – and critics debate even these placements. Literature *per se* is not modern; it is as old as the spoken word, whether recited or written down. The printing machine emerged in the 1400s, so printing *per se* is out of the modern orbit. Once again, I cite the statistic of Thomas Keymer in his Introduction to *Robinson Crusoe*, namely, that it ran into many editions, including over one hundred between 1774 and 1830. But Defoe's book had been in print since 1719: why the sudden burgeoning of production?

In *The History of the Book*, Lawrence Stone is cited on the 'conquest' of illiteracy, a conquest that in England means 'about 40 per cent of men were literate by 1675, a percentage that increased slowly until 1780 and rapidly thereafter, with two-thirds of the men and half of the women literate by 1840.'[5] Stone defines this as a 'top-down' process, education being initially confined to the most privileged in society. From these statistics, the reader can assume that literacy filtered down to the middle-classes, since the 'half' of women who could read were certainly of the better-off classes, those with money to spend and time to expend. By this assumption, the writers of gothic literature had the glory of an in-waiting female readership, even as early as 1780. And it is of no small significance that this date coincides with the proliferation of the gothic sub-genre in the years following the publication of Walpole's book. For this reason, I define modernity in publishing as 1780 and onwards. One small matter, however.

The History of the Book cites 'the number of book titles published in the decade went from roughly 14,550 in the 1800s to around 60,812 in the 1890s.' (THOB, 294) The *mass* publication of titles in the nineteenth century was no doubt due, in part, to the burgeoning Industrial Revolution: production of paper in tandem with developments in printing technology. Did Walpole aim his literary output at a definable readership or did he write his book because he sensed that burgeoning technology might pitch him into best-seller-dom? Or would he have written *The Castle of Otranto*, in any case? Since the Industrial Revolution dates from about the 1750s and Walpole published his book in 1765, disentangling cause from effect is outside the scope of this text. Besides, I do not claim to have all of the answers, merely raise questions that the reader may want to ponder; from here, I rest that

---

[5]Simon Eliot and Jonathan Rose, *The History of the Book*, (Chichester: Blackwell Publishing Ltd, 2007), p471. Subsequent references will be to this edition and will be inserted parenthetically into the text, for example "(THOB, 471)".

argument.

One important addendum is the role that the gothic sub-genre played in the emerging literature of the new (in the early 1800s) world. In his Introduction to *Tales of Mystery and Imagination* by Edgar Allan Poe, John S. Whitely provides an explanation to the reader who has ever wondered why early American literature was not the lens upon an optimistic, ebullient and out-going society that it might have been. Here, I summarise Whitely's argument by stating that the publishing industry in early 19th century North America encouraged writers to excel in short fictions, typified by writers such as Poe, Hawthorne, Melville and Henry James.[6] But art is ever a blending of imagination, reality and the available blueprints for creating it. The gothic form was already in situ, enabling these writers to explore the darker facets of life and of human nature. Even Laura Ingalls Wilder, born in 1863 and who published her 'Little House' series in the 1930s, portrayed the prairie as a dangerous and often violent place in between depictions of family togetherness and domestic peace. In the final book of the series, *Those Happy Golden Years*, Laura, now a teenaged school teacher, watches from behind a flimsy curtain (her only protection) as the woman of the house that she is lodging in, threatens her husband with a knife. This scene calls into question the sugar-coated treatment so beloved of television show and movie producers of gingham-clad matrons contentedly producing roast dinners and apple pie.

This darkness in American literature continues to this day in the works of Shirley Jackson, Stephen King and Dean Koontz. However, I have excluded short stories (with the exceptions of Henry James's novella, R.L. Stevenson's novella and Hans Christian Andersen's fairytale) from my list of primary texts. In spite of the supernatural presences in many short fictions (M.R. James and Edgar Allan Poe most obviously), the shorter form does not allow for the growth of the personality, the *bildungsroman* element that is the core of many gothic texts. The listing of my primary texts follows.

Romance of the Forest by Ann Radcliffe (published in 1791) is the gothic novel at its apogee, its heroine Adeline a 'fully rounded' personality, a young woman who grows to maturity within the confines of the author's narrative. In addition to ticking all of the boxes in my thumbnail above, Adeline's tale adds another layer to the genre, namely featuring characters that seem, at one

---

[6]Edgar Allan Poe, *Tales of Mystery and Imagination*, ed. John S. Whitely (Hertfordshire, Wordsworth Editions, 1993), px-xi. Subsequent references will be to this edition and will be inserted parenthetically into the text, for example (Poe, x-xi)".

level, to mirror one another, two brothers (the Marquis and Adeline's father) and two friends (Adeline and Clara). Yet, these characters embody different qualities, one good and one bad, one orphaned and the other having grown up within the confines of a secure family. In Chapter 9 of this text, I discuss the concept of duality and doubling.

The gothic genre was already in decline when Jane Austen was working upon her novel, *Northanger Abbey*, c. 1798-1803, though it was not published until 1817. In this book, the author presents a humorous sketch of what a gothic heroine is *not*. Catherine Morland, the heroine, is not orphaned. She grows up in an ordinary vicarage rather than a run-down castle, with a mother who did not die when Catherine was born, and a good clergyman father. Above all, Catherine is not beautiful; in fact, Jane Austen describes Catherine as having: 'a thin, awkward figure, a sallow skin without colour, dark lank hair and strong features'.[7] Yet, as often happens in art, this burlesque proves to be a way of directing us back to the original idea of the lovely heroine, and other tropes of the genre. For example, Catherine has grown up with her parents and an extensive band of siblings but early in the narrative she, in the words of Marilyn Butler, finds herself under the control of ineffective parent-substitutes, namely the Allen couple, the absent or ineffective parent being a tenet of the genre (MB, 106). By the time *Northanger Abbey* had been published and Jane Austen had died, the popularity of the gothic and its motifs had waned and the literary world was in the throes of Romantic poetry and sagas by writers such as Keats, Byron and Shelley. Although I do not include Romantic poets and writers among gothic authors, I will explain throughout the chapters why Romantic writing was the pivot upon which, three decades later, the gothic genre once more returned to popularity.

In 1844, Hans Christian Andersen published *The Snow Queen,* a parable on youth, growing sexual awareness, lost innocence and maturity. These strands entwine harmoniously to tell the story of the young boy and girl, Kay and Gerda. In this, the only one of my primary texts not to have been written first in English, the gothic elements are unmistakeable, the young girl looking for her lost friend, the castle, the journey and so forth. I have chosen to include a fairy tale because Andersen's text represents, in various points, a 'bridge' between a traditional fairy tale and a gothic text. I have chosen this fairy tale

---

[7] Jane Austen, *Northanger Abbey*, ed. Marilyn Butler (London: Penguin Classics, 1818), p15. Subsequent references will be to this edition and will be inserted parenthetically into the text, for example "(NA, 15)".

because it is not a traditional tale in the folkloric sense, and the text being as the author wrote and intended it, making the original symbolism eminently accessible to the reader. In other words, it is free of the corruption of the added and subtracted symbols by random storytellers down through the centuries, that afflicts the likes of *Cinderella* and *Snow White*. It has Bruno Bettelheim's endorsement as a 'real' fairy tale, with a happy ending.[8] The reader experiences the greater part of the narrative through the eyes of Gerda, but Andersen splits the 'maiden' and the 'beauty' role into the adolescent Gerda and the highly sexual Snow Queen.

Jane Eyre: published in 1847, contains many recognisably gothic motifs, the young woman struggling, albeit for social recognition rather than just survival, the castle, the perilous journey, and more than a hint of the supernatural. In addition, this novel contains the archetypal 'mad woman in the attic'. But Charlotte Brontë presented her readers with a unique and original blend of events that still influences literature today.

The most eminent fiction writer of the nineteenth century, Charles Dickens, grew initially famous for *The Pickwick Papers*, the novel derived from eighteenth-century picaresque fiction. As the 1800s progressed Dickens's voice darkened into social realism and portraits of psychological damage.

Hard Times, published 1861, is Charles Dickens's satire on the darker side of rigid learning systems and the pitfalls of uber-organised workplaces. It is also a fine demonstration of what the gothic novel is not. Stephen Blackpool's fallen wife is a parody of the madwoman as much as Louisa Gradgrind is the antithesis of a gothic heroine.

Following its serialisation, Dickens published *Bleak House* in 1853. This novel is structured with many events and characters, the most notable being the progress of the first-person narrator, Esther Summerson. Her new life with guardian John Jarndyce is so beset by inexplicable events that Sandra Gilbert and Susan Gubar's phrase springs to mind: 'The person who has not become anyone is haunted by everyone.'[9] The reader may wonder if Esther's

---

[8] Bruno Bettelheim, *The Uses of Enchantment: The Meaning and Importance of Fairy Tales* (London: Thames and Hudson, 1976), p37. Subsequent references will be to this edition and will be inserted parenthetically into the text, for example '(Bettelheim, 37)'

[9] Sandra M. Gilbert, and Susan Gubar, *The Madwoman in the Attic* (US: Yale University Press, 1984), p176. Subsequent references will be to this edition and will be inserted parenthetically into the text, for example "(G&G, 176)"

own lack of social nous may play a part. Amongst many subplots, the narrative tracks Esther's journey to personhood, and introduces the possibility of a 'real' ghost.

Published in 1861, Dickens's novel, *Great Expectations*, continues the theme of the haunted person. Though devoid of the supernatural, protagonist Pip becomes Dickens's character most beset by ghosts. And the novel uses the device of seeing the lovely maiden Estella through Pip's eyes, rather than making her the central character. In addition, the reader is presented with the *alter ego* of the fresh, young maiden, the mentally and physically blasted Miss Havisham.

In 1881, author Thomas Hardy published his novel, *A Laodicean*. In this lesser-known and much under-rated text of Hardy, the reader sees the heroine Paula through the eyes of a number of male narrators. An atypical gothic novel, the title is taken from a reference in the Bible, the interpretation of which takes up much of the narrative, so that it can be placed in situ as the 'mysterious document' of the gothic tale. It is a *bildungsroman* in that both George Somerset and Paula Power gain much in self-knowledge before uniting in wedded bliss – and their tale is overshadowed by the great (in the sense of 'large') and corrupting influence of Castle Stancy.

Robert Louis Stevenson's *Dr Jekyll and Mr Hyde* (1886) is an atypical gothic novel; it has no lovely maiden, perilous journey or supernatural ghosts, while Dr Jekyll's circle of friends substitute the dysfunctional family of the more typical examples of the genre. In the narrative, nature is a perverted rather than a healing force – and that is the pivot that the plot twists upon. A series of intriguing documents lays down the trail that lawyer Gabriel Utterson follows to solve the mystery surrounding his friend. However, the novel is significant in the genre because of its treatment of the duality theme, and the role of the *dis* played by Utterson.

By the end of the century, with advances in psychology, the tone of the novel had altered once again. By now, supernatural writers had accepted that the perception of the protagonists played no small part in how the supernatural was being seen, if at all. A student of psychology, Anglo-American author Henry James published his novella *The Turn of the Screw* in 1898. Its publication unleashed a critical storm that has barely died down since. Over and over, this 'mysterious document' presents the question: who or what is haunting the governess and the two children over whom she has charge – if indeed, she is haunted?

As the twentieth century progressed, optimism faded in favour of plots with darker and indeed, fatal outcomes. Mrs de Winter of *Rebecca*, by Daphne du Maurier (published 1938) finds herself trapped in the very way of life that she sought to escape from. As with Stevenson's text, the novel explores the theme of duality, the author presenting Maxim de Winter with two wives, either with natures that bear traits apposite to highlighting the contradictions in his own nature. Eventually, events at his ancestral home Manderly and his devotion to aristocracy crush and destroy his personality.

In *The Haunting of Hill House* by Shirley Jackson, protagonist Eleanor Vance tries and fails to build a new life following a family bereavement. The ghosts of this particularly frightening narrative are 'real' in that they are perceived objectively by all the characters and are not just the perception of one underdeveloped personality. In addition, Jackson invites a new device into the galaxy of literary hauntings, the *material* ghost. With the exception of the material manifestations of M.R. James' short fictions, literary ghosts had been subjective perceptions and suppositions, but all of the characters in Hill House hear the mysterious rappings, see animals that cannot be there, mysterious blood appears in one of the rooms and, in one particularly hair-raising instance, Eleanor squeezes the hand of a person *who is not there*; whose hand is she holding, indeed?

In spite of its horrible – and objective – spectre, *The Woman in Black* by Susan Hill is a postmodern comment on the genre, a study of what might happen when the tale of the young and lovely woman does not have a happy ending. The protagonist is an ageing, world-weary male rather than a young female. As with George Somerset, Arthur Kipps is an under-developed personality, able to make his own way in the world, but touched with a slight naiveity when dealing with sensitive, personal matters. At first reading, its opening is a blending of gothic burlesque in the style of Jane Austen, and the Christmas-tide stories-round-the-fire motif so brilliantly elucidated by Henry James in the opening bookend of *The Turn of the Screw*. This event pitches Arthur back into his past, to his memories of the woman in black, the ghost of Jennet Humphrye, who is a travesty of gothic heroines; a despoiled virgin, she has borne a child and died a long time before the narrative opens. Unlike other female heroines, she has failed to find a place in society, locked out by a legal system that would not recognise her as the legitimate mother of her child. 'She' succeeds in depriving other people of the notionally happy family that was denied her in life.

Lyra Belacqua of Philip Pullman's *His Dark Materials* trilogy is the 'bookend' of my work, the end to Adeline's beginning, and a heroine that many young readers may identify with. Many of the elements that pervade gothic narratives are evident in the three Pullman novels. For much of their narratives, both Adeline and Lyra spend time in convents, and are unaware of who their parents are. This lacuna of the protagonist seems to be a prerequisite of many gothic heroines. In addition, Pullman's trilogy is an unashamed *bildungsroman*. Uncertain of her family origins, Lyra sets out to rescue friends from the forces of darkness, battling through many obstacles similar to those that hampered the progress of the original gothic young woman.

It is significant that the gothic heroine strove for her personal freedom when the condition of women often precluded her from engaging professionally and financially in the wider world, for example, in the matter of property ownership. For centuries, women had been in hoc to traditional attitudes and oppressive laws that prevented their entry into the professions. This is possibly the reason that the female reader of two hundred years ago could enjoy the *symbolic* success of her heroine.

Just when it had reached its high point, the genre began to wane in popularity. Marilyn Butler suggests that this was possibly because of the shock engendered by *The Monk* (1795) by Matthew Lewis, a narrative filled with violence, rape and murder.[10] The fact is, the genre did go into decline following the publication of Lewis's book, to the point where it almost ceased. And this decline was underlined by Jane Austen's writing of *Northanger Abbey* between 1798 and 1803. But Butler's explanation seems implausible when we consider that Walpole published *The Mysterious Mother* in 1768, a narrative that features mother/son incest, and the genre flourished for another generation.

The years between 1800 and 1830 saw the rise of the (always) male Byronic hero, sensitive, self-conscious and seeking to escape society, a matter that I explore in my opening chapter, **The Gothic Narrative: Fairy Tale, Romance or Novel?** But the symbolism inherent in the gothic genre somehow resurfaced in novels post-1840, and much of it is evident in literary works

---

[10] Marilyn Butler, *Romantics, Rebels & Reactionaries* (Oxford: Oxford University Press, 1981), p95. Subsequent references will be to this edition and will be inserted parenthetically into the text, for example '(MB, 95)'

today. I stress again that this book is not a 'history' of the gothic novel, but a comprehensive exploration of the development of themes, symbols and motifs that have driven the genre in Great Britain from its heyday to the present day. Why have I sub-divided my text into chapters that delineate individual literary symbols? Irving Mallin identifies three symbols, the castle, the journey and the masquerade, all of which my text will explore with regard to the genre.[11]

A symbol is an intuitive idea that words do not adequately express, tangible and visible emblems that articulate emotion and political ideas. Unlike words, a symbol can provide a range of meaning to the person who perceives it. For example, the symbol of hearth might signify security and comfort to one subject while providing an expression of social entrapment to another. And it is this range of reactions that makes their exploration a rich and fascinating source of literary perspective, rather like watching a landscape in constantly-changing atmospheric conditions, yet remaining ever the same topography.

The majority of these symbols have been laid out by Chloe Chard: the young woman fighting for survival, trouble concerning her or another person's family, a sojourn in a dominating structure such as an old house or castle, a perilous journey, a mysterious document or series of them, a background of natural landscapes and the underlying hint of other dimensions, quite often the supernatural. Irving Malin stresses the role that the theme of deception or *masquerade* plays in the gothic novel, while I place emphasis upon the roles of the doppelganger, dualism and chiaroscuro. In addition, the presence of the 'dis', a person or persons with the ability to travel to all levels of a hierarchical society. Because more than two hundred and fifty years have elapsed since the first gothic novel was written, the genre has developed much since the dawn of the Industrial Revolution, and my chapter **The New Alchemists: Text, Time and Travel** explores the increasing presence of technology.

Chapter 1: The Gothic Narrative: Fairy Tale, Romance or Novel?: like every genre, gothic literature has a trajectory of its own, a cause and an effect, a beginning, middle and end, a point of popularity and the recognition of its demise. The genre also straddles those four recognisable mythos: tragedy,

---

[11] Irving Malin, 'American Gothic Images' in *Mosaic*, p145. (Spring 1973). Subsequent references will be to this edition and will be inserted parenthetically into the text, for example '(Malin, 145)'.

comedy, romance and satire. I attempt to allay the eternal confusion surrounding the various meanings that attach to the word 'romance'. Using the definitions laid down by Northrop Frye, I lay down the terminology used throughout the text, and outline the traits of the Byronic hero.

Chapter 2: Maid in the Mirror: the young person alienated from society is an essential ingredient of the sub-genre. Originally a female, by the nineteenth century notable authors had begun to render this young person as male, for example, Pip in *Great Expectations*. This chapter takes the reader through the original galaxy of robust heroines, followed by the vapid nineteenth-century 'angels', to the psychologically-alienated heroines of the twentieth century.

Chapter 3: The New Alchemists: Text, Time and Travel: systems of information, transportation methods and networks, and essential time-keeping, controlled mostly by males, have all had a profound effect upon the modern world. I define this archetype, the alchemist, the dominant male, that is common to the majority of gothic narratives, and explore how his character works through the genre.

Chapter 4: The Allegorical Castle: the significant dwelling – large house, abbey or castle - has ever been a site of conflict and drama. The dwelling provides a point of stasis in the narrative and a metaphor of and/or personification of whatever the protagonist is trying to break into/escape. Topics include: isolation, movement and stasis, omnipresent authority and individual consciousness, identity: masculine and feminine, imagination and reality, order and chaos.

Chapter 5: Danger in the Family: the protagonist of the gothic novel is quite often orphaned, or the parents are unknown or the protagonist is disaffected from his or her family in some fundamental way. This chapter explores how the family theme has evolved over time and how it works through even 'surrogate' family novels, how the family roles occupied by female characters in literary works have changed – or stayed the same – in tandem with social and political developments.

Chapter 6: The Lexicon of Haunting: the majority of the gothic sub-genre plots contain a suggestion of the supernatural, the notion that something lurks beneath the surface of superficial appearances. I explore the paradox by which belief in ghosts has expanded since Enlightenment, that time in history when the learned people of the day, at least, disavowed belief in ghosts, banshees, fairies and so forth. Instead, belief in the supernatural seems to have proliferated.

Chapter 7: The Journey: the journey is a tenet of the majority of tales, from the *Odyssey* to fairy and folk tales and numerous other adventure stories. In the gothic genre, the journey provides an element of movement, a riposte to the stasis of the castle theme, a vehicle for escape. The journey also behaves as a metaphor for personal development and is a staple of the *bildungsroman*. From Adeline to Lyra, all gothic protagonists make journeys, each having a different purpose. For example, Catherine Morland is obliged to leave Northanger Abbey in Jane Austen's text, while Jane Eyre practically runs away from Thornfield. Sections in this chapter include: stasis and movement, moving away from authority, the bildungsroman: the fairy-tale journey, the unfinished journey.

Chapter 8: Deceptions, Doppelgangers and the Dark Dis: this composite chapter deals with the less obvious but very potent themes that run through the genre; characters enmeshed in self-deception and the deceit of other people, and the doppelganger and duality. In *Bleak House*, Esther and Ada seem to change places, the poor young woman becoming more fortunate as the narrative draws to a close, while the wealthier woman sinks into poverty and loneliness. Duality may also offer an explanation for the Byronic hero phenomenon. The *dis* is a character with the ability to move with ease between unbreachable worlds. In classic literature, supernatural creatures, such as Satan in *Paradise Lost*, serve as the *dis*. In later literature, the *dis* was usually a servant or governess, and in more recent times, a lawyer or detective. In contemporary works, the *dis* is a character that comes in contact with all social classes, either as an observer or by becoming involved in the dynamism of the narrative, or both.

Chapter 9: The Landscape in Literature: in gothic literature, an encounter with the natural world often provides a healing experience for the protagonist and other characters. This chapter explores the theme of 'natural' healing, and questions the origins of attitudes to nature in literature, looking at how nature has been portrayed in literature before the emergence of gothic, and the development of the theme in literary works ever since. One topic questions the significance of Jane Eyre in Charlotte Brontë's text, following her escape to an idyllic wilderness free from societal judgement, yet almost loses her life in a storm. Sections include the origins of the landscape in art and literature, the female paradigm, the pastoral and the Romantic, healing and perverted nature, the landscape as metaphor: pathetic fallacy, turbulence and calm, and chiaroscuro.

Chapter 10: The Future: I provide a glimpse of the future, posing the question – though not answering – where the next generation of writer may take the genre.

Throughout the text, I have chosen to write 'gothic' rather than 'Gothic' since I prefer the adjective to the noun form of the word. I have, of course, spelled the word as 'Gothic', when quoting other writers.

To keep my text consistent, I have adopted the terminology used by Northrop Frye, with regard to 'genre', 'mode', 'phase', 'mythos', and so forth. All of these terms I have included in a **Glossary**, which the reader can find at the conclusion of the chapters.

The Gothic Narrative:
Fairy Tale, Romance or Novel?

The history of the gothic novel ♦ The Novel and the romance ♦ Mythos of romance ♦ Mythos of comedy ♦ Mythos of irony, satire and tragedy ♦ The rise of the low mimetic mode ♦ The fairy tale ♦ The Byronic hero

The history of the gothic novel

In my **Introduction**, I provided a thumbnail of what I perceive as a typical gothic narrative. With this model in mind, I consider this quotation of Northrop Frye: 'There has never been (to my knowledge) any period of Gothic English literature, but the list of Gothic revivalists stretches completely across its entire history, from the *Beowulf* poet to writers of our own day.'[12]

Is Frye's claim accurate? The first example of the word 'gothic' used with regards to English literature was Horace Walpole's novel *The Castle of Otranto: A Gothic Story*, published in 1765. At that time, 'gothic' meant something closer to 'barbarous,' a connotation that reaches back to the Dark Ages when hordes of Goths over-ran Europe, vanquishing the progress of the Roman civilization. If we accept that the Dark Ages span the period following the fall of the Roman Empire, circa 400 AD to when the Normans arrived in Britain in 1066, then Frye's assertion is arguably accurate.

No English literature was produced in the first millennium AD because the English language of the present day (unlike Latin and French) was not in existence. The Anglo-Saxons began arriving in England c. 400 AD, and spoke in the conglomeration of Germanic dialects that we call 'Old English'. They brought with them a body of recited poetry and sagas, the most notable being

---

[12] Northrop Frye, *Anatomy of Criticism: Four Essays* (Princeton: Princeton University Press, 1971), p186. Subsequent references will be to this edition and will be inserted parenthetically into the text, for example '(Frye, 186)'.

Beowulf, which was not written down until the end of the 800s.¹³ Even though the scholarly King Alfred had begun translating Latin and writing, rendering the Old English language more 'abstractive' than formerly, modern English was yet centuries away (AB, 21).

In fact, the language that we speak today, a dialect of Old English combined with Norman French, did not emerge until about 1400 (AB, 14). Its ascent began in the early 1200s, when the Norman ruling classes lost its lands in Normandy (AB, 26). And the success of Geoffrey Chaucer's poem, *The Canterbury Tales*, written between 1387 and 1400, was due in no small way to his use of this 'new' language. By this time, the Europe of the Dark Ages was a thing of the past. Modern England and indeed, Europe, was born of the demise of feudalism in the wake of the Black Death in the earlier part of the fourteenth century, and the rise of the merchant classes.

In the fifteenth century, the invention of the printing press and the dissemination of knowledge *en masse*, brought a type of order to the world that subsequent famines and plagues have since failed to vanquish. And modern English flourished as a major European language. In this respect, Frye would appear to be correct; no gothic *revival* has taken place. However, my intention is to take Walpole's text as a starting point, a spark that fired a new strand in English literature rather than a revival. The question is: what was it about Walpole's text that enthused writers and readers for the next half-century?

In the words of Marilyn Butler why did these motifs become 'favourite trappings'? (RRR, 20) To answer that question, I now look at the *mythos* of literature. Since classical times, three mythos had prevailed. In the latter centuries BC, the ancient Greeks featured comedies, tragedies and a satyr play or satire, in their festivals.¹⁴ About twenty centuries later, another mythos was attracting audiences, the romance.

Say 'romance' and the majority of people envision a story of love, either returned or unrequited, an attachment which has consequences for everyone involved with the enamoured pair. To an extent, this is relevant. But *romance* has many more contexts; in addition to the quest for marriage and sex with a

---

¹³Anthony Burgess, *English Literature* (Harlow: Longman Group UK Ltd, 1958), p17. Subsequent references will be to this edition and will be inserted parenthetically into the text, for example '(AB, 17)'.

¹⁴Sophocles, *Antigone*, ed. John Harrison and Judith Affleck (Cambridge: Cambridge University Press, 2003) p110.

desirable partner, the romantic hero bears a certain attitude, a gusto and engagement with life. Very broadly speaking, a romance is the tale of a pursuant seeking love, wealth or wisdom; sometimes, all three. Be aware also that the word 'romantic' has little to do with the word 'Roman', the name given to the highly-organized civilization that thrived around 2,000 years ago. As David Wright points out, romantic, in one sense, means looking back to a past when, it was assumed, that life was much simpler.[15] The mythos of romance was born of medieval poetry, possibly as Anthony Burgess points out, steeming from sagas such as the eleventh-century chanson de geste or song of military achievement, *Song of Roland* (AB 24). Burgess claims, because it was the older language, French was much more colourful, one that over time imbued Old English with the many descriptive words we enjoy today. Writes Burgess: 'In the *Song of Roland* we see the silver of the armour, the bright red of spilt blood, the blue of the sky' (AB 24). By the time that Sir Thomas Malory's *Morte De Arthur* was printed by Caxton in 1464, the romance of the quest was in place.

This strand of romance was the result of a growing tradition in that marriage alliances were forged for a combination of physical attraction and the deepest affection, rather than for dynastical, property ownership and the sheer necessity of breeding offspring. Medieval poetry brought us lovers like Héloise and Abelard, and Tristan and Isolde, and Paulo and Francesca. By the sixteenth century, the mythos of romance was firmly in place, with *Romeo and Juliet*, and *Anthony and Cleopatra* amongst Shakespeare's galaxy of 'romantic' plays.

The mythos of romance has also brought us picaresque heroes such as *Don Quixote* (Cervantes) and later on, *Robinson Crusoe* (Daniel Dafoe), *Tom Jones* (Henry Fielding) and *Humphrey Clinker* (Tobias Smollet), narratives centring around adventuring male characters in contemporary settings (AB, 119). Walpole's achievement was to create a sub-genre of romance with a female protagonist at the centre of the action, a heroine that encounters danger and survives, with the action usually set in times past. He pitches the action of *The Castle of Otranto* back to the time of the Crusades, when feudal lords dwelt – in fond imagination, at least – in castles and sought to keep bloodlines alive with the judicious marriages of their offspring. The action centres around Manfred, Lord of the castle.

---

[15]David Wright, *English Romantic Verse*, ed. by David Wright (London: Penguin Books, Penguin Classics, 1968), pxvii. Subsequent references will be to this edition and will be inserted parenthetically into the text, for example "(Wright, xvii)"

When his son dies by supernatural means before his, the son's, wedding to the lovely Isabella can take place, Manfred schemes to take the young woman for himself. But his progress is thwarted by the actions of handsome peasant, Theodore, whom Manfred has already condemned to death.

Friar Jerome recognises Theodore as *his* illegitimate son, and so bargains with Manfred for Theodore's life, a progress interrupted by the arrival of a company of knights. Eventually, the now-fugitive Theodore fights with a knight who turns out to be Frederic, Isabella's father. Frederic falls in love with Matilda, Manfred's daughter. But the attempt by the two fathers to bargain for each other's daughters ends in failure. Manfred inadvertently kills Matilda, thus fulfilling an ancient prophecy that renders Theodore the Lord of the castle. Of course, it ends with his marriage to Isabella, while the deposed Manfred retreats into religion.

Today, the narrative, which Anthony Burgess describes as 'as a melodramatic curiosity', seems crude and simplistic, a mixture of swashbuckling medieval hokum and teen romance (AB, 163). But this could be only because the formula has been so often repeated since then. In the decades that followed, writers like Ann Radcliffe, Clara Reeve and Matthew Lewis gained fame for tales that employed similar ingredients, imbuing readers with fear, excitement and fulfilment.

In Walpole's day, the formula was seized upon by authors who identified the growing readership of newly-literate middle class young women. Samuel Richardson had published *Pamela, or, Virtue Rewarded* and *Clarissa, or the History of a Young Lady*, novels with a woman as the central character. Like the picaresque novel, both narratives have contemporary settings and present a didactic view of how women should behave. Clarissa, in particular, following a life of imprisonment and sexual slavery, ends up dead. Contrary to this, the language of the gothic authors was never didactic but told a story at the end of which the female triumphed.

Much of the action of *Otranto* is set in an actual castle, a motif made popular by Shakespeare's plays, *Hamlet* and *Macbeth*. The feudal lord, Manfred, presents a type of picaresque jauntiness to the reader of the time, swiftly followed by a smattering of sympathy for the death of his son. But as the narrative progresses, Manfred's wickedness is revealed and the sympathy that ebbs away is replaced by interest in the two princesses. The full pot of gothic ingredients is in place, a lovely young woman, family troubles, lust and betrayal, the supernatural and death. Into its midst steps the character of Theodore, the peasant bearing strands of humility and nobility.

Walpole was looking at the Dark Ages in a new light, a time when 'free' peasants fought against aristocratic tyranny. Thus does he endow Theodore with a type of nobility. For decades, Swiss philosopher and novelist, Jean-Jacques Rousseau (1712-1778), had been discoursing on the nature of humanity and education, most notably through his work, *Emile, on an Education*, published 1762. Broadly, his argument runs that man is at his happiest and most productive when he is unfettered by the formalities of society (AB, 162). The character of Theodore would indeed seem to fit the prototype of Rousseau's natural man, inheriting Manfred's castle through intentional noble deed rather than accidental bloodline.

Anthony Burgess offers yet another explanation as to why this 'manly freespoken peasant' becomes the hero of the narrative. According to Burgess, a medieval myth arose in England, almost as powerful as the myth of Arthur, of a hero named Robin Hood, an outlaw with a band of followers who would not accept Norman rule but lived freely in the forest (AB, 25). In Theodore, Walpole rebrands as virtuous, the close-to-nature lifestyle of the peasant in contrast to that of the pampered, decadent nobility as represented by Manfred. Quite possibly, Walpole was channelling the myth of Robin Hood and transforming him into a romantic hero.

The author provides Theodore with a number of challenges so he can prove himself worthy of the status of hero. In addition to winning the hand of Isabella, he has to fight off his death sentence by Manfred, escape the castle, fight a duel with Frederic and work in tandem with the supernatural. Although set in feudal times, Manfred seeks to trump the supernatural. 'Heaven nor Hell shall impede my designs', he declares to Isabella in Book One, when he reveals his more dastardly intentions. But barely is he finished speaking when a painting in the chamber, that of his late grandfather, moves and falls upon the ground, thus enabling Isabella to escape and meet with the man who is to be her lover. Walpole may have lived during a time of philosophical and scientific progress, that is, the Enlightenment, but he was aware that many readers believed in ghosts or, at least, enjoyed reading about them. In his excellent book, *The Cock Lane Ghost*, Paul Chambers, recalls a 'genuine' eighteenth-century haunting, genuine in the sense that the incident concerned actual people, and was not simply a work of fiction. The incident concerned unexplained rapping and scratching sounds in a house in the Clerkenwell area of London between 1759 and 1761, just a few years before Walpole published *Otranto*. During its time, this activity sparked enormous public interest, a media frenzy and a landmark court case. The public needed novelty and distraction, and reportage of the Cock Lane ghost seemingly affected Walpole in a singular fashion. He had the talent and the vision to place the freeborn Theodore into a setting that appealed to the human heart, the noble, natural man fighting to win the lovely princess, grappling with a tyrant and the supernatural, by turns. With the tyrant deposed, the only tragedy is the death of gentle Matilda.

Another ingredient is its setting in 'the past', most likely in feudal times. It is difficult to explain the roseate glow of the past but one way to illustrate its appeal is to liken it to comparing two photographs of the same, notional townscape or landscape, one monochrome and the other in colour. The monochrome is a poetic evocation of muted shapes, every gradation of shade from darkest to palest grey, softening sharp edges and ironing out the more mundane details. The interrelationships of the many tones imbue the image with a sense of unity, like a piece of fine lace.

The colour image is, on the other hand, devoid of this subtle tonality. Instead, it is composed of strips of garish and even, clashing colour. It is literal, immediate and insistent. The image all but drags the viewer into this immediacy. In certain cases, this literality can provide an enjoyable experience. But it is not a subtle, evocative or poetic one. The past is, of course, the monochrome experience, even when painted in full colour by the words of the author. And the present is the full-on colour experience, even when the writer is describing the present-day world in terms of banality and monotony. It is a perceptive rather than an actual experience and the writers of the 'long ago and far away' understand this emotion perfectly: the majority of 'revival' experiences are perception rather than reality. To sum up, these mid to late-eighteenth century authors saw a readership eager for this cocktail of ingredients: the glow of the past, the suggestion of the supernatural, the presence of an authority in a stronghold or castle, all appealing to a readership of newly-literate middle-class females. Again, I stress that the language of the new gothic literature was never didactic but observed how the protagonists extricated themselves from their dilemmas, rather than morally implying what they *should* have done. In addition to these factors, Walpole's narrative straddles two popular, literary mythos, romance and comedy. Before I move on to discussion of the various *mythos*, I want to explain a little about the *novel* and the *romance*.

The Novel and the Romance

In my **Introduction**, I pointed out that much confusion exists surrounding the various meanings that attach to the word 'romance'. I have already explained a little about the *mythos* of romance. Here, I introduce the term in the context of *genre*. Say 'romance' and the majority of people envision a story of love, either returned or unrequited, an attachment which has consequences for everyone involved with the enamoured pair. To an extent, this is relevant. But the literary romance encompasses so much more than this.

What is the difference between a romance and a so-called serious novel? Very broadly speaking, a romance is the tale of a pursuant seeking love, wealth or wisdom; sometimes, all three. He (usually) leaves behind the stable society in which he lived – if indeed, he did live in a stable society – following a course through unknown territory, encountering and defeating obstacles and dangers, by turn. The hero of the romance usually triumphs and wins not only what he is seeking but draws to himself a host of other prizes. For instance, the hero that slays the dragon and finds the pot of gold also gains by default the lovely princess. In a romance, many of the characters and instances are stylized, rather than actual persons and events. The hero is often pursued by a villain and encounters obstacles that embody the forces of the universe. He may have to cross a dangerous mountain (earth), traverse a fast-flowing river (water) and find a way to bridge a chasm (air) between dizzyingly high cliffs. His final encounter might be to slay the dragon (fire) that is guarding the treasure, the princess or magic talisman or whatever he is seeking. And the outcome is usually happy and triumphant. The narrator almost never questions the right, wrong or other moral implications of what the hero does. With few exceptions, the hero of the romance does not need to justify himself to anyone but – himself. He is his own person, single-mindedly set on his quest and answerable to no one.

The novel, on the other hand, is set in a stable society, often with recognisable laws. The novel only came of age in more recent times when our modern world came into being, with laws and statutes and government. Generally, the protagonist of a novel is an individual making his way in society, trying to reconcile his individuality and personality with societal demands. Throughout, the author/narrator provides objective discourse on the behaviour or otherwise of the protagonist. And the people that he or she encounters are 'real' in the sense that they are individuals with distinguishing traits, rather than archetypes.

The person inadequately equipped to deal with these demands will find him or herself in conflict, which provides the essential ingredient that constitutes drama.

The novel heralds the coming of *realism* in literature, the nineteenth-century movement that was the precursor to modernism. Realism is beautifully nuanced by Jane Austen in her novel, *Sense and Sensibility*. The two Dashwood sisters, Elinor and Marianne, represent 'sense', that is, Elinor subduing her romantic interests to maintain her family's foothold in society, and 'sensibility', respectively, Marianne giving way to the dictates of her heart. Of course, novels do contain romance, in the sense that individuals seek love and companionship within societal strictures. Whatever the plot, the actions by the protagonist of the novel always have consequences, a mixture of advantageous and disadvantageous outcomes for the other characters. And this is why novels have endings that are ambivalent, even for the protagonist, rather than the unambiguously 'happy' ending of the fairy tale or romance. With which genre do we place the gothic narrative?

In *The Castle of Otranto*, both Isabella and Matilda find themselves in love with Theodore. That the young women are already friends compounds the problem. As in a novel, both women behave with decorum, neither wanting to hurt the other. But fate takes a hand in the plot and the narrative has a satisfactory ending. In *Romance of the Forest*, Adeline has fallen in love with Theodore but they cannot marry until he and she reach a place that is safe from the designs of the Marquis. Adeline escapes first and safely ensconced in Arnaud La Luc's home, her first duty is to her foster father, assisting him in his failing health. As in a novel, her actions have consequences for other people. Only when Arnaud is recovering does Adeline begin her quest to rescue Theodore. The happy ending affirms the tale as a romance.

The writers of gothic tales succeeded in creating a sub-genre that, although the ending for the protagonist was invariably satisfactory, as in romance, the author presented the character with a number of moral ambivalences throughout the narrative, as in a novel. One distinguishing trait of the gothic sub-genre is that the female protagonist eventually comes in contact with a so-called hero. But even these heroes can be subdivided into certain types. It is the type of hero that defines the mode of the work, of which Northrop Frye has identified five: the myth, the romance, the high mimetic, the low mimetic and the satire (Frye, 33-4).

These mimetic modes endow literary works with a recognisable type of hero at its heart, a hero that has waned or gained in popularity throughout the ages. When civilization, as we know it, was in its infancy and few people were literate, populations depended upon bards and wandering poets reciting epic poetry and enacting dramas for entertainment, c. 1000 BC (AB, 17). Three of the four familiar *mythos* emerged during this time, comedy, satire and tragedy, and these *mythos* required the actions of a particular type of hero, thus the existence of the *mimetic* modes. The easiest way to remember the difference between 'mythos' and 'mimetic' is to be aware that the word 'mimetic' is derived from the verb 'mime', which means 'to imitate'. The mimetic mode indicates the nature and actions of the hero (or heroine), mythic, ordinary person, and so on. The mythos is the environment in which the action takes place, fantastical, real world, etc.

Anthony Burgess explains how we are all possessed of an innate inclination to imitate everything about us, from the movement and sound of animals, to the actions of other people (AB, 44). When civilization was developing, the populations favoured the tales and enactments of beings who were *not* like them. This is why the earliest of the mimetic modes is the *myth*, an epic tale with a *super-hero* at its centre, stronger than other men and often bearing superpowers. In ancient Greece, the populations listened enthralled as poets recited these epics, often from memory, relaying events that lifted the listener from his or her everyday surroundings (Frye, 188).

As the world developed, the population began to pay more attention to the mode of *romance*. The hero of the romance is human. He does not possess superpowers, but operates in a world in which the known laws of nature are suspended. The romance encompasses legends, folk tales and fairy tales that were recited by ordinary people, ordinary in the sense that they were not professional poets. Because of this democratisation of tale-telling, many popular folk tales survive in slightly altered narratives. Among the best-known are *Snow White*, *Cinderella* and *Little Red Riding Hood*.

By the middle ages, a newly-literate population had emerged, most notably the clergy. Books were precious, hand-written objects that few people could access. The invention of the printing press changed all of that. For the first time in history, an individual could purchase a book from a publisher. This did not mean the end of drama or poetry, of course. The late 1500s saw a golden age of drama in London with the plays of William Shakespeare: 'England's – and the world's – greatest dramatist', who is still one of the world's most famous writers (AB, 44). In addition, individuals began to *read* poetry rather than await recitations – though these did and still do take place – and another type of hero emerged.

The hero of the *high mimetic mode* is human. Unlike the hero of the Greek epic, he is not a god but is endowed with free will to choose his own fate (AB, 44). However, a personal trait – social standing, talent – distinguishes him from the people around him and that rarity of character marks him out for an unhappy fate: the tragic hero of the high mimetic mode had emerged. In Shakespeare's play *Julius Caesar*, Cassius says to Brutus: 'Men at some time are masters of their fate./The fault, dear Brutus, is not in our stars but in ourselves./That we are underlings.' (Act 1, Scene 2). Shakespeare's *Hamlet* and *Richard II* are fine examples of the tragic hero. Over the following two hundred years, literacy increased among the population and by the end of the 1700s, the middle-class reader could simply purchase a volume from a bookshop. And the 'ordinary' middle-class reader wanted to identify with an individual as like as possible him or herself. This was in contrast to centuries of classical epics, stories from sacred books like the Bible, and folk and fairy tales. And the protagonist of the *low mimetic mode,* which I explore later, is identifiable with the novel.

First, I want to explore the various *mythos* in more depth.

Mythos of romance

Once more, bear in mind that the romantic *mythos* differs from the romantic *genre*. The mythos refers to the turn of events rather than the actually literary form, romance or novel, which is the *genre*. Within each mythos, Northrop Frye defines a number of phases that occur frequently therein. The phases are too numerous to describe in depth here, but I will outline those that typify the converging events in a gothic novel.

As explained earlier, a romance is not necessarily a love story, but a narrative that features a protagonist engaging with life with a certain, go-getting attitude. The picaresque mode is a fine example of a romance. Usually, the protagonist is seeking that which is of value, love, wisdom or wealth, a phase known as the *quest*. The gothic writers transposed this quest from a male to a female protagonist, typified by Adeline's repeated attempts to escape from the Marquis and to rescue her lover. Jane Eyre struggles to attain meaning in life, both within and outside of the strictures of society, while remaining true to her own soul. In the final pages, the reader sees her married to the man she loves.

Another phase of this mythos is the *pastoral,* where lovers meet and fall in love within lush, rural settings (Frye, 199-200). Adeline and Theodore meet in a forest, thus giving the novel its name, while Mr Rochester observes and courts Jane Eyre in the sylvan, summer-time gardens of Thornfield. However, Charlotte Brontë was a nineteenth-century writer who used the metaphor of natural surroundings in a more sophisticated fashion. As Delia Da Sousa Correa explains, the presently blighted landscape at Thornfield externalises Jane Eyre's changed fortune, that is, on discovering her lover is already married, and her heartbreak: 'A Christmas frost had come at midsummer; a white December storm had whirled over June; ice glazed the ripe apples, drifts crushed the blowing roses; on hayfield and corn-field lay a frozen shroud: lanes which last night blushed full of flowers, to-day were pathless with untrodden snow; and the woods, which twelve hours since waved leafy and fragrant as groves between the tropics, now spread waste, wild, and white as pine-forests in wintry Norway.'[16]

That Charles Dickens never intends romance to blossom between Estella and Pip in the pages of *Great Expectations*, is evident in the blasted surroundings in which they meet. As the pair walk and talk, Estella makes Pip feel as if: 'the green and yellow growth of weed in the chinks of the old wall had been the most precious flowers that ever blew'.[17] Another element of romance is the checker-board effect, defined by Frye, where every good character is balanced out by the 'moral opposite', a corresponding evil character (Frye, 195). In *Romance of the Forest*, the wickedness of Marquis de Montalt is balanced by the assumed virtue of his murdered brother, eventually revealed as Adeline's father. In Austen's text, the calculating General Tilney and his philandering son, Captain Tilney, are checked by the good-hearted Henry Tilney. What romances have in common is that good always triumphs over bad and the mythos of comedy bears a similar quality.

---

[16] Charlotte Brontë, *Jane Eyre*, ed. Margaret Smith (Oxford: Oxford University Press, 1980), p295. Subsequent references will be to this edition and will be inserted parenthetically into the text, for example '(Brontë, 295)'

[17] Charles Dickens, *Great Expectations*, ed. John Bowen (London: Wordsworth Editions, 1992), p203. Subsequent references will be to this edition and will be inserted parenthetically into the text, for example '(GE, 203)'

Mythos of comedy:

> *Comedy: 'a movement from illusion to reality. Illusion is whatever is fixed or definable, and reality is best understood as its negation; whatever reality is, it's not that.'* (Northrop Frye, 169-170).

Good triumphing over evil is an age-old trope in practically every genre of literature. The reasons are obvious: since literature is an art that records the progression of humanity, then good deeds in a narrative are bound to dominate, at least. However, this reiteration of triumphing morals can render the art form insipid and lacking in drama. Authors of comic literature have side-stepped this polarisation by placing their characters in a succession of ambivalent circumstances. In the finest comedies, a succession of social events exposes truths about the characters, their passions and their distastes, their strengths and their very human weaknesses.

Subtly handled, these ambivalences may not only make an audience/readership laugh, but illustrate profundities about life in general. These profundities are often exposed when a couple realise that they love (or hate) one another, when a person's true character is uncovered or when two people who thought that they were pursuing different interests come together in a surprising way. Northrop Frye describes this as the comic discovery, the *anagnorisis* or *cognitio* (Frye, 163).

Comedy occupies a particular place in literature. Highly subjective in perception, its potency often dwindles with changing culture. Indeed, it is a tribute to the staying power of the gothic genre that its more comic modes are recognisable by the reader of today in Henry Tilney/Jane Austen's denouement of it to Catherine: 'While they snugly repair to their own end of the house, she (the heroine) is formally conducted by Dorothy the ancient housekeeper up a different staircase, and along many gloomy passages, into an apartment never used since some cousin or kin died in it about twenty years before. Can you stand such a ceremony as this? Will your mind not misgive you, when you find yourself in this gloomy chamber – too lofty and extensive for you, with only the feeble rays of a single lamp to take in its size – its walls hung with tapestry exhibiting figures as large as life, and the bed, of dark green stuff or purple velvet, presenting even a funereal appearance? Will your heart not sink within you?' (*NA*, 150).

If the reader imagines Henry and Catherine as a brother and sister pair, Harry and Kate, and pitches them into modern times, the above paragraph could be rewritten as follows, without any loss of comedy:

> 'And when we get to the holiday house, you will be separated from the rest of us and lodged in a distant part of the building.'
> 'Harry, don't be silly: how could that happen?'
> 'Because that's what happens in one of those books you are always reading.' Harry tapped the shiny-covered paperback that sat on Kate's lap. 'The girl is always separated from the others by the creepy old housekeeper and she is taken to a chamber filled with ancient and broken furniture and the lighting is always gloomy and you will wander round, picking up items, many of them broken and you will wonder who owned them and what dark tales are attached.'
> 'Harry, will you not be so silly.'
> 'And then, she will leave you on your own, the housekeeper, I mean, and before she does, she will tell you that you are on your own for the night, that no-one will come if you call for help and she will slam the door shut.'
> 'Harry, shut up.'
> 'And then, a thunderstorm will break out and the electric will shut down and you will cower under the bedclothes for a while. And then, you will get fed up and start exploring the room with your phone torch and you will keep searching until you come across a locked door.'
> 'Harry, I told you to shut up." (ends)

However, comedy has functions other than to amuse.

Comedy often takes place in a society controlled by older people, filled with younger people yearning for freedom from 'habit, ritual bondage and arbitrary law' (Frye, 169-70). This comedy is brilliantly stated in *Bleak House*, when the eminent Judge reveals to the victors of the Jarndyce vs Jarndyce lawsuit that legal costs have devoured the assets of the disputed estate, and the characters watch dismayed as: 'bundles in bags, bundles too large to be got into any bags, immense masses of papers of all shapes and of no shapes, which the bearers staggered under, and threw down for the time being, anyhow, onto the Hall pavement, while they went back to bring out more. Even these clerks were laughing.'[18]

However, few modern writers have nuanced comedy as brilliantly as Jane Austen. In her novel, *Pride and Prejudice*, Mr Bennet declares he will never again speak to his daughter Elizabeth if she marries the odious Mr Collins,

---

[18]Charles Dickens, *Bleak House*, ed. Norman Page (London: Penguin Classics, 1971), p922. Subsequent references will be to this edition and will be inserted parenthetically into the text, for example '(BH, 922)'.

while Mrs Bennet protests that she will never again speak to her, if she does not. The existential dilemma is a demonstration of Mr Bennet's rationality over Mrs Bennet's social climbing. The scene affects the reader in the manner of the moment in *Northanger Abbey* when Catherine discovers that her fantasies over General Tilney have been unfounded, that he is not a wife murderer. And yet, the episode subtly points to a future event when the General's mistreatment of her proves that her instincts about him were not without foundation. But because the resolution of Catherine's tale has a happy ending, the reader may regard *Northanger Abbey* as belonging to the mythos of comedy.

In the more recent book, *The Woman in Black*, the roles of aged experience and youthful innocence are reversed in the opening chapters of the narrative. Narrator Arthur Kipps guides the reader from the inadvertent mocking by his step-family to a truly chilling and direful account of his supernatural experience, an instance that could be summed up by Frye as 'a movement from illusion to reality' (Frye, 169-170).

The Mythos of Irony, Satire and Tragedy

As Northrop Frye explains at length, the satirical tale is normally set in a world that is filled with injustice, the citizens forced to comply with a set of ludicrous circumstances that are permanently in place (Frye, 226). In the satire, the citizens either assume or are forced into absurd modes of behaviour. The dystopian novel belongs to this mythos, and examples include *1984* by George Orwell, *A Handmaid's Tale* by Margaret Atwood and *Never Let Me Go* by Kazuo Ishiguro. *Hard Times*, by Charles Dickens, is a fine, nineteenth-century example. The clique in power – government, army, church – usually abuse their executive powers, visiting random unfairness upon the citizens (Frye, 228). This same clique often take a high moral tone when dealing with 'their' populations. The protagonist or protagonists are usually young, idealistic people who decide to rise up against them.

One, significant factor about the satire is that its setting is seldom remote, in contrast to the 'far away' action of the gothic sub-genre, which means that it and the mythos of romance are unlikely to converge. The satirical world bears a resemblance to the 'real' world, but it is imbued with a sense of menace. For the reader, the experience is rather like eating a favourite food and finding that the taste is 'off' or trying to listen to a piece of beloved music played by a musician who is out of key. In many instances of the conclusion of a satire, the protagonist or protagonists realise that all is lost, that nothing in their world is ever going to change. At this point, the characters assume a conventional social role – in terms of their society – or masque. One example is what happens to Julia and Winston at the end of *1984*, when they decide to become conforming citizens. This pessimism is in contrast to the hopeful ending of the gothic novel. The events in *A Laodicean* by Thomas Hardy ever threaten to tip over into satire but the author's wit and delicacy saves the narrative from being yet another satirical tale. It is almost a laugh-aloud moment at the end of the narrative when Paula Power says to her now-husband, George Somerset: 'I wish my castle wasn't burnt; and I wish that you were a de Stancy'.[19] Incidentally, the masque or masquerade or deception is a strand of many gothic novels, a matter that I explore in Chapter 8, **Deceptions, the Doppelganger and the Dark Dis**, but 'deception' in the gothic novel takes place in the *course* of the narrative, only to be cast away at the conclusion, when the characters reveal their true selves. This ties in with the mythos of comedy when, to quote Frye again: 'a movement from illusion to reality.' This does not happen in true satire, which always ends with a sense of unfinished business.

From the above discourse, it would seem that satire and the gothic sub-genre never cross paths. Yet, they do. Consider the following phrase from their definition of the uncanny by Andrew Bennett and Nicholas Royle, cited by Delia Da Sousa Correa, 'a disturbance of the familiar'.[20] In the light of how I have described it above, 'imbued with a sense of menace' this phrase could, in fact, refer to the supernatural. In the eighteenth century, with the crossover from the popularity of the satire to romantic and social realist literature, the reader might discern that the presence of the supernatural in a narrative became almost a surrogate for satire, that sensing by the reader and the novel's protagonist(s) that something in the environment is out of sync with reality.

The major difference between literary satire and the supernatural is that the former is experienced on a political plane, whereas disturbance by the

---

[19] Thomas Hardy, *A Laodicean*, ed. Barbara Hardy (London, Macmillan London Ltd, 1979), p136. Subsequent references will be to this edition and will be inserted parenthetically into the text, for example "(AL, 437)".

[20] Delia Da Sousa Correa, 'Jane Eyre and Genre' in *The Nineteenth-Century Novel: Realisms, Volume 1* (London, Routledge, 2000), p109. Subsequent references will be to this edition and will be inserted parenthetically into the text, for example "(DDSC, 109)".

latter is a more personal experience. This makes sense: the rise of individualism around the time of the Industrial Revolution paved the need for a more introspective literature, and the supernatural was at hand to externalise the discomfort felt by the individual. The paradox is that the Industrial Revolution arose from the same advances in scientific knowledge that promulgated Enlightenment, a time when, theoretically at least, belief in supernatural entities ought to have been waning. Other definitions of the supernatural exist, of course, which are discussed in the chapter, **The Lexicon of Haunting**. Irony and satire are closely related, but irony in a novel or drama is usually the result of deceit enacted by one individual over another, rather than devastation by societal conformity. *Atonement* by Ian McEwan, is a good example. *Romeo and Juliet* is invariably classified as romance or tragedy, but it is actually an ironic drama, the lovers becoming victims of the mistiming events (Frye, 41). Irony and tragedy are closely linked and a tragedy invariably contains a tragic hero, which leads to an exploration of the *high mimetic mode.*

The hero of the *high mimetic mode* is human. Unlike the hero of the Greek epic, he is not a god but is endowed with free will to choose his own fate (AB, 49). He is in possession of a personal trait that distinguishes him from the people around him. Throughout much of his narrative, he is wrapped in mystery, a matter that the people about him can sense (Frye, 207). The people are aware that he is different, slightly more dignified which, in archaic terms, means 'close to the gods' (Frye, 209). Quite often this mode is expressed as the mythos of tragedy. Today, we simply recognise such people as talented or more intelligent or endowed with charismatic qualities. But writers of old approached the hero with a mixture of admiration and apprehension and in addition, they were aware of his inherent vulnerability. Indeed, the hero could be brought down simply by the envy of others; Shakespeare's Julius Caesar is such a hero. But often, the hero was in possession of a character flaw or *hamartia* that proves his undoing. Coriolanus is such a hero, who is brought down by his own pride.

Here, Manfred of Walpole's narrative would seem to be just such a hero. But in contrast to the noble Hamlet, Manfred's deeds are not heroic. The narrative gradually reveals that he had won his social position by deception. He has practically kidnapped Isabella to promulgate his familial line, is prepared to depose his wife, to have Theodore executed and the narrative ends with his slaughtering his own daughter. And even if Manfred is a 'tragic' person rather than a hero, the reconciliation of the forces of good at the end of Walpole's narrative preclude it from being a tragedy. With an understanding of the romance and the satire, it is now possible to put the *low mimetic* in context.

The protagonist of the *low mimetic mode* is identifiable with the novel, obliged to live in the 'real' world and beset by moral ambiguities. Overall, this mode of literature has triumphed. This hero has no special powers or recourse to magic talismans, which is why this protagonist is one that the majority of readers identify with (Frye, 34).

The narratives of the gothic sub-genre proved popular because it straddles (most evidently) the mythos of both romance and comedy, yet features a hero or heroine of the low mimetic. The action centres upon a protagonist that the reader could identify with, yet contained enough suspense, intrigue and pathos to stir, move and hold in thrall. In *Northanger Abbey*, Catherine finds herself quite literally, in society, when she arrives in Bath, awkward, gauche and trying to conform to the behaviours of those around her. Suddenly, romance – in the form of Henry Tilney – presents itself and Catherine expends all of her wits in pursuing her love interest. However, conflict is present in the form of the selfish demands of duplicitous companions, the self-styled (and selfish) friends of her brother. As in a novel, Catherine is aware that her actions to subvert their pernicious effects have consequences and she experiences much discomfiture in trying to resolve the conflict. But the eventual happy ending belongs to the romance.

The significance of the fairy tale

Before this chapter ends, I am going to explore one significant writing form with which the gothic sub-genre blends, the fairy tale. With more than a little help from Bruno Bettelheim, the finest writer on the subject, I present my own outline of what constitutes one of these age-old 'tales':

Although the narratives are set in the 'real' world, the reader always has a sense that the events occur in a remote place, in the distant past. The typical fairy tale subject is often, though not always, a child. But a child or adult, he is always young and unworldly. Whatever the background to his story, he is always mortal and not endowed with superpowers. (Bettelheim, 39-40)

The other characters in the narrative are types or stereotypes rather than individuals, and often are not named but referred to as 'the old man', 'the wise woman', 'the wicked witch,' and so on. Most often, the main subject is isolated and apart from parents through being orphaned, or trapped somewhere, or cast out simply because the parents are inadequate (Bettelheim, 8, 11). To escape his plight, the fairy tale hero frequently embarks upon a journey, and is helped by maintaining harmony with nature – animals, birds, trees – he never harms these but 'listens' to what they have to tell him (Bettelheim, 11). In addition to being kind, he is brave and does not shirk from the task he has to accomplish (Bettelheim, 24). Often, the tale is a parable on the 'pleasure principle', the notion that it is better to work and/or suffer in advance of gaining any rewards (Bettelheim, 33-4). Too much indulgence now can cause failure later on.

Eventually, the hero encounters a person, animal or magical being who grants him certain powers. But these powers are usually temporary and/or can only be enacted under certain conditions. The rule of three is significant in folk tales, with events happening in threes or the hero being granted three wishes, or both. Throughout the narrative, there is much emphasis on symbols, for example, earth, air, fire, water, and includes other reminders that the hero is human and not mortal, for example, by succumbing to hunger, grief, loneliness. When the challenge has been met, the magic fades and the hero and his world return to 'normal'. But *normal* here does not mean 'unchanged'. The fairy tale hero returns from his adventure and emerges a much wiser person, chastened even. Quite often, the narrative ends with a wedding 'the prince and princess lived happily together always' which, Bruno Bettelheim stresses continually, is simply a metaphor of the integration of the male and female aspects of the personality, rather than exhorting the reader to go out and win an aristocratic marriage partner (Bettelheim, 146).

By now, the reader will have recognised several parallels by the fairy tale with the gothic sub-genre and indeed, the romance: the sense of remoteness, the isolation, the youth and naivety of the protagonist, the embarkation on a journey, the connection with nature, emphasis on kindness and good works, the proliferation of symbols, the presence of the supernatural, the 'coming right' at the end, the return to the recognisable world and the happy ending (Bettelheim, 62).

I explore the majority of fairy tale motifs in the larger body of my text but here, I refer to a small number of them. In certain instances, the fairy tale narrative is so buried in layers of metaphor as to be barely recognisable, for example, in *Bleak House*. The beaten-down Caddy Jellyby seeks to escape what she believes is an inadequate family life for the glamour of a husband, and the world of dance. Ironically, she ignores the talent that brought the book's author much fame and fortune: 'I can't hardly do anything, except write,' says Caddy, her words incongruous in a narrative filled with male characters all scripting for a living, from the Lord Chancellor right down to the person who sells the paper, ink and pens, that is, Mr Snagsby the stationer. While the reader cannot blame Caddy for wanting to escape her parents' chaotic household, she does seem rather to step out of one cauldron into another – quite literally – in marrying (her) Prince Turveydrop. Indeed, Caddy's eventual fate seems to parallel that of Snow White's wicked stepmother, destined to dance forever in red-hot slippers. Viewed in this light, Caddy's 'escape' seems grotesque and absurd.

To demonstrate the vulnerability of subjects exposed by the absence of parents, I juxtapose two characters, Adeline of *Romance of the Forest*, who survived her ordeal and prospered, and Eleanor of *The Haunting of Hill House*, who did not. The La Motte family rescues Adeline from a band of brigands who have been ordered to kill her. This episode is reiterated later in the narrative when La Motte himself is ordered to kill Adeline. In an episode reminiscent of *Snow White*, La Motte tells her to run for her life – and in a forest. Even before this happens, Adeline's narrative is filled with fairy-tale episodes, most notably the Oedipal conflicts, which are defined by Bettelheim (Bettelheim, 247). Madame La Motte becomes jealous when she fears that her husband is attracted to Adeline's overt charms, a situation that places the young girl in even more danger from the rapacious Marquis. Throughout much of the narrative, Adeline is frightened. But she never once, even in her search for domestic security and stability, gives in to the orality and sensuality defined by Bettelheim (Bettelheim, 161).

Adeline is forced by the Marquis to go to his chateau, and regards with distaste and disgust the exotic fare on offer by him: '(the Marquis) now led her, and she suffered him, to take a seat near the banquet, at which he pressed her to partake of a variety of confectionaries, particularly of some liquors, of which he himself drank freely: Adeline accepted only a peach.'[21]

---

[21] Ann Radcliffe, ed. Chloe Chard, *The Romance of the Forest* (Oxford: Oxford University Press, 1986), p161. Subsequent references will be to this edition and will be inserted parenthetically into the text, for example '(ROTF, 161)'.

Within the text, Adeline's austerity is in marked contrast to the orality and sensuality of the Marquis.

By contrast, the delicious food served to Eleanor Vance by the inscrutable housekeeper Mrs Dudley in Shirley Jackson's *The Haunting of Hill House* seems almost to be intoxicating the inmates of the house, drawing them into an undefined purpose.[22] In fact, the theme of food runs throughout Jackson's text. At the outset of the narrative, Eleanor has spent her entire adult life caring for her invalid mother. With that mother dead, Eleanor is playing second fiddle to her married sister. In an uncharacteristic act of defiance, Eleanor accepts the invite of Dr Montague to take part in his paranormal study at the titular house. On the way, Eleanor encounters three females (rule of three) that illustrate what she, Eleanor might become. She collides with an old lady and to her (and Eleanor's) distress, destroys the packet of food that the lady carries. The lady reveals the food to have been 'left over', which illustrates a type of poverty that Eleanor disdains (HH, 13).

Further along the way, Eleanor stops for lunch at a restaurant where she witnesses a family with a young girl who refuses to drink her milk because it has not been served in her favourite cup 'with stars in the bottom' (HH, 21). Mentally, Eleanor supports the girl, willing her not to give in to adult pressure. For much of the narrative, Eleanor mentally repeats the phrase 'cup of stars' when she is trying to define what she wants from life. In this episode, Jackson uses the language of the fairy tale to express what Eleanor is experiencing. Eleanor's third female encounter takes place towards the close of her journey when she stops for coffee at a run-down diner and encounters a young waitress (HH, 24). Once again, the author's language expresses how Eleanor feels as she observes the conditions about her in the sordid diner with its overweight overseer, without freedom or prospects (HH, 24). But once in Hill House, with her characteristic lack of self-awareness, Eleanor slowly forgets her 'cup of stars' and succumbs to sensuality, a trait that leads to her own destruction.

Only one of my primary texts is a 'real' fairy tale, in the sense that it was written as one and contains all of the elements that I outlined above. Hans Christian Andersen published *The Snow Queen* in 1844, a triumph of the

---

[22] Shirley Jackson, *The Haunting of Hill House* (London: Penguin Classics, 2009), p64. Subsequent references will be to this edition and will be inserted parenthetically into the text, for example '(HH, 64)'.

genre that combines elements of feminism, fantasy, animism and discourse on the value of education in nineteenth-century Denmark. Indeed, Gerda is such a triumph of feminism that the reader cannot but wonder at the plethora of *Snow Queen* spin-offs today that serve to all but destroy the essence of this marvellous tale, for example, transforming the boy/girl pair into two young women as in the Disney movie, *Frozen*. This transmogrification destroys much of the metaphor in the story-line, the reasons which will unfold to the reader in the succeeding chapters. Here, I just mention that Gerda almost succumbs to the charms of the witch who feeds her cherries and milk. But Gerda regains her memory and her senses just in time to leave the witch's cottage and resume her search for her friend. This action results in a growth in personality that is the essence of the *bildingsroman,* a work of fiction in which the protagonist grows to maturity.

And the gothic sub-genre encompasses much of the *bildingsroman.* When the reader first encounters Adeline, she is a helpless elder girl in the hands of brigands. By the close of the narrative, she is a poised young woman who has survived threats to her life and who has saved other people from peril. The emotional see-saw that Adeline seems obliged to undergo amounts to no less than a concatenated passage from childhood to young womanhood. This is a personal growth experience akin to Lyra's leaving Jordan College that would never have taken place had she, Adeline, stayed in the convent.

The majority of nineteenth-century fictional heroes and heroines improve in the course of their narratives: Catherine Morland, Esther Summerson, Jane Eyre, Pip and indeed, Estella, Paula Power and George Somerset are among these. However, toward the close of the century, the tone of literature darkened and a series of protagonists became entrapped by their own follies. Eleanor's determination to get into the estate, on arriving at Hill House, is on parallel with that of a gothic heroine determined to enter mainstream life. It is her stubbornness in her refusal to leave that destroys her. In contrast to Eleanor is Lyra, who sensed her time to leave Jordan College was due. She experiences her growing up outside of the castle walls, proves herself worthy of it and eventually returns.

Before closing this chapter, it is essential to provide an outline of the literary archetype that was emerging in tandem with the gothic sub-heroine. In the latter decades of the eighteenth century, the *Byronic hero* was born.

The Byronic hero

As time passed, the romantic hero gradually became a stock archetype of the gothic sub-genre. What is a Romantic hero? Generally, he is the direct descendant of the chivalric knight and over the centuries, he has wended his way into story, song, and movie plot. He is handsome, confident and blessed with the ability to ride roughshod over life's challenges, often astride a fine horse with sword in hand or arrow quiver slung over broad shoulder. In spite of this military prowess, he never hurts anyone, except to preserve himself or to win the hand of the fair lady. Indoors he is as socially charming as he is swashbuckling in the saddle seat. Even if he is not a 'gentleman' in the familial sense, his background ever bears a tinge of mystery. He may be the illegitimate son of a nobleman, given over to peasants at birth or abandoned and saved and suckled by wolves. Or his personal qualities simply make up for any familial deficit. Whatever, he is eminently suited as the life partner of the gothic heroine, often as her ticket to society.

This is not difficult to understand; a handsome – and brave – young man proved a useful archetype in a narrative in which a villain went in pursuit of the lovely, young heroine, not least because it provided scope for a love match at the conclusion. In Walpole's narrative, Theodore fulfils this role – and readers can identify their own hero (or anti-hero) in the remainder of the narratives. But what is the *Byronic hero* and why, in the nineteenth century, did he replace traditional gallants such as the Theodore of Walpole's narrative, and his namesake in Radcliffe's narrative? Broadly speaking, the Byronic hero is attractive in a conventional, male way, brave and distinguished: most often for physical prowess, less often for cultural attainment. He tends to be youthful but old enough to have lived a little and to have endured the trials that artistically furrow his (almost always) handsome brow. Whatever his attainments, whether rich or poor, he must possess an air, an attitude of being his own person, and of a disinclination to conform to social convention. Mr Darcy of *Pride & Prejudice* is a fine example of a wealthy Byronic hero.

If a Byronic hero is poverty-stricken, he makes up for this by achieving something remarkable in the course of the narrative, usually to impress the female love interest. In *Wuthering Heights* by Emily Brontë, following his rejection by Catherine Earnshaw, Heathcliff goes away and returns three years later, an improbably rich man. Another trait is his solitariness. Never comfortable in society, the Byronic hero likes to wander in remote places, usually to brood upon whatever has blighted his life either in reality or in perception. Whatever his condition, the Byronic hero carries with him a perpetual air of mystery, and the reader – and the heroine – gain the impression that he has been hurt psychologically by an incident in his life. Much of the narrative consists of the heroine trying to pierce this fog of mystery, to get to his heart, in every sense of the word. Here, the reader may conflate the Byronic hero with the earlier-defined tragic hero. But whereas the tragic hero has had his career and/or life stopped in its tracks by unfortunate events and seeks to regain control of his life, the Byronic hero seems determined to evade sociability.

Even when the Byronic hero is finally seated at a comfortable fireside, communing with friends and spouse, the reader gains the impression that he would much rather be in isolation or travelling to a remote place. After all, would Edward Rochester have settled so happily with Jane Eyre if he had not been maimed and disabled in the fire in which Berthe Mason perished? And if Henry Tilney – a romantic hero on the cusp of the Byronic – hadn't married Catherine Morland, would he ever have become reconciled to the society into which 'roads' and 'newspapers' were encroaching, and his suspicion of the 'voluntary spies' that peopled once intimate neighbourhoods (NA, 186)? Indeed, Henry's speech pre-empts that of William de Stancy in Thomas Hardy's novel *A Laodicean*, written eighty years later: 'that (telegraph) wire is a nuisance, to my mind; such constant intercourse with the outer world is bad for our romance' (AL, 228). It could be that de Stancy's worries are at a practical level: Paula might be courting another lover? But it is just as likely that his anxiety stems from the encroachment of technology into his rural idyll. Overall, the later gothic heroine in tandem with the Byronic hero served as an element of conflict in the narrative, a method of infiltrating the Apollonian with the Dionysian.

For decades before Walpole published his book, Swiss philosopher and novelist, Jean-Jacques Rousseau (1712-1778), discoursed on the nature of humanity and education, most notably through his work, *Emile, or an Education*, published 1762. Broadly, his argument runs that man is at his happiest and most productive when he is unfettered by the formalities of society (AB, 162). The short answer to the above question is that the Byronic hero served as a saturnine foil for the contrasting sociability of the gothic heroine, without which the realistic narrative could be rendered rather insipid. The union of Catherine and Henry serves as a paradigm of the contrast between female and male wants and needs. If the reader has accepted Catherine as a gothic protagonist, then she has struggled and succeeded to join society on her own terms. Meanwhile, Henry, in his railing against 'voluntary spies' of said society and in spite of his virtues, the reader must wonder: what will their marriage turn into?

An exploration of Romanticism may provide a fuller answer, the Yale Dictionary meaning which runs: *a personal, partly spiritual apprehension of nature as environment and life-force, as envisioned by poets and painters.* On the matter of the word 'romantic', critic David Wright quotes F.W. Bateson on the use of it between 1650 and 1659, how rare it was and how its meaning varied (Wright, xii). But there may be an historical precedent for the copious use of the word at that time. The era between 1649 and 1660 was the most bloody in the history of England, an era that saw the execution of a reigning monarch and innumerable clashes between opposing Cavalier and Roundhead forces. Poets, in an era when stage plays were banned, sought to create a literature that appealed to a new sensibility, that of the *individual* striving in a hostile world.

The restoration of the monarchy saw the publication of John Milton's epic, *Paradise Lost*. Milton, a parliamentarian who narrowly escaped execution, had espoused the Puritan religion of the Roundheads.[23]

Paradise Lost is actually a rewriting of the Book of Genesis in which Milton endows all of the biblical players – God, Satan, Adam, Eve, the serpent, the angel Raphael – and others, with disparate personalities. It is also the parable of an individual – or two individuals – struggling in a highly organised environment. But the more secular message of Milton's parable was to lie dormant for another century. The decades that followed saw many writers emerge who excelled in critical essays, political pamphlets, morality plays and satires (AB, 120). The political satire bloomed for about one hundred years until Walpole picked up the baton of personal sensibility once more and published *Otranto*. Why this sudden – it seems – sea-change in literary taste?

The Glorious Revolution in 1688 saw many political changes among the

---

[23]Gordon Campbell and Thomas N. Corns, *John Milton: Life, Work and Thought* (Oxford: Oxford University Press, 2008, 'Surviving the Restoration', (pp307-320)

ruling classes, both the monarchy and the government, for example, the sudden deposition of James II in favour of his sister, Mary, and her Dutch-born husband, William. Many writers, among them William Congreve (1670-1729) and Andrew Marvell (1621-1678), indirectly attacked almost every aspect of public life, holding the rulers up to scrutiny and even ridicule. Jonathan Swift's (1667-1745) seeming fairy tale, *Gulliver's Travels* is actually a satire on the government of the time (AB, 156). With this turmoil in public life, the interests of the individual had taken a back seat. It was not until the early 1700s that the Hanoverian King George I was in place, his family the ancestors of the present British monarchy, that the rise of the new, romantic sensibility, one that appealed to individual interests, could begin. With the suppression of the Highland rebels in 1745, the mid-eighteenth century found Britain in a period of political stability. With public life, peace and a kind of prosperity in place, the individual could now focus on the, well, individual.

And that individual was not, at heart, a happy one. Remember the earlier reference to Jean-Jacques Rousseau and his assertion that man is at his happiest and most productive when he is unfettered by the formalities of society? This philosophy, in tandem with fictional heroes on the pattern of the unschooled and gregarious Theodore of *Otranto*, became a token of free-thinking writers and their readership. The idea of a peasant, answerable to no one and beneficial to all about him, surrounded by the glow of a mythic past, was subsumed into popular imagination and resurfaced in the literature of the eighteenth century.

Anthony Burgess cites the 'key year' for English Romanticism as 1798, when William Wordsworth published *Lyrical Ballads* (AB, 166). Throughout Wordsworth's lifetime, other poets with claims to the name 'romantic' emerged; Samuel Taylor Coleridge (1772-1834), Percy Bysshe Shelley (1792-1822), John Keats (1795-1821), and Lord Byron (1788-1824), which defined the emerging type of hero. To explore how and why the work of these poets captured public imagination are many and varied, and are beyond the scope of this text. But in a nutshell, it is as if the romantic sensibility that writers of a century earlier had fleetingly referred to, and that had slumbered through the decades, had suddenly awakened, nudged into life by Walpole and brought to full consciousness by Wordsworth and other writers. David Wright asserts that Romanticism was the birth of a new kind of sensibility that sprung from the desire to be an individual rather than just one of the mass of people who toiled all day to meet the demands of the new economy brought on by the Industrial Revolution (Wright, xix). It is not difficult to understand why, when unable to escape the demands of a highly-organized society, the individual sought ways to avoid the crushing impersonality of the environment. Wright also cites 'human psychology' as a tenet of Romanticism (Wright, xix). Focussing on the word 'psychology', it may or may not be that our progress in psychology took place *because* of Romanticism. But it cannot be a coincidence that, in the later nineteenth century, Sigmund Freud and William James began the body of research and writings upon which the present-day practice of psychology is based?

I state once more that the Byronic hero served as a saturnine foil for the contrasting sociability of the gothic heroine, providing the realistic narrative with the measure of conflict that is essential to drama. Here, the reader may perceive a link between the Byronic hero and what Bettelheim deems the 'animal groom' character in a fairy tale (Bettelheim, 282-285). Generally, in a typical animal groom tale, an animal or animal-like male character pays court to a recalcitrant heroine. But gradually, she gets to know him and perceives the finer human qualities underneath his more bestial veneer. Eventually, she demonstrates her love for him and instantly, he becomes the handsome prince/romantic hero of her dreams. *Beauty and the Beast* is one of the best-known examples of this type of tale, the original version which was written in the seventeenth century by Madame de Villeneuve. The motif of a female protagonist overcoming her aversion to a less-than-perfect male resurges in the nineteenth century, exemplified by the relation between Jane Eyre and Edward Rochester.

As the nineteenth century progressed, the Byronic hero faded from literature, most likely because of the moral ambivalences that arose in tandem with the infiltration of insights into psychology. The female protagonist no longer needed to do battle with her interests in conflict with that of a dark, brooding and handsome male; she had her own inner demons to deal with. Paula Power gains the fortitude to reject the morally dubious William de Stancy; Henry James's Governess's 'hero' never puts in an appearance and Eleanor Vance learns, too late, that journeys do not *always* end in lovers meeting. The Byronic hero makes a brief resurrection in the form of Maxim de Winter who thrives socially before his own actions serve to mentally crush him, and seriously attenuate the life of his young bride.

By the twentieth century, Byron-ism had become a mode of behaviour which either gender could espouse or indeed, venerate. Shirley Jackson's text takes a definitive turn when Eleanor begins her rampage and stands outside of Mrs Montague's door, pounding upon it (HH, 229). Mrs Montague invites whatever entity to come inside and the reader may wonder forever what would have happened if Eleanor had gone into the room, what words would have been exchanged if the Doctor's wife had discovered that the activity outside of her bedroom door was not a supernatural 'wronged' character from an earlier century, complete with a Baroque tale of woe, but the rather unremarkable young woman who was taking part in her, Mrs Montague's, husband's experiment. But the author affords us a clue in words spoken by Mrs Montague, a little further on in the text, just following Eleanor's rescue from the spiral staircase (and certain death) by Luke Sanderson: 'This childish nonsense has almost certainly destroyed any chance of manifestations *tonight*, I can tell you' (HH, 236). The reader must wonder: if Mrs Montague believes that she can help the dead, then why is she unable to offer counsel to the living?

Throughout the various essays of this book, I explore the ways that 'psychological' thinking has permeated fiction writing and gothic tropes, most notably in tales of the supernatural. I begin my chapter, **Maid in the Mirror**, with a discourse on the significance of the past, whether real or imagined, in the lives of many fictional protagonists.

Maid in the Mirror

Into the past ♦ Seduction, beauty and the maiden ♦ The maid in the mirror ♦ Curiosity and the maiden ♦ The Ice Maiden ♦ Madness and the maiden ♦ The adolescent sleeep ♦ Maid of the future

The chapter explores the question: how and why the feisty and vibrant eighteenth-century badass lass transformed into the vapid, Victorian housebound 'angel', wan as the dust-covers on the drawing-room furniture? In the twentieth century, the heroine transitioned once more into a neurotic though not always self-aware entity, such as Eleanor Vance who believes that she 'belongs' in Hill House and the Bridget Jones-type heroine, worrying about the size of her derrière. But the story of the maid begins with Adeline of *Romance of the Forest*, whom the reader rarely sees even looking in a mirror.

Into the past

In my Introduction, I attempt to explain our all-out fascination with *the past*, a time and place where no-one has been and yet everyone, it seems, retains fond memories of. To repeat: 'The past is ... the monochrome experience, even when painted in full colour by the words of the author. And the present is the full-on colour experience, even when the writer is describing the present-day world in terms of banality and monotony. The colour image is ... composed of strips of garish and even, clashing colour. It is literal, immediate and insistent. The image all but drags the viewer into this immediacy. In certain cases, this literality can provide an enjoyable experience. But it is never a subtle, evocative or poetic one.'

In gothic literature, the yearning for the past works at a number of levels. Horace Walpole provides the reader with a remote past, *The Castle of Otranto* being set during the French Crusades, any time between the late eleventh century and to almost the end of the thirteenth century. This combination of vagueness and remoteness adds a sense of the picaresque to Walpole's narrative, for instance the cavalier way that Manfred condemns Theodore to his execution and the ease with which, later on, the reader learns that Manfred has kidnapped Isabella.

One generation later, Ann Radcliffe also places protagonist Adeline in the past, albeit less remote. In Chapter XXIII, the date of Adeline's father's death – and her birth – is revealed as 1642, one year before the reign of Louis XIV began. The concurrence of the majority of Adeline's life with France's extravagant and despotic monarch may have been a deliberate ploy on the part of Radcliffe to add a dimension of exoticism to the narrative. But it is still a definite past with laws, a functioning judiciary and parliament. The reader receives this sense at the outset of the narrative when La Motte is fleeing Paris, away from 'his creditors and the persecution of the laws' (ROTF, 1). The trial of the Marquis towards the end of the narrative reminds the reader that La Motte has returned to these 'laws', and that the days of the feudal past, of arbitrary executions and imprisonments, are well nigh over.

The reader receives another nod to the more civilized 'present' when the author states: 'The passion of Louis De La Motte yielded at length to the powers of absence and necessity. He still loved Adeline, but it was with the placid tenderness of friendship' (ROTF, 363). The younger La Motte represents modernity; he is not going to subject Adeline to sexual coercion. About half a decade following the publication of Radcliffe's novel, Jane Austen began writing the narrative that she eventually named *Northanger Abbey* though it was not published until 1817. As Marilyn Butler explains in the 'Introduction' to the narrative, the past *is* present but treated in a very particular way (NA, xxx).

Set in a present recognisable to the early nineteenth-century reader, the author pokes sly fun at the erstwhile mania for the fictional past, targetting both readership and protagonist Catherine Morland. Austen does this subtly through the voice of Henry Tilney, whom critic Marilyn Butler describes as the 'fictional double' for the author (NA, xliv). Henry says: 'Will your mind not misgive you, when you find yourself in this gloomy chamber – too lofty and extensive for you, with only the feeble rays of a single lamp to take in its size – its walls hung with tapestry exhibiting figures as large as life, and the bed, of dark green stuff or purple velvet, presenting even a funereal appearance? Will your heart not sink within you?' (NA, 150).

Although Catherine deflects Henry's humour: 'Oh! But this will not happen to me, I am sure', the modernity of the Abbey takes her unawares. From here, the narrative leaves aside harmless fun and descends into a more insidious tone when Catherine insists upon placing her own construction upon the possible fate of Henry's late mother. The disgusted Henry responds: 'And from these circumstances ... you infer perhaps the probability of some negligence ... of something still less pardonable' (NA, 185).

The aggrieved Catherine owns up and regrets her yearnings for a Tilney family mystery. Later in the century, in his realist narrative, *A Laocidean*, Thomas Hardy created a female character who openly and earnestly longed for an 'invented' past: 'I wish I had a well-known line of ancestors' (AL, 136). The tussle between the ancient and the modern are eminently represented in Paula Power, the female protagonist of the novel, wealthy daughter of a deceased railway engineer and in possession of an ancient castle left to her by him. In the narrative, the reader initially sees Paula through the eyes of architect George Somerset, who befriends and guides her when she decides to 'restore' the ancient pile.

Susan Brownmiller places a humorous slant on the feminine penchant for the mythic past: stating that, in order to remain feminine, a woman must look to the past.[24]

Horace Walpole knew what he was doing when he transformed an old farmstead by the banks of the Thames in Twickenham into his own vision of the 'gothic' past, Strawberry Hill Villa. It was but a short step to writing his first novel. His genius lay in sensing that the eighteenth-century palate, jaded from literary satire, political pamphletting and didactic moral fiction, longed for something new. In attempting to reconstitute the past, both in literature and architecture, Walpole had invented his own, in the words of John Berger, vision of the future.[25] The joke is that the Regency woman was already living in *a* past; in a world jaded from the Baroque excesses of Europe, images of Regency England show women clad in shift dresses, their graceful and simple

---

[24]Susan Brownmiller, *Femininity* (London: Paladin Books, 1986), p62. Subsequent references will be to this edition and will be inserted parenthetically into the text, for example "(SB, 62)".

[25] John Berger, *Ways of Seeing* (London: Penguin Books, 1972), p139. Subsequent references will be to this edition and will be inserted parenthetically into the text, for example "(Berger, 139)"

lines derived from the illustrations found on artefacts from the newly-excavated Grecian ruins, no doubt made fashionable by the Grand Tour.²⁶ The towering head-dresses of the earlier 1700s were now fallen from grace and had been replaced by utilitarian styles that sat close to the female scalp and were easily accommodated underneath low-rise caps and bonnets. But even these styles eventually dated.

The artistic movement known as pre-Raphaelite began in 1848, possibly after, with the publication of Alfred Lord Tennyson's poem, *The Lady of Shalott*. Whatever its origin, the pre-Raphaelite trend in art nodded to an imagined past of long-haired maidens wandering in flower gardens and remote scenes of country cottages and castles. Like all trends, it was not to last and popularity for the 'pre-Raph' was already on the wane when John Waterhouse produced his painterly equivalent of the Tennyson poem, the *Lady Of Shalott* (Tate Britain) in 1888. But in the intervening years, an adoring public flocked to galleries and exhibitions to see paintings by William Holman Hunt, John Everett Millais and Dante Gabriel Rossetti. All over Britain, wealthy patrons commissioned architects to construct buildings with turrets, machiolated parapets and arched windows. And Hardy's Paula Power became the literary embodiment of that yearning. When Paula defends herself to Somerset against medievalism stating that she associates herself with Greek culture, her defence is quite profound (AL, 108). This association with ancient Greek culture is actually a symptom of her inner tussle between the established church and her own 'pagan' brand of Christianity, one of the many pairs of conflicting forces in the narrative. But it matters not to the reader and indeed, not to Paula.

What is more insidious and dangerous is Paula's attempt to chain herself to a scion of the ancient family that once owned the castle. Her love interest is William de Stancy who, in a moment of irony, appears when Paula is gazing longingly at a portrait of his look-alike ancestor. It is but one of the moments when the story-line of *A Laodicean* threatens to fall into satire, a mythos that the subtle and skilled Hardy just about steers the narrative clear of: but Hardy was writing in an environment much changed since Austen's day. The forward-looking Austen simply wasn't interested in 'the past', either chronologically nor as the fount of an individual's ills of the present (NA, xxx). Hardy's

---

²⁶John Summerson, *The Classical Language of Architecture* (London: Thames and Hudson Ltd, 1963), p95. Subsequent references will be to this edition and will be inserted parenthetically into the text, for example '(Summerson, 95)'

contemporary, Charles Dickens, took a different view of matters when he presented (arguably) the most psychologically-damaged character in fiction, Miss Havisham.

Today, the name of this unhappy literary character is almost a cliché, jilted twenty years before the narrative opens on her wedding day and insisting upon wearing her bridal gown and veil ever since, in the vicinity of the uneaten and rotting wedding feast, a disquieting metaphor of her own mentality. Dickens paints a picture that haunts the reader as much as protagonist Pip. Even when out of her company, Pip fancies that he sees: 'A figure all in yellow white, with but one shoe to the feet, and it hung so, that I could see that the faded trimmings of the dress were like earthy paper, and that the face was Miss Havisham's, with a movement going over the whole countenance, as if she were trying to call me' (GE, 54). Few readers would wish for such a fate, so was the author merely being theatrical in his creation of Miss Havisham – or was he sending out a warning? David Lean, director of the 1946 movie based upon the novel, hits upon a truth when he depicts Estella in danger of succumbing to the same fate as her foster mother, on the failure of her marriage to Bentley Drummle. A warning to young women: don't live in the past. Contrary to Dickens's literary ending, Pip's love saves Estella.

But in book or movie, Miss Havisham and Estella have that modicum of personal choice that ever accrues to the well-to-do. Far more cruel is the fate of Mrs de Winter in Daphne du Maurier's novel, *Rebecca*. The beginning of the narrative is actually the end of the story, and the reader perceives the female narrator acting as companion and carer to a ruin of a puzzled-looking man.[27] The narrative progresses to the back story and the reader learns with shock that the man is actually the companion's husband, the protagonist herself formerly a companion to a wealthy woman. Mrs de Winter simply cannot escape the past, not her own nor her husband's, nor that of his late wife. Even the fancy-dress ball that takes place at Manderley serves as a metaphor of the yearnings of the county set that eagerly flock to it. At every turn, she is reminded of whom she is *not* by Maxim's sister, by Maxim's grandmother and of course, by the insidious Mrs Danvers, that is, she is not the late, glittering Rebecca. Presently, the narrator falls to masquerading feelings of what it may have

---

[27]Daphne Du Maurier, *Rebecca* (London: Virago Press, 2003), p5. Subsequent references will be to this edition and will be inserted parenthetically into the text, for example "(R, 5)"

been like to *be* Rebecca (R, 226).

The rebuke that Maxim delivers is just one of many that Mrs de Winter receives throughout the narrative. Among the more sinister episodes is that of Mrs Danvers hoodwinking her into believing that she can win Maxim's admiration by dressing as an ancestor of the de Winter family. With his subsequent disgust and disdain of his new wife, the reader may feel that he deserves his bankrupt, dispossessed state revealed at the beginning of the narrative. And in a metaphorical way, he is depicted chain smoking, that is, destroying himself with the same element with which Manderley has been destroyed - by fire.

Seduction, beauty and the maiden

In *Romance of the Forest*, the reader perceives the figure of Adeline for the first time, through the eyes of La Motte: 'A habit of grey camlet, with short flashed sleeves, shewed, but did not adorn, her figure: it was thrown open at the bosom, upon which part of her hair had fallen in disorder, while the light veil hastily thrown on, had, in her confusion, been suffered to fall back. Every moment of farther observation heightened the surprize of La Motte, and interested him more warmly in her favour' (ROTF, 7). Whether or not the eighteenth-century Radcliffe took time to research the details of seventeenth-century dress hardly matters. The question to ask is: why do writers dwell so much on the details of their protagonists' dress? In his book, *Ways of Seeing*, John Berger explains how the female creates an aura about herself of clothing, hairstyle, voice and even household accoutrements (Berger, 46). In summary, the female protagonist may manipulate other people's image of her through her dress. Berger's argument is broadly that the female creates her own subjective version of herself to present to other people. And she creates this version with visual and audial contrivances, clothing, voice deliverance and even, the décor of her immediate surroundings.

In *Northanger Abbey*, Mrs Allen is obsessed with muslin and Isabella is passionate about bonnets. In *Jane Eyre*, the young women of Lowood Institution are cruelly denied their womanhood by being forced to contain their maturing bodies within clothing more suited to that of the young children: 'Above twenty of those clad in this costume were full-grown girls; or rather young women: it suited them ill and gave an air of oddity, even to the prettiest' (JE, 47). Manager Mr Brocklehurst denies even the right of the young women to full heads of hair: 'the young persons before us has a string of hair twisted in plaits which vanity itself might have woven: these, I repeat, must be cut off' (JE, 64). To explore his attitude towards the more extravagant adornment of his own daughters would be to diversify; here, his words can be construed as an echo of his fears of the budding sexuality of the poverty-stricken Lowood pupils. Subsequently, Charlotte Brontë provides the reader with a commentary on the changing details of Jane's dress, from her time as a pupil at Lowood to the dress code required by Rochester while she is governess at Thornfield, to his and Jane's tussle over the nature of the garments that she allows him to adorn her with upon their engagement, to the metaphorical destruction of her wedding veil by Berthe Mason.

In Hardy's narrative, William Dare is aware of the importance of context when he is trying to raise his father's interest in the prospect of marriage to Paula Power. So, he lays a scheme to have William de Stancy observe Paula when she is at her most apparently nubile, that is, when she is exercising in her gym. The scheme works and de Stancy observes: 'the clouds, till that time thick in the sky, broke away from the upper heaven, and allowed the noonday sun pour down through the lantern upon her, irradiating her with a warm light that was incarnadined by her pink doublet and hose, and reflected in upon her face' (AL, 197). George Somerset is ever aware of the details of Paula's clothing 'a straw hat having a bent-up brim lined with plaited silk' while Maxim de Winter subverts every attempt by his new bride to go shopping for clothes (AL, 108), (R, 68). Indeed, Mrs de Winter spends the earlier months of their marriage dressed in the worn old suit that she was wearing when they first met. She soon discovers that glamorous feminine clothing puts him in mind of his detested, late wife. On arrival at Hill House, Eleanor Vance contrasts her own dismal attire and attempts at fashion with the glamour of fashionable Theodora (HH, 41). Of course, this displacement of physical beauty by sartorial devices was possibly an attempt by writers to avoid confusion with the changing nature of beauty throughout the ages, as humorously documented by Susan Brownmiller when she quotes 'the Gothic ideal' (SB, 8). The ideal that Brownmiller alludes to is, of course, the medieval notion of beauty. But whether medieval or eighteenth century gothic, the question of whether Walpole, Radcliffe or Reeve, et al, were aware of either 'Gothic ideal' is a moot one: even within accepted definitions, the concept of physical beauty was just too subjective and nebulous for the realist writers of the nineteenth century to grapple with.

Whether contrived or natural, it does beg the question: how did the cult of beauty begin? Until the middle of the eighteenth century, beauty had been the preserve of Renaissance artists in their depiction of the Madonna, and of angels and saints. Society and aristocratic beauties abounded but this quality had no currency among the middle classes. The typical, seventeenth-century depiction of a middle-class woman was of a blunt-featured creature dressed in plain linen, with woollen stockings and stout leather shoes. The reader has only to look at the paintings by seventeenth-century artist, Pieter de Hooch, to appreciate this. For example, *Woman and a Maid with a Pail in a Courtyard* (c. 1660), shows a middle-class woman seated serenely while her young maid mops the black and white tiles of the courtyard. Although the women are of different social classes, their proximity in the image indicates that they share the same values, cleanliness and industry.

Being privately alluring to her husband was another matter, but her required public profile was a combination of piety, honesty and a capacity for domestic labour. In the eighteenth century, the excavations of Pompeii and Herculaneum and other ancient ruins, sparked off new ideals. The rebirth of classicism gave rise to the cult of the aesthete, spreading a new sensibility outside of an elite minority. Renaissance architects and writers, among them Antonio Palladio, laid down the correct proportions of buildings, and the Greek Golden Section laid down ideal measurements for geometric curves (Summerson, 13). In the age of Enlightenment, beauty became a science as much as an art, and artists set out to define it. William Hogarth published his book, the *Analysis of Beauty* in 1753, and in it, he lays out the principles by which, to quote Ernst Gombrich, 'an undulating line will always be more beautiful than an angular one'.[28] I repeat the description of Adeline's clothing: '(the dress) was thrown open at the bosom, upon which part of her hair had fallen in disorder, while the light veil hastily thrown on, had, in her confusion, been suffered to fall back'. No sharp edges in evidence here.

In the longer term, developments in aesthetics equipped writers with a sophisticated vocabulary by which to describe beauty. One use that writers found for the *concept* of beauty is referred to in my section on the mythos of romance, namely the checker-board effect, where every good character is

---

[28] E.H. Gombrich, *Art & Illusion: A study in the psychology of pictorial representation* (London, Phaidon Press Limited, 1960), p464.

balanced out by the 'moral opposite', a corresponding evil character. This device is a less intense variation of the one that the reader encounters in fairy tales, the dichotomy of the beautiful princess and her ugly relatives. In *Northanger Abbey*, the 'almost pretty' Catherine encounters the lovely, flirtatious and shallow Isabella. In *Bleak House*, the fair and privileged Ada Clare – a name that means 'light' – befriends the dark Esther, whose origins are lost in obscurity (Frye, 101).

In the opening chapters of *Northern Lights*, Lyra is seduced by the glamour of Mrs Coulter.[29] Eventually, Lyra's eyes are opened to the true nature of the woman that fosters her. In the longer term, the cult of the visual promulgated the occurrence of another device in literature.

The maid in the mirror

The modern woman who does not field a mirror amongst her possessions, either personal or household, is very unusual indeed. So accustomed are we to associating mirror-gazing with the feminine, that it is shocking to be aware that mirrors, as we know them, have only become ubiquitous in recent centuries. Paradoxically, the earliest mirror-gazer in literature was the male Narcissus of Greek mythology who fell in love with his own image as he gazed into a pond. I cite John Berger's argument, namely that, while the male unconsciously seeks to influence the actions of other people by their objective opinion of him, the female creates her own subjective version of herself to present to other people. And she creates this version with visual and auditory contrivances, modulated voice and evocative clothing, thus the constant requirement for the feedback inherent in a mirror. Unlike the wicked Queen in *Snow White*, Narcissus is not looking for information or approval 'who is the fairest?', he simply *is*. Right through the nineteenth century, the Byronic hero wanted to reflect in the adoring and imploring eyes of the females surrounding him. Gilbert and Gubar cite from a poem 'The Buried Life', by Matthew Arnold exploring how the poet expresses the wish to read the soul of the female he is addressing, but the reader may surmise that what the poet really wants is to see his own reflection (G&G, 402). In *The Tenant of Wildfell Hall* by Anne Brontë, Arthur Huntingdon objects to his wife Helen's

---

[29]Philip Pullman, *His Dark Materials* (London: Everyman's Library, 2011), p61. Subsequent references will be to this edition and will be inserted parenthetically into the text, for example "(HDM, 61)"

piety, claiming that her devotion to the Almighty must mean that she can't be that dedicated to *him*.

Shakespeare brought mirror-gazing to apotheosis in Richard II, when he externalises the monarch's inner turmoil by making him perform a long and eloquent speech in front of a glass mirror, which he then shatters: *Hath Sorrow struck/So many blows upon this face of mine/And made no deeper wounds?* (Act 4, Scene 1). Like Narcissus, the monarch is not seeking approval but is conducting a heart-searching dialogue with his innermost self. A century later, John Milton promulgated the narrative of the female-as-vain in *Paradise Lost*, the rewriting of Genesis, when the newly-fledged Eve gazes into the water and ponders upon what she sees: 'What there thou seest fair creature is thyself'.[30] In *Romance of the Forest*, the *reader* becomes the mirror, the author relaying information at intervals of what Adeline looks like: 'She was now in her nineteenth year; her figure of the middling size and turned to the most exquisite proportion; her hair was dark auburn, her eyes blue, and whether they sparkled with intelligence, or melted with tenderness, they were equally attractive' (ROTF, 29). In *Adam Bede*, George Elliot's anti-heroine Hetty Sorrel takes delight in privately dressing up in purchased baubles and posturing in front of a strip of mirror, a contrivance that says much about the subject's role in the narrative.

The passivity of Henry James's Governess is projected in her first encounter with a full-length mirror: 'the long glasses in which, for the first time, I could see myself from head to foot.'[31] As I explained earlier, the heroine *is becoming* while the Byronic hero *is*. But the Governess is not constructing a new nature; she is learning about herself as she has always been. The reader becomes aware of this when the Governess perceives a person staring through the window at her: 'it was as if I had always been looking at him for years and had known about him always' (TOTS, 142). Faced with herself, the Governess has a choice: create a new (and better?) self or see herself as she is now.

Perhaps the most profound use of reflection takes place in *Northanger*

---

[30] John Milton, *Paradise Lost*, ed. John Leonard (London: Penguin Classics, 2000), book 4:460-468. Subsequent references will be to this edition and will be inserted parenthetically into the text, for example '(PL, 4:460-468)'

[31] Henry James, *The Turn of the Screw and Other Stories* (New York: Oxford University Press, 1992), p124. Subsequent references will be to this edition and will be inserted parenthetically into the text, for example '(TOTS, 124)'

Abbey, when Mrs Morland hands a broken Catherine, still smarting from her experience at Northanger Abbey, a book of moral essays, entitled *The Mirror*, which the older woman believes will do Catherine 'good' (NA, 225). Following her humiliation, Catherine must now use a literary looking device to construct a better self, in the 'mysterious enclosure' or mirror, that Gilbert and Gubar speak of (G&G, 144). Throughout the nineteenth century, mirrors occurred more frequently in literature, possibly because of the publication of *The Lady of Shalott* in 1834. By then, the mirror had ceased to be a 'magic' object and became a device that showed the viewing subject a truth about him or herself – in many cases, *the* truth. In *Bleak House*, Esther Summerson sees her mother, Lady Dedlock, for the first time and experiences the disquieting sensation of seeing a 'broken recollection' of her own face (BH, 304).

Inside of Hill House, Eleanor Vance sees her own reflection on the polished floor, a suggestion by the author that Eleanor is about to become enmeshed into the personality of the house, its 'personality' suggested by the anthropomorphism of an earlier scene. Upon seeing her reflection, Eleanor thinks: '*I don't like it here*', suggesting that events in the house are going to show her a side of herself that she might not like (HH, 37). Again, it occurs to the reader that Eleanor might try to construct a more forthright self, but Eleanor does not.

In certain instances, the mirror does reflect a 'new' self, one that the subject may not always like to see. Following her deception of Mrs Coulter's, Lyra Belaqua contemplates her own image in a glamorous looking-glass, the author's way of indicating that Lyra's life will never be the same again (HDM, 70).

Curiosity and the maiden

Susan Brownmiller, bolstered by the result of a Broverman and Broverman survey, presents women as 'buffeted on the high seas of emotion', a bundle of contradicting instincts, by turns scared and fearful, followed by happy and hopeful, deeply in love and just as deeply in despair (SB, 161-2). Whether this picture is accurate or not is eminently arguable. What is evident is that literature has ever presented us with the woman *as led* by emotion rather than logic and reason, and one emotion stands out from the others: curiosity.

Of curiosity, Edmund Burke wrote in his book *A Philosophical Enquiry into the Origin of Our Ideas of the Sublime and Beautiful,* 'Some degree of novelty must be one of those materials in every instrument which works upon the mind; and curiosity blends itself more or less with all our passions' (Burke, 27). Coming from the pen of the same author that wrote '(perfection) in the female sex, almost always carries with it an idea of imperfection. Women are very sensible of this; for which reason, they learn to lisp, to totter in their walk, to counterfeit weakness, even sickness', this area of his polemic is surprisingly free of gender association (Burke, xviii). Most significantly, the *Enquiry* provided a blueprint for novelists of the time on how to excite emotion in both the reader and how to elucidate it in characters. The first literary woman that many young readers encounter is the biblical Eve, derivative of Adam and ever his inferior (Berger, 48). In classical literature, the reader sees Pandora, the young maiden who was unable to help opening a certain container and unleashed upon the world all of the ills that we have encountered since.

Psyche was unable to resist gazing upon the face of lover Eros, and thus found herself cast out into the world (Bettelheim, 291-295). And Eurydice could not help looking back when lover Orpheus was rescuing her from the Underworld, and she thus found herself condemned to spend six months of every month there. Her fate echoes that of Lot's wife of the Bible who was also unable to help 'looking back' when fleeing the burning Sodom, and was transformed into a pillar of salt (SB, 169). Right down through literary history, readers and perusers of fiction have been presented by curious females, eliciting information from perhaps where they should not, from the Sleeping Beauty's curiosity about a spinning wheel causing her to prick her finger and fall into a deep sleep, to Goldilocks developing a fascination with the accoutrements of Baby Bear, to Little Red Riding Hood straying off of the path laid out by her elders and thus finding herself gobbled by a wolf. In the nineteenth century, Alice of Wonderland fame follows a white rabbit and finds herself descending to the fantastical world that has since given rise to literary cliches.

But even writers of realist literature found a use for the curious woman. Catherine Morland spends her first night in Northanger Abbey wondering about the mysterious documents in the trunk at the foot of the bed. Later in the narrative, she wanders about the Abbey, straying into a space for which she is 'forbidden' to enter, seeking to acquaint herself with details from the life – and possibly death – of the late Mrs Tilney. Indeed, her actions almost lose her the love of Henry Tilney. Almost. In *The Turn of the Screw*, Henry James's Governess broadly hints that she spends much of her time in the village near Bly, digging for information about the former servants of the house (TOTS, 152). This situation causes her to make deductions that eventually lead to disastrous consequences.

Certainly, literature is filled with curious males: Mr Guppy cannot help exploring Esther Summerson's past – but he is a man in love. Arthur Kipps carefully combs through the lumber in Eel Marsh house, seeking out the information that will help him solve the mystery of the deceased Jennet Humphrye – but he is a lawyer at work. And Dr Jekyll, like Dr Frankenstein before him, seeks to uncover the secrets of life and nature: 'I was driven to reflect deeply and inveterately on that hard law of life which lies at the root of religion' (DMJH, 42). But these are practising scientists. In summary, the investigating fictional male is possessed of an agenda that places him above mere curiosity. The exception would seem to be Mr Rochester, who takes great interest in Jane Eyre's sketches. But throughout the episode, the reader gains the impression that Rochester wants to impress Jane with his thoughts: 'These eyes in the Evening Star ... how could you make them look so clear ... the planet above quells their rays' (JE, 126). And his manner changes abruptly when he perceives Jane neglecting her duty and orders her to 'take Adele to bed' (JE, 126). In the guise of a gypsy woman, he cross-questions her – but only to probe her feelings about *him:* 'Is it known that Mr Rochester is to be married?' (JE, 200). I have already cited Gilbert and Gubar's theory on why the dominant male may take an interest in a female, that is, any curiosity the male shows is but seeking to know what *she* thinks about *him*.

One century later, the level-headed Mrs de Winter cannot help venturing into spaces unbidden by her spouse, the hidden cove off of the beach and eventually, into the late Rebecca's bedroom, where a revealing encounter with Mrs Danvers occurs. At the outset of *His Dark Materials*, protagonist Lyra is all curiosity as she hides in the chamber where the Master of Jordan College is conducting a meeting. The intelligence gained by Lyra tips the narrative into its subsequent events. And the (female) reader is complicit in this curiosity.

In the gothic sub-genre, the female reader is invited to enter the secret world of the protagonist, sharing her wonderment and terror by turns. The Byronic hero, on the contrary, shuts us out of his world. Earlier, I explained that the major difference between the Byronic hero and the gothic heroine is the female's eagerness to find a place in society, no matter how indifferent the world seems (G&G, 402). If the hero was to assume the heroine's zest for life, he would lose his mystery, the glamour that keeps the reader – and the heroine – at arms' length. In summary, the reader is complicit in the world of the gothic heroine, sharing her emotion, invited to empathize with but not to envy her. The Byronic hero, by contrast, is set up for envy, an emotion that transmutes as sexual attraction to women. In his narrative, the Byronic hero is in a position of power while the heroine is ever in subjugation to another person's. Edmund Burke writes: 'When danger or pain press too nearly, they are incapable of giving any delight and are simply terrible; but at certain distances, and with certain modifications, they may be, and they are delightful, as we every day experience' (Burke, 34). In describing Adeline, Ann Radcliffe writes: 'Her features, which were delicately beautiful, had gained from distress an expression of captivating sweetness' (ROTF, 6). The distress that Adeline shows through the eyes of La Motte renders her even more attractive to him and indeed, the reader. But the distress of the Byronic hero had a rather different agenda.

'What the deuce to do now?' shouts Mr Rochester, when his horse slips on the ice (JE, 112). The reader can no more imagine Rochester remaining silent as he catches sight of Jane, than they can see Mr Darcy fretting over the colour of the Pemberley carpets or Heathcliff suffering the flavour of burnt soup at Wuthering Heights. Yet we can perfectly well imagine Darcy charging new wife Elizabeth with the refurbishing of his mansion, or an angry Heathcliff flinging a spoon at whatever female happened to be in sight. I remind the reader of what John Berger claims about its being the woman who carries the aura of her environment with her. If something is out of synch in his environment, it is the woman who is either the blame or remedy or both. And indeed, right to the end of the narrative, Rochester regards the practical Jane as an enchanted figure who steps inexplicably into his life: 'When you came on me in Hay Lane last night, I ... had half a mind to demand whether you bewitched my horse' (G&G, 352). Presumably, the hitherto self-sufficient Rochester can accept needing help from a socially-insignificant woman, only if she has practised magic upon him and his surroundings. Even *without* a rifle aloft and a horse at his side, the Byronic hero exuded power. As the nineteenth century progressed, this premise obliged the heroine to assume another quality.

The ice maiden

'Her beauty, touched with the languid delicacy of illness, gained from sentiment what it lost in bloom. The negligence of her dress, loosened for the purpose of freer respiration, discovered those glowing charms, which her auburn tresses, that fell in profusion over her bosom, shaded but could not conceal' (ROTF, 87)

In the above paragraph, Ann Radcliffe uses phrases such as 'glowing charms' and 'auburn tresses' to evoke the colour and drama surrounding her heroine. By contrast, in the words of Sandra Gilbert and Susan Gubar, the Victorian woman is pale of complexion and 'Passive, submissive, unawakened' (G&G, 615-6). By now, the reader may wonder how the glowing eighteenth-century heroine might have transformed into this 'passive, submissive' creature? Before she retreated into her Victorian parlour, the gothic heroine was a *tour de force* in literature. She was healthy and vibrant, crossed class boundaries, leaped convent walls, fought off villains and unsuitable suitors, possibly not so much to preserve her virtue as to pursue a healthy sex life with an attractive man of her choice. At the outset of the narrative, Adeline eschews the emotional frigidity of the convent for the luxuriant and fertile forest. When she runs away from the designs of the Marquis, it is not so much an escape from him as a running towards an eligible youth. Adeline is a woman who knows what she wants, a point that Jane Austen may have missed when she satirised Catherine Morland at the outset of *Northanger Abbey*: 'a thin awkward figure, a sallow skin without colour, dark lank hair, and strong features' (NA, 15).

A few pages later, Catherine is 'almost pretty', her passport into society (NA, 17). But the Victorian age is not yet dawned and Catherine is eminently qualified as a gothic heroine. Sterility in the narrative is represented by the boutiques of Bath and the hot-houses of Northanger Abbey. By contrast, Woodston (the forest), Henry's house, with its litter of puppies, is all fecundity and fertility, and points towards Catherine's future. In Andersen's fable, Gerda saves her friend Kay from the icy wastes of the north. Their return to the south in 'summer, glorious summer' is an apt metaphor of their ripening sexuality. The Snow Queen is an interesting creation, all frosty beauty and bewitching glamour, and her putting Kay 'under her coat' is an obvious sexual metaphor. When he finally arrives at her palace, he has been 'reborn' as her offspring.

The icy glamour of Philip Pullman's Mrs Coulter seems rather to echo that of the Snow Queen as she takes Lyra away to her London palace, not out of love for her daughter, but to glean information for her own ends. And it is unsurprising that the HQ of the General Oblation Board, site of the fiendish, child-cutting apparatus, is located in the icy wastes of the Arctic circle. Metaphorically, Lyra succeeds in destroying it by fire and explosion. At Gateshead, Jane Eyre dreads an afternoon in the frosty air and longs for the comfort of the fire, a condition that is repeated at Lowood. At Thornfield, she by turns rescues Mr Rochester from ice and fire and ultimately, proves to be the moderating force in his life. Concurrent with fiery, feisty young women battling for their rights to live and love is the Victorian angel – as defined by Gilbert and Gubar – ministering compassion and philosophy by turns, before dying or turning to religion or comforting the bereaved. These angels range from Agnes Wickfield of *David Copperfield*, to Helen Burns and Charlotte de Stancy, and Rachel from *Hard Times*, whom Stephen Blackpool deems 'th' Angel o' my life'.[32] And yet, Dickens – in this most masterful of satires – by rendering the true angel – or demon – of *Hard Times* a male, almost succeeds in turning the genderal tables: 'the lightest of porters, fit colourless servitor at Death's door' (HT, 222). The subject is young Bitzer, former model pupil at Thomas Gradgrind's school. I say 'almost succeeds' because the task of this 'colourless servitor' is to summon Louisa Gradgrind to her dying mother's bedside, and she duly consigns the matriarch to eternity. Dickens does the same narrative – nor its readers – no favours when he establishes the character of James Harthouse: 'rather taken by the novelty of the idea, (a career in business) and very hard up for a change, (he) was as ready to 'go in' for statistics as anything else' (HT, 158). If the author had endowed Harthouse with a few ennobling qualities – that of engaging Louisa with the world of intellect and imagination, perhaps? – this might have given the author (and Louisa and Sissy Jupe) a real problem. Far safer to cast him as the archetypal Victorian cad. Dickens, in withdrawing from this challenge, turns a fine satire into a morality tale. It smooths the way for Sissy's self-righteous 'saving' of Louisa from a certain type of social disgrace – and it consigns Louisa forever to the realm of vapid, self-abnegating angel: 'Such a thing (marriage and children) were never to be' (HT, 313).

---

[32] Charles Dickens, *Hard Times*, ed. David Craig (London: The Penguin English Library, 1969), p189. Subsequent references will be to this edition and will be inserted parenthetically into the text, for example '(HT, 189)'

What is it about the nineteenth-century fictional female that enables her to move close to the liminal world and either stay there or return unscathed to 'this' world? According to writer Jay Griffiths, death was not always the isolated activity that it is today, but that persons often died in full view of assembled family members (JG, 262). Griffith also claims that this isolation, this throwing a cloak of secrecy over what was once a natural transition, has led to the progressive 'eroticisation' of death (JG, 264). Without dwelling too much upon the definition of 'eroticisation', which I take to mean the twinning of a lovely young woman with a macabre figure or the instance of death itself, I look once more at the Lady of Shalott and the popularity of Tennyson's poem. While she lay dying, we learn that the Lady was 'Lying, robed in snowy white' and that 'her blood was frozen slowly', and that she was 'Dead-pale between the houses high'. But no matter; Sir Lancelot looked at her and said 'She has a lovely face'. In *Hamlet*, the lovely Ophelia immolates herself in a river, surrounded by flowers. And German artists of the Renaissance, in their imagery routinely twinned a macabre figure with the young maid.

But why the resurgence of the trope? It could be that the growing number of social realist authors in the nineteenth century, combined with their penchant for didactic and moral writings, wanted to appeal to a certain type of reader. Here, I refer to a theme introduced in the previous chapter, that of the Byronic hero in conjunction with the animal groom character in a fairy tale. As Bettelheim argues, the man-disguised-as-animal proved a useful theme in introducing the young reader to the hairy topic of adult sexuality. With the resurgence of the theme in the nineteenth century, exemplified by the relation between Jane Eyre and Edward Rochester, perhaps the Victorian reader had to be coaxed into believing that good might come to a character who *gave in* to his or her physical urges? Whereas the eighteenth-century author placed his or her heroine in the softening aura of the distant past, the social realist author tended to place his or her protagonist in the recent present. I quote from Radcliffe again: 'those glowing charms, which her auburn tresses, that fell in profusion over her bosom, shaded but could not conceal' (ROTF, 87). Radcliffe's prose enables the reader to almost *see* Adeline in full colour. Would the reader who eagerly consumed Victorian moral tomes have accepted just as readily a *contemporary* robust and sexual Adeline or even

---

[33]Michael T. Wilson, "Absolute Reality' and the Role of the Ineffable in Shirley Jackson's *The Haunting of Hill House*,' *Journal of Popular Culture*, p115.

Catherine, who preferred playing cricket to nursing dolls? On the contrary, the nineteenth century saw a return of the popular fairy tale trope in which the errant character is punished by being turned to stone or frozen: Dickens informs us in *Bleak House* that the unhappy Lady Dedlock 'fell into the freezing mode' (BH, 57).

Another reason could be that within the confines of the home, since the female already had access to the mysteries of birth, it was not a massive leap in imagination to hand over the keys to the gates of the next life. Or it could be, as Michael Wilson put it, the woman of the house was a surrogate *for* the house?[33] Again, I remind the reader of John Berger's assertion, that the man perceives the woman's environment and external ornamentation, clothing hair and domestic surroundings, as an extension of her personality (Berger, 46). It is no surprise then, when General Tilney asks Catherine how she might alter the furnishings of Woodston (NA, 200). Esther Summerson delights in the trivial details of Bleak House: '(the household articles) agreed in nothing but their perfect neatness, their display of the whitest linen, and their storing-up, wheresoever the existence of a drawer, small or large, rendered it possible, of quantities of rose-leaves and sweet lavender' (BH, 116). Shortly afterwards, John Jarndyce entrusts Esther with the housekeeping.

Only the less comfortable and more unhappy protagonists never take a practical hand in their dwellings. Mrs Jellyby's neglect of her home causes much distress to her husband. Mrs de Winter never alters the parlour at Manderley which with the dark panelling and heavy curtains is all masculinity (R, 76). When she accidentally breaks a small porcelain ornament in the drawing room, a minor household crisis ensues. On her first night in Hill House, Eleanor Vance wonders how such an ugly place could be so comfortable (HH, 91). The reader has already witnessed Eleanor contemplating 'her reflection in the polished floor of Hill House', the suggestion that she eventually becomes enmeshed into the fabric of the house. In a later scene, Theodora forbids Eleanor from clearing cutlery from a dinner table, and causes Eleanor not a small degree of discomfort (HH, 122). Whether she is inclined to keep house or not, the gothic heroine *is becoming*, and the majority of later heroines remain vapid and insubstantial almost to the end of their narratives when, if successful socially, they take on a robust materiality. If not, immolation is imminent.

But maybe even materiality has its limitations. On the first night in Hill

House, Eleanor is delighted with her new surroundings and thinks of herself as belonging with her companions (HH, 60).

But as the imagined connection fails and her alienation grows she gradually transforms into a wilful individual, rampaging wantonly through the place where she had earlier tried so hard to create a good impression. Was her behaviour the expression of her true nature or was her 'breaking out' the results of constraints placed upon her by unrealistic expectations?

Madness and the maiden

In his article 'The Freudian Reading of the Turn of the Screw', Robert Heilman vigorously defends the supernatural narrative of the events of James's text against the Freudian reading put forward by Edna Kenton in 1924 and Edmund Wilson a decade later. Heilman defends the Governess against a case of 'repressed passion'.[34] He states that her emotion is well out in the open, that in Chapter 1 of the text, she emphatically declares her love for the Master. Heliman argues that her love for the Master is essential to the plot because it is the device by which the author prevents the Governess from writing to the Master about the state of Miles. Whether Heilman is 'right' and Kenton is 'wrong' is not at issue here. What is at stake is the reliability of the Governess's testimony. Once more, Heilman defends this and states that though she is 'the sensitive, acute governess' and he presents her as lucid and believable (Heilman, 438). The question is: why is a highly emotional woman considered out of order?

Feminine lack of mental soundness has thrived in literature since Ophelia's death in *Hamlet*. An angry Jane Eyre is locked in the Red Room and her *alter ego* Berthe Mason is forced to dwell in an attic, a trope echoed in *Hard Times* by Stephen Blackpool's crazed wife. Even Paula Power of *A Laodicean* does not escape the taint that attaches to emotional/hysterical heroines: '(The train) rushed past them, causing Paula's dress, hair, and ribbons to flutter violently, and blowing up the fallen leaves in a shower over their shoulders' (AL, 123). The incident in Hardy's text takes place when Paula and George Somerset go to look at a railway tunnel, which has been built by Paula's

---

[34] Robert B. Heilman, 'The Freudian Reading of *The Turn of the Screw* in *Modern Language Notes, 7* (November, 1947) 433-445, p436. Subsequent references will be to this edition and will be inserted parenthetically into the text, for example "(Heilman, 436)"

late father. In a Freudian analysis, the sudden appearance of the train could be a metaphor of the late engineer, with Paula thrown into agitation by her imagining what he would think of her in the company of a male companion. Or it could be the agitation Paula experiences while in close proximity with George? Whatever, it is *Paula* who experiences emotion – and it is her fluttering ribbons and laces that behave as metaphors of this. As explained in a previous section, the female uses clothing among other accoutrements to create her own subjective version of herself to present to other people.

In his analysis of Shirley Jackson's novel, *The Haunting of Hill House*, Richard Pascal explains how by the twentieth century, the Victorian family had swiftly microscoped from a group with a shared solidarity at least into a collection of wanton individuals, each with his or her own agenda, a paradigm of which takes place in the narrative.[35] From this point of view, it is not difficult to pinpoint the reason for Eleanor Vance's near lunatic rampage towards the end of Jackson's text, that is, her belief that the house wants her, and that it is her mission to outwit the people whom she earlier claimed as friends.

A nineteenth-century writer has given her voice to this matter: 'Women are supposed to be calm generally: but women feel just as men feel (JE, 109). Charlotte Brontë's comment, through the voice of Jane Eyre, seems to sum up the situation. In a world driven by the female's untrammelled emotion, what is the reader to think? The argument hinges around Brontë's word 'supposed'. Here 'supposed' may be used as a verb, as in the minds of other people. Or it could mean women's behaviour in the obligatory sense, as in 'You are supposed to stay quiet.' In neither case is the notional female a winner. Either her actual behaviour is the product of the notional others' imagination. Or she is obliged to attune her behaviour to the standards of others. In neither scenario does she enjoy the freedom of expression that, socially at least, men have access to. In literature and often, in reality, men do not necessarily feel more. But they do have social licence to one emotion: anger. On the other hand, a man is not supposed (a loaded word) to give vent to femine emotions like grief. The exploration of reasons are outside

---

[35] Richard Pascal, 'Walking Alone Together: family monsters in *The Haunting of Hill House*' in *Studies in the Novel*, 46.4 (Winter 2014), 464-85, p476. Subsequent references will be to this edition and will be inserted parenthetically into the text, for example "(Pascal, 476)"

of the scope of a work of literary analysis. But I will assert that yes, men and women do experience similiar emotions, both in type and depth. It is only societal expectation that diversifies these feelings into 'male' and 'female'. And expectations in literature run parallel to those in society. In creating Jane Eyre and Berthe Mason, Brontë gives voice to this dissent.

Could this *denial* of anger be a source of the madness experienced by Miss Havisham, Berthe Mason and even, Rebecca? Because not one female protagonist of my literary line-up ever betrays anger. In Walpole's narrative, Isabella and Matilda coolly discuss their both falling in love with Theodore. In *Romance of the Forest*, Adeline faints, cries, is afraid – but she is never angry. Catherine, Jane, Esther, Paula, the Governess, Mrs de Winter and Eleanor never *show* anger[35] but they do witness it. As explained above, it is Paula's clothing that expresses her feelings, not her words or actions. Indeed, the reader never sees her lose her cool, as modern terminology puts it. Even when she discovers that William Dare is the illegitimate son of William de Stancy on the morning of her and de Stancy's wedding day, her most turbulent reaction is: 'Now please leave me' (AL, 397).

By the twentieth century, matters had changed. In Jackson's text, the sight of Theodora's face, thin with anger, frightens Eleanor (HH, 49). But Theodora is not *the* heroine; in addition to her propensity to anger, Theodora is prone to a peculiar kind of oral incontinence, a kind that heroines tend *not* to suffer from. For example, being hungry renders her angry, the 'mean and nasty' emotion that, according to Susan Brownmiller, no woman is supposed to display (SB, 163). It is a paradox then, that the gender who is 'tossed and buffeted on the high seas of emotion' is the one most likely to suffer aesthetically when she betrays her feelings. But perhaps emotion manifests in other ways. Miss Havisham has perversely worn her wedding dress for twenty years, while the rejected Berthe Mason, the prototype madwoman in the attic, experiences bouts of insanity. Rochester claims her illness is hereditary but the reader may wonder to what extent her condition results from the external responses provided by a husband who never actually wanted to marry her (JE, 305).

Mental illness manifests in the ways that female protagonists regard food. Gilbert and Gubar cite Christina Rossetti's poem *Goblin Market*, a narrative that illustrates the consequences to the young woman who succumbs to temptation and eats forbidden fruit – or food – as actually referring to the danger inherent in the feminine propensity for oral gratification (G&G,

573). The biblical allegory is obvious, of course. What is less obvious are the social rites that initiate a young woman into a family's acceptance by *her* acceptance of the fruits or foods that they offer – and her measure of resistance or acceptance is often a measure of her acceptance of them socially, and a particular member romantically.

Adeline refuses to eat the exotic desserts offered her by the Marquis, in his chateau (ROTF, 161).

Following her breakdown as a child, Jane Eyre is unable to eat the fruit tart offered her by Bessie (JE, 20). Catherine Morland readily dines on the food offered at Northanger Abbey, a feast that is slightly soured the next day, when she discovers the source of the earthly delights (NA, 168). The witch in *The Snow Queen* feeds Gerda upon cherries in the hope that Gerda will forget her greater purpose, that is, to find Kay. In *Rebecca*, the narrator constantly contrasts the sumptuous fare that she enjoys at Manderley with the frugal and unappetising rations that Mrs van Hopper allotted her when she was but a poor companion (R, 76). When she and Maxim are expelled from their paradise, ie, Manderley, the narrator stresses that once again, she – together with her spouse – have reverted to eating plain bread and butter for afternoon tea, a statement of their changed social status. Eleanor Vance readily tucks into the sumptuous fare that Mrs Dudley provides at Hill House. Once more, the reader can detect a fairytale narrative in Jackson's text, the food that the toxic housekeeper cooks and serves seeming like the poisonous apple in *Snow White*, seducing her to Hill House in a way that the others seem immune from.

The adolescent sleep

In his analysis of fairy tales that involve the heroine taking an extended sleep, such as Snow White and the Sleeping Beauty, Bruno Bettelheim writes much about the periods of inactivity or sleep or even seeming death in many adolescent characters, periods that precede, upon awakening, feats of progress and achievement (Bettelheim, 214). In *The Snow Queen*, this 'long period of inactivity' runs analogous to Gerda's period of forgetfulness when she is in the power of the witch that woos her with food and comfortable living. When she reawakens to her purpose, Gerda resumes her quest for Kay, stronger and more purposeful than ever.

In *Romance of the Forest*, Adeline experiences several periods of inactivity, the first following her rescue from the brigands' house by La Motte and another, just as she arrives in Switzerland. Following her recovery, Adeline meets Arnaud La Luc, her new 'father' and the person who curates her final, enlightened state of being. On arrival at Moor Cottage, Jane Eyre falls into a prolonged stupor. In *Bleak House*, the mother-less Esther contracts smallpox and almost loses her eyesight – and her life. It could simply be the author's practicality; he needed to physically disfigure his protagonist in order to disguise her true identity. But Dickens may have had a more profound message than that. Esther is indeed metaphorically 'blind' to a number of situations, not least the selfishness and hypocrisy of the people around her. It is no accident that her mother acknowledges her – albeit in private – while Esther is in recovery, a kind of fairytale reawakening.

In *Great Expectations*, Pip undergoes a physical chastening and is nursed back to health by foster father Joe, before he recovers – a less selfish person, at least. George Somerset emerges from a fever to find Paula soliciting him (AL, 422). This incident presages the situation in Hardy's later novel, *Tess of the D'Urbervilles*, when Angel Clare recovers from a life-threatening illness and returns to England a better man, full of forgiveness for his spurned wife. In Hardy's earlier text, another sleeper is Charlotte de Stancy. Charlotte does not grow personally following her illness: instead, she almost seems to regress, taking the curious child-like and indeed, the reader might discern, *childish* decision to renounce her sexuality and become a nun. It is as if in this renunciation, Charlotte hopes to atone for her brother's sexual 'sin'. What the author effects is the transfer of her energy to Paula, whose vision clears, enabling her, Paula, to identify her true love.

Tellingly, Catherine Moreland undergoes no inactive period. It could be that Jane Austen was so determined to avoid literary cliches that she refused to entertain the instance of the adolescent sleep in her earliest plot. Or it could be that the plot mechanics did not allow for such an instance. Whatever the truth, her later works do allow for instances of rejuvenating illness, chiefly in the persons of Jane Bennet, Marianne Dashwood and Louisa Musgrove. It is as if Austen eventually recognized that enforced inactivity is essential to the character development of the protagonist. Catherine shows no such development. Instead, her trip to Northanger Abbey infuses her with the restless curiosity referred to earlier, curiosity about the trunk at the foot of her bed and about the contents of the ebony cabinet.

In *The Turn of The Screw*, the endless vigilance of the Governess keeps her awake at night, an action that ends in tragedy: 'I waited and waited' (TOTS, 166). The theme of awakening runs throughout *The Haunting of Hill House*. In her former home, Eleanor's sleep is constantly disturbed by her demanding mother knocking on her bedroom wall. This disturbance is paralleled by the nocturnal incidences at the titular house. Near the end of the narrative, Eleanor reveals her thoughts, her longing for peace and calm (HH, 195). When Eleanor takes her final drive to destruction, the reader can't help but feel that she has gotten her wish, that she is at last at peace because, as the author reminds us, in the final words of the narrative whatever entity dwells in the house is still there 'alone'. In other words, Eleanor is gone peacefully to eternity. (HH, 246). The reader may surmise that it is the protagonists who take time out to 'sleep' – Adeline, Esther, Jane, Pip – who survive their environments, while it the restless protagonists – Eleanor, the Governess – whose narratives end tragically.

By the end of *Romance of the Forest*, Adeline has borne children, a sign of her social success. If the heroine has not been successful, that is, has not entered into society, she is annihilated either physically or personality-wise. On the contrary, the Byronic hero *is* and carries the baggage and soil of his spent lifetime – but survives. The unsuccessful gothic heroine dies or causes death. This feminine vapidity in contrast to the robust male could explain why the idea, at least, of the supernatural, haunts the pages of many a gothic narrative.

By the time Shirley Jackson became active as an author, the development of the two modes, gothic heroine and Byronic hero, had spanned two centuries. This progression enabled her to use the protagonist of her narrative, *The Haunting of Hill House*, as a paradigm of these modes. To reframe the modes, a gothic narrative is one in which the (usually) female subject seeks to break free of the restraints that have hampered her from social fulfilment, whatever the context. A narrative featuring the Byronic hero is one in which the (usually) male subject seeks to break free of society itself. Sensing that she is failing in her aim to join society, Eleanor transmutes into a destructive Byronic character.

Maid of the future

The fates of Mrs de Winter and Eleanor Vance indicate that the post-nineteenth-century woman bears a type of neediness, the *need* to care for someone, a relative or a male lover. In reality, this is expressed by the large number of female contenders for the occupations of carer, nurse and teacher. This emotion is seen as morally good but if the subject herself fails to win a parallel dimension of emotional fulfilment, as Esther Summerson eventually does, personal or physical annihilation can result. Caring for another person or people is seen as a 'good' emotion when it provides the protagonist with a dimension of personal fulfilment, as opposed to the passivity of Eleanor Vance and Mrs de Winter. We see this at work in two fantasy narratives.

The Snow Queen, by Hans Christian Andersen, is the most astonishing triumph of feminist writing produced in the nineteenth century, a status it holds to this day. The young Gerda leaves home and hearth to go in search of her young friend Kay, who has left town in the company of the older, bolder and considerably colder titular character. That Kay should prefer this other woman in preference to his more homespun friend Gerda could be a sign of his growing sexual awareness and burgeoning adolescence, but that matters not here. The fact is, Gerda conducts her search with no help other than from a clutch of talking animals, and using nothing other than her own eloquence and intelligence to escape the clutches of a witch and abduction by a band of robbers. Witness part of the Finland woman's speech to Bac the reindeer: 'I can give her no more power than what she has already. Don't you see how great it is? Don't you see how men and animals are forced to serve her; how well she gets through the world barefooted? She must not hear of her power from us; that power lies in her heart, because she is a sweet and innocent child! If she cannot get to the Snow Queen by herself, and rid little Kay of the glass, we cannot help her.'

Nor do they need to: Gerda marches boldly into the icy castle and fighting off treacherous animated snowflakes meanwhile, pulls Kay out of his glass-induced trance and brings him home to where it is 'summer, glorious summer'. One and a half centuries later, Lyra, in her disdain of her icy mother and her subsequent release of the children from their Arctic prison, echoes the actions of Gerda. In essence, Lyra is a more developed Gerda, albeit in a fantasy rather than a fairytale narrative. She assumes Gerda's bravery as she works her way across the frozen wastes, anxious to rescue her stolen friends and all the while combatting her adversaries. Like Gerda, Lyra is free of mirror-gazing vanities and the only time that the reader sees her perusing a looking-glass is when she is pondering her changing personal nature rather than arranging her hair. It is almost metaphoric that the narrative of *The Snow Queen* begins with the *destruction* of a mirror.

How has self-absorbed Byronism manifested in the other narratives, between the successful Adeline, Gerda and Lyra? The answers to that question will emerge in the following chapters.

The New Alchemists:

Text, Time and Travel

In the beginning ♦ The learning enigma ♦ As dreams are made on

I explore the archetype, the alchemist, the dominant male, that is common to the majority of gothic narratives, and I explore how his character works through the novels of the genre. Invariably an older, rather powerful male, he may be a father figure or a sage, well or ill-intentioned, whose actions and/or advice have a direct bearing upon the outcome of the narrative. Over time, the nature of his potency has shifted from mystical power to scientific, paternal and legal, to the present-day politician and industrialist. This shift has been effected by changes in technology, systems of transportation and essential time-keeping, documenting methods and networks of information, systems controlled mainly by males.

In the beginning

Until about the time of Renaissance, a certain breed of wise man thrived in the courts of rulers and emperors. Epitomised by John Dee in the court of Queen Elizabeth I, who was variously described as an astronomer and astrologer, alchemist and occultist, this male served his monarch in amorphous functions raging from teaching, forecasting and healing. In fiction, he is typified by Shakespeare's Prospero. In the scientific expansion that followed the Renaissance, this wise man fragmented into various and definable roles; mathematicians and biologists, lawyers and industrialists. This fragmentation was almost complete by the time that Walpole penned *The Castle of Otranto*. And the alchemist is an archetype that is traceable in the gothic sub-genre.

He is usually an older and influential male, learned in a particular discipline that he uses to good or ill effect. Almost never the protagonist or hero, 'good' alchemists include Arnaud La Luc, Joe Gargery and the Master of Jordan College. 'Bad' and ineffective alchemists include John Jarndyce, Thomas Gradgrind, Dr Jekyll, Abner Power, Dr Montague and Lord Asriel. In certain narratives, the alchemist manifests only as part of the back story but is never seen by the reader, such as Jane's Uncle Eyre, who provides her with her fortune. Paula Power's late father was a modern alchemist, a metallurgist whose success as an engineer manifests throughout the narrative as the rail network and the wealth that Paula enjoys. And this effectiveness is in marked contrast to the uselessness and meddling of Paula's Uncle Abner.

Whether his intent is 'good' or otherwise, the alchemist always conveys a sense of stability and timelessness, the sense that he will ever pervade the heroine's life, legitimising and authenticating her course through the narrative (or meddling and obfuscating) with signed documents and technical marvels, communication networks and the punctuating of time. Whether these facilities are insidious or beneficial is arguable by the reader and definable only within the context of the narrative. In *Northanger Abbey*, Henry Tilney, in his diatribe against the 'open' society, has no problem equating roads and newspapers (technology and communication networks) with spies (NA, 186). If, as Marilyn Butler asserts, the reader hears the voice of the author through the words of Tilney, then Jane Austen seems almost to regret the demise of the arcane society that she seeks to burlesque.

The ancient crafts of mining and metallurgy had been shrouded in mysticism for aeons and only gained social kudos when the 'captains of industry' of the Industrial Revolution channelled the wealth of the earth into the more worldly currency of pounds and pence (JG, 40). In awareness of the connection between the two occupations, William Blake famously renders his character Urizen, as a quasi-mystical metallurgist, with a pair of dividers in his hands as he creates the world, a trope that Philip Pullman transfers to Lord Asriel when he portrays him as having 'a pair of brass dividers' on his desk (HDM, 698).

The effort of manufacturing called for an organisation of labour, labourers and their time, and the new industrialists were championed by the time-keeping technology that had already reached a degree of sophistication by Blake's day. In parallel, the transportation of goods required adequate thoroughfares, roads and later on, railways. Production *en masse* led to an increased flow of capital, profit and taxation, which required a sophisticated scheme of documentation. Before the advent of electronic text, the document may have been considered a non-technical item. But the signed document enabled its scribe to place a situation *in time*, such as the lawyer that establishes Adeline's year of birth. With sophistication comes obligation, thus the angry voice of Boythorn in *Bleak House* when he senses his guests coming in 'late' on the stage coach, and the impatience of John Thorpe and General Tilney, to be first and the quickest – at everything. And nineteenth-century authors voice another type of anger.

Once more, the reader must imagine Jane Austen speaking through the words of Henry Tilney, then it might be she who is looking askance at the effects of progress made by encroaching industry upon village life when he declares: 'every man is surrounded by a neighbourhood of voluntary spies' (NA, 186). Maybe Austen had every right to be aggrieved at 'voluntary spies' and 'roads' that she perceived as tainting her environment. However, she seems unaware that the public coach was essential for conveying Catherine home safely when General Tilney had her ejected from the Abbey, and in Radcliffe's narrative it was only La Motte's intervention that extricated Adeline from the remote brigands' house. Throughout the nineteenth century, geographical mobility continued as essential to fictional plots.

In *Bleak House*, the chief characters make numerous journeys between Hertfordshire, London and Gloucestershire. Jane Eyre almost loses her life when she abandons the public coach at the crossroads, and wanders into a wilderness. In James's text, young Miles *does* lose his life when the Governess fails to communicate with her employer about the condition of the young boy, or at least take him to London in company with Flora and Mrs Grose. In Jackson's text, Eleanor Vance fails to take the natural route out of her toxic environment, and thus destroys herself.

Rotund and comely the gothic heroine may have been, but she did require the perceptively male pointers of dated documents, reliable conveyances and a network of roads and thoroughfares to take her out of isolation and into society. But to use these facilities is one matter; to become involved with them is another. In today's world, there is doubtless very little difference between the treatment of technology by men and women, but writers of fiction still use technology to differentiate between male and female protagonists. Throughout Philip Pullman's narrative, the alethiometer is strongly associated with the female, Lyra. It is round in shape and consists of an anchor, an hourglass, a skull, a bull, a beehive (HDM, 72). By manipulating the dials and interpreting the pictures, the owner can decipher what is taking place in her world. Lyra spends much of the narrative guarding this precious item, which has been given to her by her then guardian, as it assists her in finding the missing children and in other quests. Will Parry eventually acquires a knife, a vicious item that cuts off two of his fingers and almost costs him his life. Yet, he becomes lord of the knife and gains the power to 'cut' in and out of the web of the parallel worlds that the children find themselves wandering about in. The gendered symbolism of the round alethiometer and the sharp knife cannot be lost on the reader. Nor can the reader fail to notice the parallels of the 'subtle' knife with the ferocious cutting equipment used by the General Oblation Board to separate the children from their souls or daemons. At the end of the narrative, Will's knife shatters (AS, 1080) and Lyra's alethiometer loses its mystical powers (AS, 1063). The vanished powers render both children in the situation of fairy tale heroes who revert to everyday life; Lyra returns to Jordan College where a life of privilege awaits her – but she is the denizen of the fantastical world. Will returns to 'this' world to become an ordinary schoolboy and potentially, a student.

Authors have not been kind to female characters who supersede the 'male' roles of documenting and organising and keeping time, except in domestic matters. Even the information that Lyra channels through her alethiometer takes on a quasi-mystical function rather than serving as an intellectual activity that she masters. In their book, *The Madwoman in the Attic*, Gilbert and Gubar cite the 'masculine cosmic Author' and debate the phallic nature of the pen and discuss it as a reason why writing is perceived as a 'male' business (G&G, 7). From the sceptre to the sword and the rifle, the male has ever been perceived as the instigator of law, politics and war, and the documentation that goes with it. And the gothic heroine is drawn towards the document that might point her in the direction of her origin, or lead her to her fortune or simply show her the inside of another mind.

Quite often, this device acts as a surrogate male force in the feminine world of gothic intrigue. In *Romance of the Forest*, the words that Adeline reads from a document that she finds in the Abbey are the writings of her dead father. This surrogate parent proves to be her mainstay throughout the narrative, eventually establishing her as heiress to a great estate. In the same way, Will Parry discovers the character of his father, who has only ever lived in his imagination, through the words that he reads from the pages of letters that he, Mr Parry, has sent from another world to Will's mother. Though she is unwell, Will leaves her to go in search of his father.

This presence of the written word as male surrogate is so potent that by the nineteenth century, the protagonists were inclined to disdain any scripting that did not have its origin in male authority. Catherine Morland reacts with scorn when she finds that the alluring documents that emerge from the locked trunk at Northanger Abbey are nothing but laundry lists (G&G, 135). And this scorn is not confined to the female protagonist. In *The Woman in Black,* lawyer Arthur Kipps describes a number of the documents that he finds: 'cantankerous letters to all and sundry – all of which was usual for such a female client'.[36] Arthur experiences similar disdain when he sorts the documents that he finds at Eel Marsh House: 'There were accounts from department stores in London ... Only the letters themselves I reserved for later perusal. Everything else was waste' (Hill, 136).

In *Bleak House,* without exception, all of the lawyers, clerks and law writers, from the Lord Chancellor to the very poor Nemo, are men. And the effects of legalities upon women are devastating. The first appearance of Lawyer Kenge in Miss Barbary's house is an intrusion of male legalities into female domesticity (BH, 66). In the same episode, Miss Barbary reads aloud from the Bible, excoriating the 'illegitimate' child in her care, the Bible being a document supposedly written by men and endorsed by a male deity. Miss Barbary's death soon follows. Esther, Ada and Richard meet Miss Flite, the old maid who has spent her golden years attending the Inns of Court daily with 'her little bag of documents', anticipating a judgement on the long-running Jarndyce v Jarndyce case, which has ruined and impoverished her (BH, 105).

It is Lady Dedlock's reaction to a fragment of writing that alerts Lawyer Tulkinghorn to investigate her link with Captain Hawdon, and thus uncovers Lady Dedlock's secret. For the remainder of the novel, characters by turn pursue and conceal documents and pieces of writing. The gentle and inoffensive George Rouncewell, friend and colleague of the late Captain, is forced – at the risk of financial ruin – to hand over a piece of the Captain's handwriting to Tulkinghorn, and thus seals Lady Dedlock's fate. When Tulkinghorn meets

---

[36] Susan Hill, *The Woman in Black* (London: Profile Books, 1983), p33. Subsequent references will be to this edition and will be inserted parenthetically into the text, for example '(Hill, 33)'

his end – deserved, the reader might argue – anonymous letters directed at the various people involved in her life seek to incriminate Lady Dedlock for his murder. Tulkinghorn's death might have saved her reputation, but a packet of letters written by her and signed 'Honoria' finally brings about the events that lead to her downfall. Lady Dedlock is literally the author of her own undoing.

Throughout the text, the constantly scribing Mrs Jellyby rises little beyond a figure of fun. The detritus of her efforts to become involved in a social project, that is, heaps of letters, fills her house to the detriment of family comfort, even throughout mealtimes: 'Richard, who sat by (Mrs Jellyby), saw four envelopes in the gravy at once.' (BH, 89) Once more, the male world of administration and correspondence intrude into the domestic, feminine realm. The reader is reminded of this dichotomy when Caddy tells Esther: 'As to Pa, he gets what he can and goes to the office' (BH, 95). Mrs Jellyby's husband is entitled to escape to the office – where he presumably does his scripting without challenge but *her* writing is the cause of family chaos, a pointer to the polarisation between the administration/male and domestic/female roles of the nineteenth century. Just as the map-makers of the sixteenth and seventeenth centuries used their paper charts to delineate conquered territories, the marriage certificate of the legal service was paper proof over the ownership of the female body, her name changing to that of her husband, his right to sexual services, and so forth.

Themes of colonisation, ownership and inheritance run through *Jane Eyre*. The titular character's name is, as Gilbert and Gubar point out, an allegorical name, as its sound reveals Jane's eventual status of *heir* in the narrative. Her wealth comes to her via a male relative whom she has never known in her lifetime. And its bitter under taste is the prevention of her marriage by the actions of the same relative to lover Rochester, who is still legally married to another woman. Rochester suffers as much and arguably, more than Jane does, when legalities – instigated by and large, by men – usurp his plan to satisfy the longings of his heart.

In *Great Expectations*, a series of legal manoeuvres enhances the life of protagonist Pip, endowing him with the financial means to lead a fashionable life. It comes as a bitter shock to Pip when he discovers that his benefactor is not the wealthy Miss Havisham, the lady who had engaged him as a playmate for her ward, Estella, when they were children, but the miserable criminal whom he helped earlier in life. Success in business has enabled Magwitch to manifest as the regular cash payment via the legal system that is represented by lawyer Jaggers. Miss Havisham longed for, yet was denied the legal tie of marriage. Her lover's jilting of her on their wedding day unhinges her to a sub-existence of unbridled, destructive emotion.

In *A Laodicean*, George Somerset follows the humming wires of the telegraph and encounters Paula Power in her castle. William Dare postures as George Somerset by sending Paula a note that she believes the architect has sent, and dishonestly extracts a sum of money from her. And it is the tattoo on Dare's chest that gives away his relation to William de Stancy to Mr Havill, thus opening the way for blackmail (AL, 168).

In *Dr Jekyll and Mr Hyde*, Henry Jekyll writes his own life, quite literally, through a series of documents uncovered and relayed by friend and lawyer, Gabriel Utterson. Interestingly, even though Dr Jekyll changes into Mr Hyde and back again throughout the narrative, one thing about him remains the same: his *signature*, which eventually reveals the identity of Hyde to Utterson. Before the conclusion of the narrative, the deceased Lanyon and Jekyll tell their respective stories via documents. In his narrative, Jekyll writes: 'one part remained to me; I could write my own hand' (DJMH, 51).

In *The Turn of the Screw*, the Governess, a girl of nineteen, is elevated to occupying a 'state room' by virtue of her literacy, on arrival at Bly. When Miles – the male, the avowed master of the documents, though yet a child – clandestinely takes control of a letter written by her, he comments 'there was nothing there' (TOTS, 232-233). The only writing that the reader witnesses young Flora producing is 'nice 'round O's", as T.J. Lustig points out, a series of nothings (TOTS, xvii). And Mrs Grose, the housekeeper, is seemingly unable to read at all; with regard to the headmaster's letter, she says 'Such things are not for me, Miss' (TOTS, 128). The Governess eventually produces the manuscript of her story, but it is framed in Henry James's wider narrative, via a male agent. Oscar Cargill argues the point that, in spite of her illiteracy, the housekeeper is more perceptive than the Governess.[37] And is Cargill criticising – if he is criticising anyone – the Governess and her assumed learning, or just the Governess?

---

[37]Oscar Cargill, '*The Turn of the Screw* and Alice James' in *PMLA* (June 1963), 238-249, p241. Subsequent references will be to this edition and will be inserted parenthetically into the text, for example "(Cargill, 241)"

In *The Haunting of Hill House*, Luke Sanderson uncovers an illustrated diary written by former owner Hugh Crain. Crain was the fanatical Victorian *pater familias* who built Hill House and endowed his shocking pictorial document to his daughter to save her from hell, a diary that the twentieth-century characters regard with horror. Meanwhile, Doctor Montague, the 'author' of the paranormal experiment, who is writing a book, is taking responsibility for charting all measurements and recording all the emotional responses by the participants. Yet, throughout the narrative, protagonist Eleanor feels disinclined to even read. And Dale Bailey refers to 'the phallic emblem' of Hugh Crain, the novel's deceased patriarchal figure, meaning the library that is situated in the tower of Hill House.[38] For much of the narrative, Eleanor is unable to even enter it.

Gilbert and Gubar explain in relation to Emily Brontë's novel *Wuthering Heights* that Edgar Linton's power lies in the collection of documents, books, wills, testaments and so forth, that he can bequeath to his (male) successors, that he does not have to be the conventional strong handsome outdoor type to be a hero (G&G, 281). How did the scripting male, represented by wills and documents, usurp the male with the 'conventionally masculine body'? Until recent centuries, the 'king' was always the strong man, the man who could triumph in battle, by mastery of whatever prevailing technology, sword, bow and arrow or rifle. As recently as 1690, King James II fought William III for supremacy on Irish territory. The custom of military prowess survives in today's younger Royal family members routinely joining the army and navy, and excelling at horsemanship. But as far back as the seventeenth century, the day of the warrior hero was well nigh over.

In popular portraits, French monarch Louis XIV is portrayed in an extravagant wig, copious lace about his throat and wrists, silken clothing glinting above shining, buckled shoes. And his palace of Versailles is a tribute to the triumph of parlour culture, furnished with sofas and curtains and china cabinets, the lords and ladies partaking of the spoils of colonial trade, cups of tea and coffee poised in bejewelled hands, with sugar-decorated confections on the side. It took another century for such luxuries to descend to the

---

[38]Dale Bailey, 'June Cleaver In The House Of Horrors: Shirley Jackson's The Haunting Of Hill House' in *American Nightmares: The Haunted House Formula in American Popular Fiction*, University of Wisconsin Press, 1999, p42. Subsequent references will be to this edition and will be inserted parenthetically into the text, for example "(Bailey, 42)

middle classes and by the nineteenth century, the 'gentleman' bore other qualities of refinement and privilege, such as the law practising Edgar Linton. But echoes of the past run through Radcliffe's narrative: '(Adeline) looked round in surprise, and saw a young man in a hunter's dress, leaning against a tree, and gazing on her with that deep attention, which marks an enraptured mind' (ROTF, 76). Later, Theodore appears again: 'There now entered another stranger, a young Chevalier, who, having spoken hastily to the elder, joined the general group that surrounded Adeline. He was of a person, in which elegance was happily blended with strength, and had a countenance animated, but not haughty; noble, yet expressive of peculiar sweetness' (ROTF, 87). Of course, the hunter and the Chevalier prove to be one and the same.

The distinction between hunter and Chevalier mattered not in the eighteenth century – or even now. Hunting and horsemanship were interchangeable activities and to an extent, still are. Both pursuits bespeak a life spent mainly out of doors and in possession of its attributes, a ruddy complexion, a fit body and developed muscle. And such qualities are presumed attractive to the female of past and present.

But as the literary female grew progressively plainer, from the lovely eighteenth-century Adeline to plain Jane Eyre, mousey Eleanor Vance and insignificant Mrs de Winter, the male morphed also. Even by the beginning of the nineteenth century, the handsome, healthy soldier of Radcliffe's day had dwindled to the philanderer Captain Tilney, Henry's brother. Their father's rank, General Tilney, is a nod to the past in the world that he is modernising quickly. In *Pride and Prejudice,* the atavistic longing for a uniformed lover is represented in Lydia Bennet's elopement with debauched army officer, George Wickham. The reader may see the same decrepitude in the absurd self-pity of soldier William de Stancy in Hardy's narrative: 'Here am I, a homeless wanderer' (AL, 369). By the nineteenth century, literature was revealing the darker side of male nature.

The learning enigma

One of the deeper paradoxes concerning men, women and literacy is that while literacy is required of men, it is invariably the woman's job to *teach* it. In spite of male authority with the pen 'the cosmic author', all of the teachers in my array of primary texts are female. Catherine Morland recounts the challenge experienced by her mother when faced with teaching her large family.

Catherine tells Henry Tilney: 'You think me foolish to call instruction a torment ... if you had ever seen how stupid (little children) can be for a whole morning together, and how tired my poor mother is at the end of it, you would allow that to *torment* and to *instruct* would sometimes be used as synonymous words' (NA, 105). The italics are the author's own, more than a hint at the darker side of learning. Erstwhile teacher Esther Summerson struggles to instil the craft of basic writing into Charley Neckett's reluctant hand: 'It was very odd to see what old letters Charley's young hand had made; they so wrinkled and shivering and tottering; it, so plump and round. Yet Charley was so uncommonly expert at other things and had as nimble little fingers as I ever watched' (BH, 482). Matthew Pocket tutors Pip for the world of business and law but, thanks to the efforts of Mr Wopsle's great-aunt and her niece, Biddy, Pip is well literate when he arrives in London. Basic teaching, it seems, is ever the role of the female. However, correspondence with the wider world is frowned upon.

Although she is obliged to tutor two young children, Henry James's Governess is forbidden to write to her Master. Yet, she struggles to decipher the rather cryptic letter that Miles's headmaster has sent to that same Master, who refuses to open it himself. Several critics, including Jacqueline Bannerjee, have questioned the motive of the older, wiser subjects controlling the situation that take no active part in the narrative. But the reader must ponder the question: even if 'Miss' had been an experienced, older and more confident individual, wouldn't the despairing young Miles still have expressed his wish: 'I want to see more life ... I want my own sort!' (TOTS, 191-192).

Bannerjee explains that, even in James's time, the governess system had been outdated and that James's narrative could have been a criticism, at a certain level of families who insisted upon subjecting their children to archaic systems of learning in the modern world.[39] If James is criticising anyone in his narrative, who is it: the male relative who has abandoned the children to an inexperienced young governess, the Governess herself or the outmoded system

---

[39] Jacqueline Bannerjee, 'The Legacy of Anne Brontë' in Henry James's *The Turn of the Screw* Published online: 13 Aug 2008, 532-544. p543. Subsequent references will be to this edition and will be inserted parenthetically into the text, for example "(Bannerjee, 543)"

[40] Joseph Firebaugh, 'Inadequacy in Eden: Knowledge and *The Turn of the Screw* in *Modern Fiction Studies*, (Spring 1957), 57-63, p60. Subsequent references will be to this edition and will be inserted parenthetically into the text, for example '(Firebaugh, 60)'.

of education? Perhaps James's text is, after all, a fable on the importance of an adequate system of learning rather than upon sexual frustration or on the existence – or not – of ghosts? Joseph Firebaugh roundly criticises the headmaster for 'withholding knowledge' from the Governess and for refusing even to discuss what has happened.[40]

But by the twentieth century, compulsory learning systems for all children of the developed world were in place, so to learn or not to learn ceased to be an individual choice or an accident of elevated birth. It is interesting that, at the conclusion of *His Dark Materials*, even though the narrative falls within the realm of fantasy, the Master of Jordan College sets aside an individual learning program for the 'aristocratic' Lyra. The reader may wonder to the extent the less well-connected females of Lyra's world (where very little of the action takes place) have access to learning?

In the meantime, writers have used the activity of writing to subtle and metaphorical effect. In the final pages of *Great Expectations*, the reader learns that Biddy has married Joe Gargery, has transferred her literacy to him and that they are the parents of young children. It is a fine and poignant fate for the kindest of characters. And yet, the reader cannot be certain that Dickens is not indulging in a spot of word-play here. As blacksmith, Joe is master of the forge, a noun that transforms into the verb, *to forge*, that is, to imitate another person's signature, the author's way of indicating that Joe is perhaps occupying a role that he has usurped from someone else – Pip?

In the *The Woman in Black*, Arthur Kipps represents the world of man-made rules and regulations. He is a lawyer's clerk, a man learning to deal with legal matters, the same legalities in the form of a conventional marriage that held Jennet Humphrye back from being the custodian of her own child. It is no wonder then, that her evil avatar enacts revenge on this custodian of the law, depriving him of *his* child. Mrs Drablow, the woman to whom Jennet Humphrye handed over her baby, had no qualifications as a mother except that she was married, a state expressed by a legal document. Jennet Humphrye expresses her rage and bitterness at legal matters by attacking Arthur. It is interesting that Arthur's eventual family is a *step* family, that is, a legal construct. When in later life, Arthur is forced to reminisce on the darker events of his past, he realises that the only way to exorcise his ghosts is to write down them down and thus pave the way for a type of personal healing. Through these narratives, we see ways in which documents can heal or hinder. But overall, the condition of literacy, which today we are in danger of taking for granted, endowed its *male* custodian with a type of privilege. The unprivileged male was another matter.

'Foreign language, dear boy,' says Magwitch in *Great Expectations*, now in the guise of Provis, when he asks Pip to read to him. For all of the convict's improved finances, he has failed to gain the literacy that would enable him to take part in wider society. Reading even more deeply into the matter, Magwitch is unable to read the legal edicts by which other, learned men have condemned him to exile and inexorably, to death. His dying before the sentence – a loaded word here – can be carried out, is the final and tragic reclamation of his human dignity. Joe Gargery has been emasculated by his own father, a character whose violent behaviour deprived Joe of an education. His attitude to learning is the product of a blighted childhood, beaten by his father and prevented from attending school. His strange mix of disdain and reverence of the learning process is reflected by other characters, epitomised in 'the greasy memorandum book' of Mr Wopsle's great-aunt, and the books with dead insects mashed between their pages, and is coupled with Joe's reverence of virtuosity: 'poetry costs money' (GE, 39). Eventually, he is tutored into reading by Biddy, whom he marries. Together, they conceive the children that he failed to father when he was married to Pip's sister, a hint that literacy may have facilitated his manhood. Meanwhile, the unease with the learned female continued.

In Daphne du Maurier's novel, the titular Rebecca's neatness with documents is in odd contrast to her exotic love life. Erotic and lovely by any standards, Rebecca has run Manderley with chilling, clerical efficiency. Mrs de Winter takes good note of the morning room where Rebecca undertook her administration, furnished with meticulously-labelled pigeon-holes in which letters and various other documents could be classified. She also recognises the handwriting in the book of poetry that Maxim had given her (R, 94). These writings and others – a signature on a book of poetry – set up a strange, sexual ambivalence that throughout the narrative, surrounds the memory of the ultra-feminine Rebecca. This counterpoint seems almost to reach back to when the learned female was deemed 'unfeminine'. Indeed, the instance of Rebecca's clerical neatness points at the efficiency with which Esther Summerson organised Bleak House. According to Harold Skimpole: 'When I see you, my dear Miss Summerson, intent upon the perfect working of the whole little orderly system of which you are the centre, I feel inclined to say to myself – in fact, I do say to myself, very often – that's responsibility!' (BH,

587). Indeed, Skimpole's disdain of 'responsibility' seems almost in accord with a certain, post-Enlightenment strand of thinking that bore a disdain of organised knowledge. In *Romance of the Forest*, Arnaud La Luc has no plans for the formal education of his daughter Clara: 'I cannot repeat it too often; let your lessons to youth consist in action rather than words: they must learn nothing from books which may be taught by experience' (ROTF, 249). Chloe Chard suggests that in denouncing formal education for his daughter, La Luc is voicing sentiments expressed in 'Emile' by Jean-Jacques Rousseau (ROTF, 249).

This discomfort with formal learning continues into the nineteenth century, often expressed by writers with regard to the unsuitability of education for the female. In *Hard Times*, in the final moments of Mrs Gradgrind's life – the wife of a man who has spent his life dispensing 'facts' – her daughter Louisa hands her a pen, which Mrs Gradgrind struggles with and fails to wield: 'It matters little what figures of wonderful no-meaning she began to trace upon her wrappers. The hand soon stopped in the midst of them' (HT, 225-6). In *David Copperfield*, Dora Spenlow's great service to her spouse is to *hold his pens* as he works. Like Mrs Gradgrind, Dora literally fades away. In *Wives and Daughters*, Dr Gibson tries to persuade daughter Molly to remain illiterate. Perhaps this disdaining of the female who strikes out to achieve an education wider than mere teachable literacy might be palatable if knowledge of *the word* was not used in a more insidious fashion by learned males.

'She's a woman; nothing more', George Somerset tells the minister Woodworth, in Hardy's text (AL, 92). The subject of the conversation is heiress Paula Power. In Chapter 7, the reader sees Somerset and a minister of the non-conformist church to which Paula belongs, disputing what form the age-old ritual of baptism should take. Somerset champions – he thinks – Paula, arguing for baptism following soon after birth, while Woodworth upholds the teaching of his own church. But the 'true' views on the subject held by either man do not matter here. What is significant is the manner in which they stand arguing, while Paula is seated detachedly in a nearby summer house: 'an interest in his off-hand arguments was revealed by the mobile bosom of Miss Paula Power, though she still occupied herself by drawing out the necklace' (AL, 88). Nor need the thread of the actual argument concern us; when it is finished – that is, put on hold by the events of the narrative – Paula claims that the discussion has interested her and refuses to let Somerset dismiss it as 'a useless, unbecoming, dull, last-century argument' (AL, 91). But the argument is not picked up again in the text, which gradually transforms into a more conventional love story. And the phrase 'mobile bosom' cannot have escaped the reader, the author's suggestion that, even when dealing with architecture or religion, the female is driven by emotion. And most often, the mysterious – yet decipherable – document is presented as a vehicle to express that conventionally feminine emotion, curiosity; again, I refer to Catherine's impatience in finding the truth about the documents in the trunk.

Twinning the female with curiosity is not inevitable, of course. The female has no more of a penchant for the emotion and the capacity for the solution of a riddle than the male – witness Krook's endless endeavours in seeking documents and tracing letters on his shop wall, in *Bleak House*. Krook has memorized the words he has seen written down in court because, as he explains to Esther: 'I can neither read nor write' (BH, 107). His arcane occupation is prescient of that of the pre-literate Joe Gargery, who had learned to form 'J' and 'O' from looking at his limited reading material, namely the Bible and religious pamphlets (GE, 38). And a difference of opinion might arise between readers and critics who insist that it is Lady Dedlock's curiosity about a fragment of Captain Hawdon's writing, rather than other persons' curiosity about the bundle of letters that she had directed to him earlier in life, that brings about her downfall. What is certain is that following the turn of events, she does indeed open a Pandora's box one summer evening when she says innocuously to Mr Tulkinghorn, her husband's lawyer: 'Who copied that?'(BH, 61). Her own, personal downfall is not far away.

It is difficult to pin-point when this unease with tutoring the under-dog, whether woman or working-class male, began. What is intriguing is the unease with formal learning that 18th and 19th century authors expressed in a world where numeracy and literacy were obligatory for the achieving male. Hans Andersen begins *The Snow Queen* by explaining that the mirror made by a sprite breaks and causes all the subsequent trouble in the world 'for he kept a sprite school' (http://www.online-literature.com/hans_christian_andersen/972/).

Andersen's unease with formal education is expressed in the way that Kay, now corrupted by the shards of broken glass in his eye and in his heart, can only remember the multiplication table when he is in the power of the Snow Queen. Just as Andersen began writing his tales, Denmark had been one of the least developed of European countries. In the early 1800s, the Danish 'Golden Age' began, heralding a renaissance in the arts and sciences, which included the works of Andersen and the philosopher Soren Kirkegaard. Perhaps Andersen felt that progress in orthodox education was taking place too quickly, drowning the finer instincts of Danish youth, with traditional myth quashed in favour of the rationalities of mathematics? This disdain, almost a fear of schooling, is evident in the Princess whom Gerda encounters on her search for Kay: 'The Princess ... she has read all the newspapers in the whole world and has forgotten them again - so clever was she.' Andersen's contemporary, Dickens, had concerns of his own with nineteenth-century learning systems. And these concerns are expressed throughout his novel, *Hard Times*, published 1854, at the height of the Industrial Revolution.

The author describes the upbringing of Thomas Gradgrind's children: 'Almost as soon as they could run alone, they had been made to run to the lecture room. The first object with which they had an association, or of which they had a remembrance was a large black board with a dry Ogre chalking ghastly white figures upon it' (HT, 54). Dickens himself had had an enriching educational experience at the school in Rochester that he attended as a youth, when his unhappy blacking factory days were behind him. The real problem was, he did not see enough schooling. I repeat the words of Joe Gargery: 'poetry costs money' (GE, 39). There is no mistaking the bitterness of these words, oozing from the pen of an author whose own formal schooling had been cut short by family poverty. Like Andersen, Dickens defends the power of the imagination over hard facts. He portrays Pip tortured and bullied by the manner in which Uncle Pumblechook forces him to engage in a long-running game of mental arithmetic while the boy struggles to eat his breakfast: 'And after each figure was disposed of, it was as much as I could do to get a bite or a sup before the next came' (GE, 46). Dickens satirizes learning by rote through the character of Wackford Squeers, headmaster of Dotheboys Hall in *Nicholas Nickleby,* and through Paul Dombey's unhappy learning experiences in *Dombey and Son.*

The reader may also witness this twinning of villainy with mathematical potency in Thomas Hardy's text, in the scene where George Somerset encounters the less-than-honest William Dare in a Monte Carlo casino: 'Allowing out of that one chance in every thirty-six, which is the average of zero being marked, and two hundred and four times for the backers of the other numbers, I have the mathematical expectation of six times at least, which would nearly recoup me' (AL, 300). Perhaps, just perhaps, as male literacy and numeracy, at least, burgeoned, and thus these skills became less potent, the 'strong' man in society ceased to be the lettered one, surrounded by documents, wills and bills? Perhaps, the male was slowly becoming aware of a new and emerging power?

As dreams are made on

In the more distant past, technology was initially allied to magic, for example, mirrors through which subjects could see far-off events, flying carpets, doors that opened on approach or command. And among more recent forms of technology are those implements that measured time, clocks and watches, thus giving their owners the illusion that they could control it also, the owners being mainly the church and wealthy individuals.

As with technology, time and magic were formerly perceived as interlinked, for example, the three wishes of the fairy tale. Prospero is the magic practising protagonist of William Shakespeare's play, *The Tempest*, a word that itself means 'time'. But Shakespeare's first 'time lord' is found in his earlier play, *As You Like It*. The plot involves group of people who seek refuge in a forest from the political forces that surround them. Rosalind, under the guise of Ganymede, is one of the escapees, bringing his/her 'dial' into the Forest of Arden with him. Presently, he explains its workings to Jacques, one of the resident characters, who consequently deems him 'a motley fool' for doing everything by the hour (Act 2, Scene 7).

Ganymede is, of course, neither motley nor a fool: he is simply fugitive from the world of luxury and privilege, and he has access to the hot-tip technology of the time or, to put it another way, to hot-tip *time* technology. According to Jay Griffiths, Shakespeare had set out to remind us that 'there's no o'clock in the forest' (JG, 14). The sixteenth-century playwright, whose works are filled with references to the flow of time, would have been ever conscious of the implications in the frenetic atmosphere of mercantile London in contrast to the slower pace of life in his native Stratford-Upon-Avon. And the Forest of Arden is even further removed from this. Awareness of the material benefits that accrue to the time-wary eventually results in a bitter outburst from the similarly exiled Orlando: 'in this desert inaccessible/Under the shade of melancholy boughs/Lose and neglect the creeping hours of time

... Let gentleness my strong enforcement be/In the which hope I blush and lose my sword' (Act 2, Scene 7).

In his story, *The Masque of the Red Death*, it is doubtlessly a nod to Shakespeare that leads Edgar Allan Poe to christen the Prince of the castle, Prospero. As described by Irving Malin, the rooms of Prospero's castle are painted in various colours, one being black. The clock in this room chimes every hour and when it does, the guests are obliged to cease dancing and talking until the chiming stops (Malin, 147). Prince Prospero has, in effect, with his ability to control his guests, deemed himself a time-lord. Whatever Shakespeare's (or Poe's) opinion on the matter of organization, time-keeping and material wealth, not even he could hold back the progress that led to the Industrial Revolution, circa 150 years following Shakespeare's writing. Indeed, no philosopher can hold back economic progress, it seems, not even the watch-averse Jean-Jacques Rousseau and those others alive at the time when the machinery was springing into action.

The progress of technology is traceable through literature, even folk literature. Every child knows the story of Cinderella, the young lady who was obliged to leave the grand ball at the stroke of midnight. Yet few people know that this ticking clock is but a recent development in a very ancient tale. This anecdote to the tale was added by Charles Perrault (1628-1703) during his employment with the Minister of Finance to the French monarch Louis XIV (Bettelheim, 252). Bruno Bettelheim points out the other versions of the beloved fairy tale in which the young Cinderella is *not* subject to such a time-sensitive diktat but uses her own judgement as to when to leave the ball. Curiously, the progress of Louisa Gradgrind's marriage to Josiah Bounderby renders her a type of perverse Cinderella. It is actually a time deadline, set by her husband, that destroys the legal tie between them: 'if she don't come home tomorrow by twelve o'clock at noon, I shall understand that she prefers to stay away' (HT, 265). Ironically, the subject of his rage is the daughter of Thomas Gradgrind, he of the 'deadly-statistical clock' (HT, 238).

The time-obsessed Louis XIV, who famously dubbed himself 'the Sun king', placed clocks of every shape and make in his newly-built palace of Versailles: gold, silver, enamel, porcelain, all superbly crafted and embellished with precious stones. In identifying himself with the star that controls *our* time, the extravagant Louis sought to control the daily activities of the courtiers that surrounded him. And remember Adeline, born in the first year of Louis's reign, racing against *official* time to save lover Theodore from execution? One century later, at the outset of the Industrial Revolution, two philosophers took polar-opposing views on matters of time. 'Time is money,' declared Benjamin Franklin (1706-90), in his tome, *Advice to a Young Tradesman*, published 1748. He was an American statesman, philosopher, scientist and polymath. On the other side of the Atlantic, his contemporary Jean-Jacques Rousseau (1712-78) 'refused to wear a watch'. Jay Griffiths describes Rousseau 'a lover of freedom' but like Shakespeare, neither man could hold back nor control the changes that were sweeping the world. (JG, 25)

In *Great Expectations*, Joe Gargery represents an older, pre-industrial, male power. Illiterate at the outset of the narrative, Joe is indicative of the blacksmith of old, the artisan who carried out a quasi-mystical role in ancient communities, forging useful and even precious metals from rock and stone.

Estella's rejection of Pip and her lampooning of the blacksmith's trade is quite profound, indicative of her rejecting the archaic world in favour of the world of fashion and, in the context of the narrative, the idle gentleman, Bentley Drummle – who impatiently whips his horse. But industry may have won Estella: if Pip's foster father had been an industrialist, a person who organised the manufacture and sale of metal goods, rather than a beater of horse-shoes, what would Estella's attitude have been to him then? As Pip and Herbert Pocket discourse humorously: 'a gentleman may not keep a public-house, may he? ... but a public-house may keep a gentleman' (GE, 154). Ironic when it is the proceeds of a defunct brewery that has kept Estella and her guardian, in comfort.

If the young Pip, Joe Gargery, the forge and the occupation of blacksmith represent the old, eighteenth century, the grown-up Pip, Miss Havisham, Estella and Mr Jaggers stand for the progressive, modern nineteenth century. It might seem that Miss Havisham, in her retro wedding dress, seated amid the ruined bridal feast and the stopped clocks of Satis House, which itself is a halted brewery, all stand for the past? This is arguable, but it is equally in order that Miss Havisham represents a new type of sensibility. New, that is, in a world where steam power was rapidly replacing the old, clockwork world of eighteenth-century automata. Throughout the eighteenth century, music was composed to beat out time. Dickens alludes to this when Herbert Pocket christens Pip 'Handel' in honour of the composer of *The Harmonious Blacksmith*, among many great works. The most popular eighteenth-century dances had been the minuet – the name indicative of a unit of time – and the bagatelle, where dancers beat out time with their feet, by musicians playing to a notional metronome. As long as the clock ticked and everyone moved or worked or sang or danced in *time*, society would hold together.

Clockwork as a source of power was already obsolete by the 1860s, when Dickens was writing *Great Expectations*. Even before the young Queen Victoria was crowned, Romanticism had taken its grip on art and literature. Feeling and even, sentiment was driving the world. By now, the *waltz* had replaced the minuet. Dancers moved across the floor in great, analogue sweeps, rather than beating out time, eighteenth century fashion. As a jilted bride, Miss Havisham embodies this sweeping tide of emotion. The old brewing industry may have given her a degree of wealth but her new self is driven by a warped and over reaching passion, the overweening rage that causes her to bring up her ward, Estella, to enact revenge on all men. By the 1860s, horse power had much dwindled and now, steam drove the biggest engines, steam, the by-product of fire, the same fire that, in actuality, almost consumes Miss Havisham. Indeed, her desperate wrestling with Pip for survival is an allegory of temperance in collision with feeling. And the Pip that emerges from combat is the new – as in morally renewed Pip – a phoenix rising literally from ashes. His act of valour, stemming from his better nature, saves her life *temporarily*, giving her room to apologise to him for ruining his life – and that of Estella, now married to the irascible Bentley Drummle. All of the eighteenth-century time marking could not reduce man to a mechanistic, uber-logical creature of reason. Humanity is tempered with emotion. But a world ruled by emotion is not *benign*. For Miss Havisham, who dies soon afterwards, it is too late. To feel is fine, the author is telling the reader, but this tide of nineteenth-century passion must be tempered with more logical instincts. In the narrative, Pip has yet to endure another fiery encounter in the form of old adversary, Dolge Orlick, who resolves to burn him to death. On this occasion, good feeling – in the form of friend Herbert Pocket – saves Pip – in the nick of *time*. In *Bleak House*, Mr Turveydrop (senior) claims that his function is to see 'that deportment is not wholly trodden underfoot by mechanics' (BH, 381). The irony, of course, is that Turveydrop's 'deportment' may at least be as rigid and artificial as any of the industrial machinery that he disdains.

If we accept that Dickens set *Great Expectations* in 1812, then the events in it and *Northanger Abbey* are not far apart. While a very young Joe Gargery was beating iron at his forge, Catherine Morland was preparing to leave Bath for Northanger Abbey. It is then she becomes aware of the General Tilney's obsession with time and time-keeping: 'The bustle of going was not pleasant – The clock struck ten while the trunks were carrying down, and the General had fixed to be out of Milsom-street by that hour' (NA, 147). On the remainder of the journey, Catherine witnesses his 'angry impatience at the waiters' when the travelling party stops to dine at a staging inn (NA, 148). At Northanger, the General takes out his watch and declares with surprise, that it is 'twenty minutes of five!' (NA, 153). Henry's sister Eleanor tells Catherine that: 'the strictest punctuality to the family hours would be expected at Northanger' (NA, 153).

Such adherence to time-keeping would be excusable in modern times, at least in an urban setting. General Tilney was a military man and he was used to controlling squadrons of soldiers and directing commands at officers. But the General was *not* a workaday man; he was a wealthy nobleman who had no obligation to be out of Milsom-street by any particular hour, except by his own dictate. The next morning, the General takes Catherine on a tour of the kitchen grounds of the Abbey, where she is surprised to see amid the growing spaces: 'a village of hot-houses seemed to arise among them, and a whole parish to be at work within the inclosure' (NA, 168). It is evident that General Tilney is producing exotic fruit on an industrial scale for the Abbey consumption, and is employing an army of workers – local people, in fact – to do it for him. In other words, the uber-wealthy, ex-military man is now a quasi-industrialist.

Earlier in the narrative, John Thorpe's obsession with time measurements pre-empt those of General Tilney. However, Thorpe's obsession is more likely to result from an expression of sexual prowess than the control exercised by the socially-elevated General: '*Three*-and-twenty' cried Thorpe; 'five-and-twenty if it is an inch.' A little later, John says: 'It is now half after one; we drove out of the inn-yard at Tetbury as the town-clock struck eleven; and I defy any man in England to make my horse go less than ten miles an hour in harness; that makes it exactly twenty-five' (NA, 44). Just where, over two hundred years ago, did the notion of such precision in matters of time and distance, come from?

Today, visitors to the village of Northill in Bedfordshire can see the clock made by Thomas Tompion in the early 1700's, on the tower of St Mary's Church. And the clock is distinguished by having only one hand, telling the hours. Tompion died in 1713, before the onsct of the broader sweep of the Industrial Revolution, which brought with it the need for more precise timings of production and people. To try to work out whether industry happened because of the advent of the minute hand on the clock in the later eighteenth century, or whether the production of the minute hand came about because of industrial necessity, is outside of the sweep of this narrative. But it is evident that General Tilney needs the precision of the industrialist in his life. Like the old soldier that he is, General Tilney controls – in fact, he bullies – his family. With help from the staging post system, marking the stirrings of the industrialization of travel, journeys are timed almost to the minute. Tilney regards his time as valuable and he has no regard for that of anyone else, shown by his rudeness to the waiting staff of the inn that they stop at. This regimentation is inherent within the private life of the Abbey, the split-second timing of the meals, the hot-house vegetables and fruit cultivation in the kitchen garden.

General Tilney controls not only the timings of the meals, but the lives of his grown-up children, denying them the freedom to express their personalities and to carve out individual paths in life. Captain Tilney, Henry's older brother, goes into the military in the wake of his father. Eleanor Tilney is obliged to conduct an affair of the heart, in secret.

By the mid-nineteenth century, awareness of time keeping was well established in literature. In *Bleak House*, Esther Summerson, Richard and Ada arrive in Lincolnshire, having enjoyed an idyllic, sleepy journey from their Hertfordshire home: 'Late in the afternoon we came to the market town where we were to alight from the coach – a dull little town, with a church-spire, and a market-place, and a market-cross, and one intensely sunny street, and a pond with an old horse cooling his legs in it, and a very few men sleepily lying and standing about in narrow little bits of shade. After the rustling of the leaves and the waving of the corn all along the road, it looked as still, as hot, as motionless a little town as England could produce' (BH, 298).

With words like 'still', 'hot' and 'motionless', Dickens has done his utmost to evoke atmosphere of a sleepy, English village on a summer afternoon. Yet, a few paragraphs later, Mr Boythorn, the host of the young travellers, pours cold water on the scene with the statement : 'Twenty-five minutes! Twenty-six minutes!' replied Mr Boythorn, referring to his watch ... With two ladies in the coach, this scoundrel has delayed his arrival six and twenty minutes. Deliberately! It is impossible that it can be accidental!' (BH, 298). Since neither of the two ladies, that is, Esther and Ada, seem ruffled by this notionally late arrival, it is difficult to discern why the host seems so put out by the situation. It could be because he was kept waiting. But bear in mind that Boythorn is a man of means who does not need – like so many characters in the novel – to work for a living. Later, the three guests and the reader learn that Boythorn is in perpetual dispute with his neighbour, Sir Leicester Dedlock, over a right of way to his estate. Boundaries and time-limits are interrelated, it seems, with the power to stir unmitigated anger in the breasts of their espousers. Yet, it is man who sets deadlines and by implication, has the power to mitigate such artificial limits.

Rather than win her heart, John Thorpe's technical marvel of a buggy endangered Catherine's life. Dr Jekyll did not succeed in leading the life he wanted by chemically altering his personality. Jennet Humphrye's son is destroyed by the technology of the day. Eleanor Vance destroys herself in her own motor car (HH, 245). With the fallibility of such man-made items, the reader might say, as Prospero did: 'We are such stuff as dreams are made on' (*The Tempest*: Act 4, Scene 1). And technology has yet another way of subverting the lives of the female subjects. Although it is perceptibly the male who invents and makes things, Jane Austen rightly foretold that the consumer of the future was to be the woman. While it is General Tilney who shows most delight over his 'modern' kitchen furnaces, it is Catherine whom he chooses to notionally redesign his son's house, Woodston.

One hundred and fifty years following the publication of *Northanger Abbey*, the familiar advertising, marketing and consuming culture was in full swing. In Shirley Jackson's text, Eleanor and Theodora witness an eerie night-time picnic on the lawn of Hill House (HH, 177).

The picnic, its description using words like 'blue, 'gold' and 'scarlet', is reminiscent of the techni-coloured advertising world of the 1950s, taunting one woman with what she so desperately wants, a husband and children, a 'normal' happy family by the standards of the time. And the other woman, Theodora, is a nonconformist who has avoided conventional marriage and motherhood. Since this technicolour tableau of happy family life fills Theodora equally with terror, it points out what she does *not* want.

The alchemists today are the advertising brandlords, the founders of tech and retail giants. And the new gothic heroine is the woman eagerly purchasing items that will make her prettier and happier. And the women that the alchemists appeal to are no *less* fictional than the gothic heroine because essentially, in today's world of marketing and advertising, *all* women are fictional, notional constructs of needs and wants driven by telegenic images of extravagant modern living, consumables such as food and clothing, and desire for luxury and status symbols, cars and houses.

But the alchemist is almost never the Byronic or romantic hero. Whether inventing or building, time-keeping or record-taking, the alchemist's engagement with the material world excludes him from this role. The Byronic hero seeks to distance himself from material reality. Whether he succeeds or not is another matter, but that is his intent. From this deduction, the reader may identify a proto-Byronic hero in the character of Henry Tilney. With his railing against the 'voluntary spies' in the neighbourhood of Woodston, the reader can only hope that, when the sun finally set on his and Catherine's wedding day, with the curtains of the fire-warmed rooms drawn against the outer world, that the well-built roads brought only the guests that the happy couple welcomed, and that the circulating newspapers informed their readers of exclusively good news (NA, 186).

The Allegorical Castle:
A repository of fantasy and reality, statis and movement

What is the castle? Past, present and future ♦ Establishing atmosphere ♦ Movement and statis ♦ The remote conundrum ♦ Omnipresent authority and individual consciousness ♦ Identity: masculine and feminine ♦ Order and chaos

Dwellings are anthropomorphic and the castle features strongly in gothic sub-genre. Its role is varied: a place to escape from, a place to seek refuge, the *alter ego* of a powerful (or powerless) character, or an overweening personality that dominates the other characters. As modern literature focuses increasingly upon the individual, the dominance of architecture in literature is set to continue.

What is the castle? Past, present and future

In her article about Charlotte Smith's novel, *The Old Manor House*, published 1793, Deborah Russell states that in the earliest gothic narratives, the large house or castle was a metonym for nationhood.[41] Overall, the role of the castle has changed in conjunction with the changing nature of the family, that is, from a political system in the eighteenth century to a nineteenth-century family dwelling to the many variations on the single-person dwellings that proliferate in our times.

By the twentieth and twenty-first centuries, the larger type of family house has become a dwelling in which to house a number of individuals rather than the traditional family, all with different and often, conflicting purposes. And it is Russell who points out that it is only in fantasy, for example, Lyra returning to Jordan College, has *the castle* become a place of family reconciliation

---

[41]Deborah Russell, *Domestic Gothic: Genre and Nation in Charlotte Smith's The Old Manor House* (Correspondence: School of English, Queen's University Belfast, John Wiley & Sons Ltd, 2013), pp771-782, p775.

(Russell, 780).

One continuing theme of eighteenth and nineteenth-century gothic literature is the image of the female protagonist striving to emerge from the murk and gloom of an ancient pile and into the comfortable and lamplit parlour of a family dwelling. A century later again, the heroine supposedly seeks to brush the cobwebs and dust from her modernistic home, to clean the scurf marks from her bathroom enamels and wall tiles. She probably works to pay the rent or mortgage on her personal space and can choose who to invite in for dinner. But is the liberated literary heroine of today any more 'free' than Catherine was, when she finally retreated to Woodston with Henry Tilney, or Adeline, when she settled in Leloncourt with Theodore La Luc? Judging by the fate of Joanna Eberhart in Ira Levin's *Stepford Wives*, it would seem, not necessarily. Why do so few modern narratives, Mills and Boon novels aside, bear traditionally happy endings for the female protagonist? To try to answer this question, I explore the symbol of *the castle* in the primary texts.

Though its narrative is populated with multitudinous dwellings, the undoubted castle of *His Dark Materials* is Jordan College, where the least of the action takes place. However, it remains an important symbol for both the reader and protagonist, Lyra Belacqua, a place that she leaves at the outset and returns to in the final pages of *The Amber Spyglass*, the third book of Philip Pullman's trilogy. She is older and wiser than at the outset of her adventures, and not a little chastened. In the manner of a fairy-tale heroine, she has lost her mystic powers. She has lost her parents, but only in the physical sense, never having found any emotional connection with either Mrs Coulter nor Lord Asriel. But throughout the narrative, she finds a host of new friends and forms poignant bonds with characters that she will most likely never see again, notably Mary Malone and Will Parry. When she returns to Jordan College, Lyra is ready to treat female scholar, Hannah, with a new respect. Indeed, Lyra is prepared to become a scholar herself, to learn to do academically what had formerly manifested as a mystical power. But the reality for the reader is that Lyra's happy ending is the conclusion to a fantasy.

Lyra's triumphant return to Jordan College echoes that of the conclusion of Hans Andersen's fairy tale, *The Snow Queen*. During the narrative, Gerda leaves her cosy urban home and following many adventures, arrives at the Snow Queen's chilly palace, filled with 'cutting winds'. She rescues her friend Kay, and they return to their home again. Like Lyra, she – and indeed, Kay –

have grown to maturity on their adventures and it is once again 'summer, glorious summer'. The author leaves us in no doubt that Gerda's life will be one of cosy domesticity and familial happiness, the nineteenth-century dream for fictional men and women.

In returning to a college rather than a home, twentieth-century Lyra represents the new woman; she will not be trapped in domesticity, whether in grandeur or austerity. Unlike Jane Eyre running away from Thornfield, she did not flee Jordan College at the outset but left it willingly to find a better life. Unlike Paula Power, she has not lost her castle, but found her proper place within it. Unlike Arthur Kipps, who experiences elements of his childhood in the nursery of the faraway Eel Marsh House, or Estella wandering about the ruins of Satis House, Lyra is not delving back into her past but looking forward to a bright and fulfilling future. In contrast to Eleanor Vance, who refused to leave Hill House, Lyra sensed her time to move out was due. She made her journey to maturity outside of the castle walls, proved herself worthy of it and subsequently returned.

Again, I point out the reality of this 'happy ending' being the conclusion to a fantasy. However, this fact should not obfuscate the significance of the role of the castle in gothic literature. Jordan College is the quintessence of what *the castle* represents in the typical gothic narrative, a place where the heroine finds herself lost or trapped in and uncovers information that serves as a pointer to her past – and her future. Of course, Lyra inhabits other castles; Mrs Coulter's swanky London apartment, the 'stinking palace' of Iofur Raknison, (HDM, 312), the toxic headquarters of the General Oblation Board, the cave in which she is kept captive by Mrs Coulter and at least one of Lord Asriel's seemingly limitless succession of laboratories and operational centres. But Jordan College is identifiable as *the castle*.

Establishing atmosphere

Overall, the presence of a castle establishes atmosphere in a narrative. It is usually in a remote location – though not always – in a place that the protagonist is bound to journey to or as with Lyra, journey from. Within its walls, tensions exist, often the result of male-female dichotomies and/or the conflict between the will of those in authority and the desires of a particular individual. The typical castle fields cavernous areas that suggest secrets awaiting discovery. In parallel, the castle can function as a vehicle for one or more characters to project imaginative scenarios upon. Not every castle bears all of these attributes but in a gothic narrative, the castle will always prove a point of stasis for much of the action to revolve around.

From the outset of their narratives, authors needed to establish the 'personality' of their castle. In his *Philosophical Enquiry into the Sublime and the Beautiful,* Edmund Burke wrote much upon evoking the sublime: 'A mode of terror, or of pain, is always the cause of the sublime' (Burke, 109). Among his statements pertaining to building are: 'a perpendicular has more force in forming the sublime, than an inclined plane' (Burke, 59), and 'I think then, that all edifices calculated to produce an idea of the sublime, ought rather to be dark and gloomy' (Burke, 66). Doubtlessly, Ann Radcliffe knew of his philosophy when she described the sensations of Adeline and her party when they first encounter the Abbey in the forest: 'The greater part of the pile appeared to be sinking into ruins, and that, which had withstood the ravages of time, shewed the remaining features of the fabric more awful in decay. The lofty battlements, thickly enwreathed with ivy, were half demolished, and become the residence of birds of prey. Huge fragments of the eastern tower, which was almost demolished, lay scattered amid the high grass, that waved slowly to the breeze' (ROTF, 15).

As the eighteenth century turned into the nineteenth, publishers made more use of visual imagery, engravings in particular of buildings, to impress atmosphere upon readers. In his article, 'Gothic visions of classical architecture in Hablot Knight Browne's dark illustrations for the novels of Charles Dickens', Dominic Janes delineates the architecture of Chesney Wold, the aristocratic Dedlock mansion in *Bleak House,* as illustrated by Hablot Knight Browne. Janes stresses the significance of Chesney Wold being the frontispiece of the original volume of the novel, rather than the titular Bleak House. He cites critic Michael Steig as stating that this illustration engenders a 'lack of human connection.[42] The reader can perceive this through the strict social hierarchy within its magnificent walls, and the loneliness of Lady Dedlock: '(who is childless) looking out in the early twilight from her boudoir at a keeper's lodge, and seeing the light of a fire upon the latticed panes, and smoke rising from the chimney, and a child, chased by a woman, running out into the rain to greet the shining figure of

---

[42]Dominic Janes, (2014) *Gothic visions of classical architecture in Hablot Knight Browne's dark illustrations for the novels of Charles Dickens,* Gothic Studies 16 (2), pp33-51. ISSN 2050-456X, p10. Subsequent references will be to this edition and will be inserted parenthetically into the text, for example "(Janes, 10)

a wrapped-up man' (BH, 56).

By contrast, Janes describes Bleak House as having 'actual warmth' (Janes, 10). The reader can perceive this in the account of the house rendered by Esther Summerson just following her arrival: 'It was one of those *delightfully irregular* houses where you go up and down steps out of one room and into another, and where you come upon more rooms when you think you have seen all there are, and where there is a *bountiful provision* of little halls and passages and where you find still older cottage rooms in unexpected places, with *lattice windows* and green growth pressing through them. Mine, which we entered first, was of this kind, with an up-and-down roof, that had more corners in it than I ever counted afterwards, and a chimney. There was a *wood fire* upon the hearth paved all around with pure white tiles, in every one of which a miniature fire was blazing' (BH, 115). The italics are of my choosing and I have selected the phrases that stress what the author is trying to convey and what the protagonist feels, that is, a sense of her host's generosity and the house's antiquity. Only the 'pure white tiles' convey a rather chilly modernity, but this may not have been so in Dickens's day.

Therapists and writers, most notably Betty Edwards in her book *Drawing on the Right Side of the Brain*, have written much upon the anhropomorphism of the dwelling, with eyes for windows and other openings for ears, mouth, and so on. Several authors metaphorise the impending destruction of its owner through architectural descriptions. As Irving Malin points out, a building may look fine and sound, but a dwelling with the merest signs of dereliction may suggest that its occupier has a deficiency in some way, possibly an inability to cope with life (Malin, 146). Through the subtlety of the prose in *Dr Jekyll and Mr Hyde*, R.L. Stevenson beautifully nuances the relevance of architecture to the text. Initially, we learn of the laboratory: 'A certain sinister block of building thrust forward its gable onto the street. It was two storeys high; showed no window, nothing but a door on the lower storey and a blind forehead of discoloured wall on the upper; and bore in every feature the marks of prolonged and sordid negligence. The door, which was equipped with neither bell nor knocker, was blistered and distained' (DJMH, 4).

It is only later in the text that the reader learns that this is the out-house in which Dr Jekyll is obliged to carry out his experiments. Here, the sense of impending doom is heightened by use of words and phrases like 'sinister', 'blind forehead', and 'prolonged and sordid negligence'. His work only reveals itself when his migrating personality causes havoc among his circle of friends. As Stevenson's narrative progresses, the reader learns a little more of the laboratory building: 'There are three windows looking on the court on the first floor; none below; the windows are always shut but they're clean. And then there is a chimney; which is generally smoking; so somebody must live there' (DJMH, 6). This indicates to the reader that the building, though neglected, is not unoccupied. Significantly, the activity seems centred on the first storey, a metaphor indicating that the occupier is engaged in a type of intellectual activity. The author completes the puzzle when he provides a description of Dr Jekyll's actual dwelling place: 'Round the corner from the by-street there was a square of some ancient, handsome houses, now for the most part decayed from their high estate, and let into flats and chambers to all sorts and conditions of men, map-engravers, architects, shady lawyers, and the agents of obscure enterprises. One house, however, second from the corner, was still occupied entire; and at the door of this, which wore a great air of wealth and comfort ... Mr Utterson stopped and knocked' (DJMH, 12). From this, the reader gains an awareness of Jekyll's wealth, but the indication that nearby dwellings are falling into decay points to the tenuousness of his social position. And the reader may find it disquieting that neither Richard Enfield nor Gabriel Utterson recognised the rear entrance of the laboratory as belonging to Dr Jekyll at the outset of the narrative, when Enfield was recounting the tale of Mr Hyde injuring the young girl, a matter that the men acknowledge. As Enfield states: 'And by the way, what an ass you must have thought me, not to know that this was a back way to Dr Jekyll's' (DJMH, 25). But their initial lack of recognition is metaphorical in that Utterson is about to encounter a facet of Dr Jekyll that he had never known. The fact of the survival of his laboratory at the end of the narrative could indicate that Utterson will never make neither Lanyon's nor Jekyll's letters known to anyone else, with Jekyll's reputation surviving intact.

In Jackson's text, the anthropomorphism of the language conveys Eleanor Vances's shock at encountering Hill House: its malicious anthropomorphism akin to meeting an unpleasant personality (HH, 34). The rational Dr Montague senses its personality also when he tells Eleanor to leave the house if she feels that it is overwhelming her (HH, 124). Here, I suggest to the reader that the castle may be, in many narratives, a surrogate for the Byronic hero. I repeat my sketch of this archetype from earlier in the text:

'he tends to be youthful but old enough to have lived a little and to have endured the trials that artistically furrow his handsome brow. Whatever his attainments, whether rich or poor, he must possess an air, an attitude of being his own person, and of a disinclination to conform to social convention ... never comfortable in society, the hero likes to wander in remote places, usually to brood upon whatever has blighted his life either in reality or in perception. Whatever his condition, the Byronic hero carries with him a perpetual air of mystery, and the reader – and the heroine – gain the impression that he has been hurt psychologically by an incident in his life. Much of the narrative consists of the heroine trying to pierce this fog of mystery, to get to his heart, in every sense of the word.'

If we substitute the word 'heart' with 'hearth', the reader may grasp the wider meaning of this. Although not necessarily 'remote', the castle most often wears an air of brooding distinction, of solitariness that make it the overweening personality in the narrative.

Movement, stasis and social isolation

The castle occupies a particular place in fiction, a place of security, rest, ease, grandeur, authority, isolation, remoteness and even, entrapment. In addition, the castle behaves as a fixed point, a stasis around which the wider action takes place. While the heroine and other characters have freedom of movement, the stiff, upright castle, complete with turrets and spires, is as fixed as a tent pole, establishing tension between aristocratic authority and the personal – and usually conflicting – plans of individuals. But though static in the landscape, the castle is a hub of seething emotion, of love and hate, pity, fear, wonder and fulfilment. In any narrative, significant dwellings establish the *stasis* that is central to the fictional plot. Shirley Jackson writes of Hill House, at the opening of *The Haunting of Hill House*, placing emphasis upon how sturdy and 'upright' the structure is, a matter she stresses once more at the close of the novel. (HH, 3) Here, the author is suggesting that it is only the human intruders that awaken the malevolence that is the sleeping giant of Hill House. By the twentieth century, the transformation that slowly saw the castle or dwelling morphing from an allegory for nationhood, or simply a theatrical background against which a wider drama took place, into a vehicle with a personality of its own that warped everyone around and inside of it, was complete. This warping effect has been typified in recent years by the publication of *Our*

House by Louise Candlish, in which the desire to hold on to a lovely home wraps the entire progression of family life. One important milestone of this transformation took place in the nineteenth century.

In her 'Introduction' to Thomas Hardy's *A Laodicean*, Barbara Hardy states that the buildings that the characters inhabit and indeed, that they wish to live in, is indicative of their passions and inner yearnings; this is fairly easily observed (AL, 27). Castle Stancy is at the heart of this narrative. It is the centrifugal force around which all the characters rotate; are corrupted, purified or tested in some way. It is the castle that leads George Somerset to Paula Power, the castle that holds Paula in its medieval spell, that sparks the rivalry between George Somerset and Havill, and triggers the rest of the story's events. It is desire to possess the name of the castle that subverts Paula emotionally, leading her to prepare for an injudicious marriage. The situation is comically burlesqued by William de Stancy himself with his antics involving the ancestral sword and suit of armour, upon their first meeting. But from where has Paula's state of mind sprung? Because what Paula is not, is the traditional, isolated gothic heroine.

The remote conundrum

In her essay 'World Building in Horror, Occult and Fantasy', Marion Zimmer Bradley states that the gothic novel is now 'vanishing'.[43] The reasons she states are broadly, the proliferation of technology and ubiquity of transport and police forces. Bradley's quotation is grounded in reality, but the reader may wonder why, in a world of sophisticated communications (our world), that vulnerable groups are still stalked, abused or worse (Bradley, 72).

In today's world, the castle is expressed by the tall buildings, often made of glass, that the anxious young person arrives at, ready to take on the challenge of a new job. The pater familias male is often a senior employer, superficially providing guidance to the new-comer, but often a 'guidance' that compels the junior to alter his or her personality in favour of providing an innocuous screen for questionable corporate activity. One fine example of such a

---

[43]Marian Zimmer Bradley,'World Building in Horror, Occult and Fantasy Writing' by in *How to Write Tales of Horror, Fantasy & Science Fiction*, ed. by Williamson, J.N. (London: Robinson Publishing, 1987), p71. Subsequent references will be to this edition and will be inserted parenthetically into the text, for example "(Bradley, 71)"

narrative is *The Firm*, a 1993 movie based on a novel by John Grisham, where a fresh-faced young lawyer serves as a front for tax fraud. And the imprisoning in the tower or dungeon has been displaced by the pressure on the young protagonist to suppress his or her talents in favour of carrying out the work of the corporation.

I assert that the gothic genre continues to flourish in the fables of psychological isolation rather than physical remoteness. Eleanor Vance could at any time have chosen to leave Hill House but she did not. The Governess could have chosen to leave the haunted Bly with Mrs Grose and Flora, but she did not. And more terrifying, what of Arthur Kipps, whose gothic experience continued *after* he left the location of supernatural activity? The new gothic writer is dealing with another kind of isolation, a state that is chimeric rather than actual; we can see this happening in the later novels of the nineteenth century. To illustrate this, imagine how different the narrative might have been if Shirley Jackson had written her novel in the smartphone era. Instead of seeing writing on the wall, Eleanor would simply have received the chilling texts to help her to 'come home' on her telephone – and would they have been any less frightening? And would she have been any less likely to blame the other house inmates of trying to terrorise her out of the place?

Paula Power, in spite of her wealth and social status, is isolated in the narrative. The only friend of her own age is Charlotte, who bears the family name that she desires herself. In this frame of mind, Paula could equate with Catherine Earnshaw of *Wuthering Heights*. But Catherine's lust for Heathcliff eventually defeats her quest for social respectability, Paula never stops longing for an ancestral name, not even when she eventually marries George Someset: 'I wish my castle wasn't burned and I wish that you were a de Stancy' (AL, 437). And this identification with an actual building may lead to another condition.

In the chapter, **The Lexicon of Haunting**, I present the cases for Bly being haunted or not haunted. Here, I question: *how* does a house become haunted? Is it a kink in the fabric of the building itself, the supernatural manifesting from the mortar and brick, like sweat oozing from pores in the skin? The insubstantial ghosts seem unable to exist without a solid bastion to dwell within: 'This tower was one of a pair – square incongruous crenellated structures – that were distinguished for some reason, though I could see little difference, the old and the new' (TOTS, 136).

It may actually have something to do with way the 'big, ugly antique but convenient old house' is built, its two towers attracting ghosts the way that spiders seek solidity upon which to spin their vapid webs (TOTS, 127). Right from the Governess's arrival, the very anatomy of Bly aids and abets its haunting. The layout of the house heightens her emotion. In Bly, she experiences air and light, a freedom she has never known. She sees herself in a full-length mirror for the first time and reads novels that have been forbidden to her, in her family home. In her narrative, she drops hints at a troubled background: 'disturbing letters from home, where things were not going well' (TOTS, 141). Perhaps *that* is her trouble? Perhaps Bly is absorbing her emotion together with that of the people who have lived – and died – there? Perhaps that is why Henry James takes pains to emphasise its solidity? On her first night, she hears an unknown child crying in the passage-way just outside her room. She first sees – the reader can assume – Quint upon one of the towers. Then, she sees him peering through a window pane at her and again, she encounters him climbing the staircase towards Miles's room. If Miles and Flora are indeed trying to 'meet' the ghosts, once more, the fabric of Bly aids them, such as in the incident of Miles playing the piano while Flora takes flight to the outdoors. But, as Shoshana Felman asserts in her reference to Sigmund Freud 'unrest in a home is often a symptom, and that symptom might spring not necessarily from an unhappy individual but the conflict between two forces.'[44]

Omnipresent authority and individual consciousness

When Arthur Kipps arrives at Eel Marsh House, the author's language indicates that he is about to encounter an authoritative presence: 'I looked up ahead and saw, as if rising out of the water itself, a *tall, gaunt* house of grey stone with a slate roof, that now gleamed *steelily* in the light. It stood like some *lighthouse* or *beacon* or *Martello tower*, facing the whole, wide expanse of marsh and estuary ... isolated, *uncompromising* but also, I thought, *handsome*' (Hill, 74). My italics underpin Susan Hill's intention, the presence of the house bearing the impression of a stern, military male 'uncompromising', 'handsome', guarding whoever is or was in the house –

---

[44]Shoshana Felman, 'Turning The Screw of Interpretation" in *Yale French Studies*, (1 January 1977), 94-207, p110. Subsequent references will be to this edition and will be inserted parenthetically into the text, for example '(Felman, 110)'.

Mrs Drablow? Arthur? And it seems to have worked because, aside from the one poltergeist incident in the nursery, the majority of unseemly happenings take place *outside* of the house.

Edward Said has written upon how metaphor is written into the very word, *author*, 'with which writer, deity, and *pater familias* are identified' (G&G, 4). The chapter, **The New Alchemists: Text, Travel and Time** explains how, until very recently the majority of 'authorising' texts, wills, deeds, pledges and so on, were written and signed by men. In the gothic sub-genre, this authority extends to one character wielding jurisdiction in a building of note, a situation that identifies it as the castle. The custom of rendering a domestic dwelling a name (identity? personality?) has endured through the ages. In certain narratives, the identity of *the castle* may be ambivalent. Irving Malin refers to the 'authoritarian tensions' represented by the castle within the gothic narrative (Malin, 146). Meanwhile, Delia Da Sousa Correa cites the castle as 'consciousness' (DDSC, 108). The castle may be firm and upright, a point of stasis, but emotions and prejudices and desires seethe within. As discussed above, as a dwelling, Bleak House endears itself to the reader and the protagonist, rendering it difficult to imagine it a place of 'authoritarian tensions'. But, according to Dominic Janes, what was at least as important as the symbolism of the actual institutions, were the politics of access, of entering and leaving, of seeing out from the inside and of looking in from the outside (Janes, 13).

If the reader accepts the advocation of these two critics, then the castle in a narrative is a place of authority, where a character may only enter – or in certain cases, leave – with permission of its owner. And this places both Bleak House and Chesney Wold as contenders for the status of castle, since both dwellings bear 'authoritarian tensions' within their walls. One of the more disquieting aspects of *Bleak House* is the failure of John Jarndyce to acknowledge Richard Carstone as his foster son. Richard, it might seem to the reader, is the obvious relative to whom Jarndyce could bequeath his bounty. Instead, Richard is forced to subsist on a scanty allowance while chasing the rainbow of a 'profession' from the limited array of occupations open to the Victorian gentleman. Yet Jarndyce only too readily admits to Esther that it is Richard's lack of stability in earlier life that has made him such a restless, incurious creature: 'How much of this indecision of character … is chargeable on the incomprehensible heap of uncertainty and procrastination on which he has been thrown from his birth, I don't pretend to say' (BH, 218). A less authoritarian character would give Richard the sense that Bleak House is *his* home. Later on, the reader makes the disquieting discovery that Jarndyce is planning on establishing a family of his own in Bleak House, plans that he fails to carry through. But it is his disquieting *intentions* that may have deprived Richard of a permanent home. The most poignant aspect of the novel is that in the narrative, the only dwelling that Richard ever takes authority over is the few dingy rooms that he shares with Ada, in which he manages to father his child before Richard dies. Just before the conclusion of the narrative, Jarndyce's handing over of Esther – without asking her first – to Allan Woodcourt, all within an eerie replica of Bleak House, is a sign that his sexual authority over her is not yet concluded.

In *The Castle of Otranto*, Manfred has the power to imprison Theodore. In Radcliffe's narrative, the La Motte family live as squatters in the Abbey until the Marquis de Montalt bids them welcome to stay, the same dwelling in which Adeline is eventually imprisoned. General Tilney invites Catherine to Northanger Abbey – and expels her again. Only select persons are allowed into Satis House, which is ever presided over by a vigilant gate-keeper. Berthe Mason is confined within the attic of Thornfield, at the behest of husband Rochester. Following her arrival at Bly, the Governess positions herself as chatelaine of the house, finding herself unexpectedly 'at the helm' of 'a great drifting ship' (TOTS, 127). Eventually, she is guarding the children against the ghosts that *she* believes haunts *it*. Curiously, it could be the *lack* of authority that stirs up activity at Bly? The receipt of the headmaster's letter throws the Governess into a mental spin: 'it gave me a second sleepless night' (TOTS, 128). Such tension can only exist within a solidly-constructed environment, such as a hammock needing two bastions from which to swing. The Governess perceives this tension before even Quint's first appearance: 'Oh it was a trap – not designed but deep – to my imagination, to my delicacy, perhaps to my vanity; to whatever in me was most excitable' (TOTS, 134).

Though she is neither owner or hereditary servant, Mrs Danvers appoints herself as guardian of Rebecca's legacy at Manderley. And though the text doesn't explicitly state it, it implies that it is Mrs Danvers who ultimately destroys the house, probably – from the point of view of the reader - because of Maxim's failure to dismiss this 'efficient' servant (R, 85). Dudley the caretaker acts as gatekeeper of Hill House, his wife guards the household treasures (HH, 101). But it is its eventual owner, Luke Sanderson, who tells Eleanor to leave (HH, 238). The chapter **Maid in the Mirror** explores the notion of woman as angel of the house, the birth/death agent who is incomplete outside of the domestic sphere. Here, the reader may wonder: would Hill House have manifested its poltergeist if Dr Montague arrived to carry out his investigation more subjectively, with only Luke Sanderson as a companion?

The chapter **The Lexicon of Haunting** explores various types of supernatural manifestations and their implications in literature for both the heroines of yesteryear and of today. Here, I simply state that the titular house feeds on nervous energy which both Eleanor and Theodora have in abundance. On arrival at Hill House, Eleanor lights a cigarette with trembling fingers, while in a later episode indoors, she senses Theodora as 'nervous and alert' (HH 35, 125). Meanwhile, Eleanor thinks of herself as having been swallowed by a 'monster', the monster of course being the house (HH, 42). As Eleanor slowly succumbs to its malevolence, the psychic Theodora learns to disarm the enemy and place herself outside of the situation with doses of well-aimed humour, stating how the following year, she will go on holiday to another, quiter place. Eleanor does not possess this facility. If Dr Montague and Luke had arrived in the company of 'just Theodora', the poltergeist may have manifested by eventually dying for lack of energy (HH, 42). Eleanor – and indeed, the others – suffer because she has both too little and too much imagination, enough to imagine the monster swallowing her whole, but not enough to fight her way out of its mouth.

In *A Laodicean*, the castle does not align itself with any personality but takes on an identity of its own, a pernicious, almost malevolent identity, yet without the supernatural manifestations of Hill House or Bly. Castle Stancy quite literally entraps George Somerset for several hours while its presence intrudes upon Paula, all but obliging her to fulfil a union with a person of lineage, which she can add to her accomplishments. And Paula does indeed almost fall into the trap of marrying William de Stancy, not evil in himself but deceptive in the insidious way that the impending union has been brought about.

On arrival at Manderley, Maxim and Mrs de Winter occupy separate sleeping chambers, initially. Eventually, they unite physically, but only after the events of the novel pull the pair closer together – has Mrs de Winter passed the test set her by the *house*, rather than its owner? It is as if Mrs de Winter is obliged to prove herself to Manderley, rather than Maxim, before being classed as fit for the position of mother to the future heirs of the estate. Because it is a male character who is most often in 'authority', while the female struggles to exercise her will, the authoritarian/individual consciousness dichotomy does extend to that of the contrast of male and female.

Identity: masculine and feminine

In their essay, 'The Parables of the Cave', Sandra Gilbert and Susan Gubar explore how the darkness and spaciousness of the cave acts as a metaphor of femininity, that is, the womb, in literature: a place to refresh the psyche, replendish vitality and to 'give birth' to something new (G&G, 99). In reality, the castle is the natural successor of the cave and in fiction, this parallel of the castle with the cave, and the cave with the uterus, ordain the castle as a paradigm of femininity. The cave/basement is at the lowest point of a dwelling, with quarters of increasing sophistication as the building moves upwards. And it is not surprising that (usually male) scholars and sages are described as working in an ivory tower, that is, the highest point of a building.

The cave as a dwelling represents a beginning or *the* beginning of man's evolutional journey from a collection of curious individuals living in caves, to the creation of a sophisticated society living in a highly designed dwelling, that is, the castle. In the gothic sub-genre, this sophistication tends to be remote from the rest of organised society. But whether the castle is at a remote location or in the centre of an urban setting, such as Jordan College or Dr Jekyll's house, the heroine/protagonist usually has the opportunity – or the obligation – of exploring its darker corners, the attics and cellars and other locked rooms. As Marilyn Butler explains, it is in this darkness that new beginnings are found (NA, xxix). Nor is it surprising that *the dream* is intrinsic to many gothic plots: just as dreaming occupies the liminal world between waking and unconsciousness, the gothic protagonist is often pointed to the nexus of his or her dilemma in the course of dreaming, for instance, once in the Abbey, Adeline dreams of the tortures her father endured before he died.

Seeds germinate and mammals gestate in darkness. Fairy-tale characters like Hansel and Gretel, and Little Red Riding Hood get lost in the darkness of the forest before they find their way home or are rescued by someone else. Aladdin finds his treasure, that is, the lamp when he is lost in a cave, before he becomes a rich and successful man. Literature and indeed, reality, is filled with instances of characters finding the solution to their problems in the downtime of dreams. The Count of Monte Cristo is confined in a prison cell for twenty years, while he gains the strength to get revenge upon his enemies. Whether metaphorical or a plot device, the cave has long featured in literature and this is eminently true of the gothic sub-genre. In *The Castle of Otranto*, Theodore takes refuge in a cave before he and Isabella find one another. Adeline finds the truth about her origins when she explores a cellar in the Abbey. Catherine Morland, however, is frustrated in her attempts to discover the 'truth' about Northanger Abbey because she cannot access its most obscure spaces, a situation that informs her of an existential truth about her environment.

Without being told, the reader already knows that Esther Summerson is *not* going to find clues to her origins within the orderliness of Bleak House: '(The moveables) agreed in nothing but their perfect neatness, their display of the whitest linen, and their storing-up, wheresoever the existence of a drawer, small or large, rendered it possible, of quantities of rose-leaves and sweet lavender' (BH, 116). But it is no surprise when Esther first hears the voice of her mother in the darkness of the keeper's lodge of Chesney Wold, where she, Ada and John Jarndyce take shelter during a storm: 'Lady Dedlock had taken shelter in the lodge, before our arrival there, and had come out of the gloom within. She stood behind my chair with her hand upon it. I saw her hand close to my shoulder when I turned my head. 'I have frightened you?' she said' (BH, 309). Over the following months, the consciousness of both women moves out of the shadows as they discover their relationship to one other. This fertility of darkness is further contrasted by the sterility of the clutter in Bleak House – whether ordered or disordered. Yet the darkness that Esther is consigned to during her near-fatal brush with smallpox bears fruit. Metaphorically, she is united – emotionally, at least – with her mother, not long following her recovery.

Omnipresent authority and individual consciousness

The parallel between Paula's father and Castle Stancy is apparent from the beginning of *A Laodicean*; he bought and bequeathed it to her, after all. But Paula never *identifies* with the castle; indeed, it is she who tries to 'rebrand' herself by marrying a descendant of its former owner, almost as if to prove herself worthy of occupying it. And when at the conclusion, she declares to George Somerset, her statement is half-ironic and half-amusing (AL, 437).

The reader can laugh with her because her castle *is* burned and she is *not* a de Stancy. She is upset, but not psychologically damaged at the destruction of the pile in which she never felt quite at ease, it having belonged to her father and in need of, from *her* judgement, restoration. This frisson of annoyance is in contrast to the number of male characters who identify unequivocally with their piles. Although it is the male who exercises authority over the more political areas of the castle, its entrances and exits, generally it is the male who collapses mentally and morally and physically when he loses possession of this female avatar. From this point of view, the castle is often his surrogate/mother wife.

When Shakespeare's King Lear relinquishes his castle, he loses his authority. In *Jane Eyre*, when Thornfield is burned down, its owner Edward Rochester is damaged with it, possibly the destructor Berthe Mason's intentions. Within the walls of Manderley, Maxim de Winter is a member of quasi-royalty, ruling his castle, his wife and other family members, and their servants. He describes Manderley as 'his little kingdom'. He states Manderley is the driving force in his life, that this type of love for a place, a plot of land and buildings upon it, have never been put into words by any preacher or church (R, 306). With his *raison d'etre* gone, that is, an ancestral pile to provide heirs for, Maxim loses both manhood and motivation. We see him at the beginning of the narrative, which is actually the end of the story, a pathetic invalid being nursed by his wife. She describes the hotel that they had been living in as free of 'atmosphere' and the better for it (R, 4). With its stark interior, the place does come across to the reader like an eerie hospital where Maxim – she assures us – is notionally recovering from the loss of his erstwhile social status (R, 4). But the reader cannot fail to see through her forced cheeriness. Without the author spelling it out, the reader knows that Maxim and Mrs de Winter are not going to have any children. Mrs de Winter is reduced once more to her status as paid companion, and in this instance, is caught in a situation that, unlike her job with Mrs Van Hopper, she will never escape from, until the death of either her or Maxim – most likely that of Maxim. Maxim has held up under a number of traumas, the discovery that his lovely, witty Rebecca is a serial adulterer, the arguable necessity of his shooting her and dispensing with her body, and the final ordeal of her corpse returning to land and threatening to drag him down to the status of murderer and to the penalty of death. But he cannot bear up under the loss of his ancestral home. He has travelled much but has always returned to his boyhood home. With its destruction, his motivation, personality, everything goes.

In Susan Hill's text, Arthur Kipps is in possession of his castle at the outset of the text: 'pretty little cottage' which the author proceeds to describe in all its solidity and certainty: 'the house was already mine, bound to me invisibly (Hill, 6). But Arthur's certain world is shaken by the mere instance of his step family telling ghost stories around the fire: 'I fought a bitter battle within myself ... my expression which I knew began to show the first signs of discomfiture' (Hill, 161). Soon afterwards, Arthur proceeds to tell his tale. A riposte to the 'pretty little cottage' is Eel Marsh House, a brooding pile caught in the liminal stretch of land at the end of a causeway, reachable only at the ebb of the tide. In keeping with the castles of the other narratives, entry is by invite only. Outside its walls, the raging titular character, the woman in black, terrorises and wreaks vengeance on descendants of the tribe that have robbed her of her birthright, that is, lawyers and their clerks.

However, one female character does form an emotional connection with 'her' notional pile. Dale Bailey cites the Cult of True Womanhood as identifying women 'with the house, often with specific rooms' (Bailey, 33). And Bailey claims that Eleanor Vance has internalized this ideology, which is the root of much of her disturbance at Hill House. The reader may conclude that the acceptance of this ideology is the cause of Eleanor's destruction.

Order and chaos, imagination and reality

In *Romance of the Forest*, the Abbey is the place where Adeline begins her adult life, achieving a kind of freedom following the strictures of the convent. It is in the Abbey that she 'hears' the voice of her late father through the documents that she unearths in the cellar. And it is there that she is faced with both the benevolence and the treachery of the La Mottes, and is forced to face the truth about the wicked designs of the Marquis. But it is in the Abbey that Adeline meets her lover and future husband, Theodore, and wins the loyalty of the serving man, Peter. The emotional see-saw that Adeline seems obliged to undergo amounts to no less than a concatenated passage from childhood to young womanhood. In literary terms, she is the subject of a *bildingsroman*, a personal growth experience akin to Lyra's leaving Jordan College that would never have taken place had she stayed in the convent. In spite of its darker side, the Abbey is the pivotal point that orders the chaos of her life.

In Jane Austen's text, the titular Abbey plays a rather different role. Catherine is the naive product of a vicarage upbringing, and in a very short time she is transported from there to fashionable Bath and from there to Northanger Abbey. From the beginning, the Abbey of her imagination is not the one she faces in reality and presently, she is forced to shed her swiftly-acquired delusions about life: 'The visions of romance were over. Catherine was completely awakened. Henry's address ... had more thoroughly opened her eyes to her late fancies than all their several disappointments had done' (NA, 187). It might have been a growth experience, but her tutor/lover Henry Tilney has problems of his own in dealing with even with the *idea* of the encroaching industrial realities of the rapidly-changing Britain. By the conclusion of the narrative, with their retreat to Woodston, Catherine and Henry have regressed rather than progressed. This latter vicarage is slightly grander than the scene of Catherine's up-bringing, yet the place will only ever fulfil mundane domestic yearnings.

In *Bleak House*, the progression of events confounds the reader's expectations at every turn; in a typical gothic narrative, the young woman arrives at the remote house to be greeted by the trusty housekeeper. At the titular house, Esther discovers that *she* is that housekeeper. Unlike Adeline and most unlike Catherine, for whom certain parts of their respective Abbeys are *verboten*, Esther is not only *not* denied access to any part of the house, she is actually given its keys on the night of her arrival: 'The large bunch is the housekeeping, and the little bunch is the cellars, miss' (BH, 118). Whatever are Esther's thoughts and feelings, she will not be, as Lisa Appignanesi puts it in her Introduction to Gilbert and Gubar's text: 'immured in a great house in which all the keys to doors or escape belong to a cruel husband or father' (G&G, xxi). Not alone does this accessibility bring Esther into jarring contrast with the majority of gothic heroines, it adds a tinge of sadness to the thoughts of the orphaned young woman who, though a model of practical good sense, would naturally be curious to lift the veil of obscurity from her own origins. In describing her thoughts on that first night in Bleak House, Esther writes: 'I wandered back to my godmother's house, and came along the intervening track, raising up shadowy speculations which had sometimes trembled there in the dark, as to what knowledge Mr Jarndyce had of my earliest history – even as to the possibility of his being my father – though that idle dream was quite gone now' (BH, 131).

Unlike many a gothic heroine, Esther is never going to wander along corridors, wondering what secrets lie behind the locked doors. No mysteries or haunting ghosts lie in wait at Bleak House; instead, it seems little more than a repository of colonial junk, filled with objects that are not imbued with particular significance: 'you lost yourself in passages, with mangles in them, and three-cornered tables, and a native Hindoo-chair, which was also a sofa, a box and a bedstead' (BH, 115). The prescence of this junk renders the house another example of the displacement that J. Hillis Miller refers to 'naming one thing in terms of another' that fills the text and leads the reader to wonder what might be taking place (BH, 13) Certainly, Bleak House is several social notches above Krook's rag-and-bottle shop, which is also filled with seemingly useless objects. Yet, Krook's shop – which has a claim to be yet another symbolical castle of the narrative - is the place that contains a vital clue to Esther's past, namely, her father. Dickens exercises his authorial mastery by not even hinting at this when Esther and her companions visit the shop: 'The only other lodger,' (Miss Flite) now whispered, in explanation; 'a law writer. The children in the lanes here, say he has sold himself to the devil' (BH, 106). As in *Romance of the Forest*, order eventually emerges from this chaos.

At the outset of *Great Expectations*, protagonist Pip takes a back seat in projecting his imagination upon Satis House. Throughout, the gates of the house are opened and shut by a keeper and only authorized persons are allowed to enter, a matter that fills him with a delight that he never expresses. Because of this access, Pip has the privilege of indulging the fantasies of persons who long to know what is inside of it, a matter that he teases even his gentle foster father with: 'And we all had cake and wine on gold plates. And I got up behind the coach to eat mine, because she told me to' (GE, 57). Initially, Pip is repentant but as he grows older and moves away from Satis House, his imagination begins to expand and project itself into yearnings for his future: '(Miss Havisham) had as good as adopted Estella, she had as good as adopted me, and it could not fail to be her intention to bring us together. She reserved it for me to restore the desolate house, admit the sunshine into the dark rooms, set the clocks a-going and the cold hearths a-blazing, tear down the cobwebs, destroy the vermin – in short, do all the shining deeds of the young Knight of Romance and marry the Princess' (GE, 197).

It is Pip's absence from Satis House that stimulates his imagination; by contrast, it is the arrival of Henry James's Governess at Bly, that causes her to project her imagination onto its walls as she becomes acquainted with its interiors and exteriors. Curiously, her opinion of Bly seems to morph in accordance with whoever she happens to be in company with. When little Flora shows her around, the Governess declares: 'I had the view of a castle of romance inhabited by a rosy sprite, such a place as would somehow, for diversion of the young idea, take all colour out of story books and fairy-tales' (TOTS, 127). The Governess's initial reaction to Bly is quite utilitarian: 'empty chambers and dull corridors on crooked staircases that made me pause and even on the summit of an old machicolated square tower ... a big ugly antique but convenient house embodying a few features of a building still older, half displaced, half utilised' (TOTS, 127). But as events unfold, the Governess begins to fantasise: 'Was there a secret at Bly – a mystery of Udolpho or an insane and unmentionable relative kept in unsuspected confinement?' (TOTS, 138). The reference to Ann Radcliffe's 1794 novel underlies the Governess's thinking and indeed, that of the author.

According to Dale Bailey, Eleanor's bid for a new life is bound to end in failure because she is unable to stop projecting her imagined new life upon the brutal reality that is Hill House. Unable to live in the style she desires, Eleanor tries to render 'her dream apartment' as Hill House itself (Bailey, 44-45). Sensing that this stance is headed for failure, Eleanor even begs to return home with Theodora (HH, 208-9). And when this fails Eleanor's despair is palpable and her descent into madness seems inevitable.

Catherine's fledgling romance with Henry Tilney almost perishes when he discerns her fantasies involving his family and ancestral seat. *Bleak House* is filled with characters whose lives, like that of Richard Carstone, are quite literally up in the air, and one possesses a name that reflects that – Miss Flite – as with a number of their notional castles. And like Richard, several of them perish.

The misfortunes experienced by Maxim de Winter exacerbate because he cannot adjust his castle, Manderley, to accommodate the idea of the 'new woman'. As Sally Beauman puts it in her Introduction to the book: 'Maxim de Winter kills not one wife, but two' (R, 439).

One of Lyra Belacqua's survival tactics is to never succumb to any sentiment about the myriad palaces and fantastical laboratories that she visits. At the conclusion of the narrative, she is rewarded, fairy-tale fashion, by returning in triumph to her true castle, Jordan College. Indeed, her future is so filled with promise that this is an appropriate place to remind the reader of Bruno

Bettelheim's adage on the ending of the typical fairy tale, a metaphor of the integration of the male and female aspects of the personality, rather than exhorting the reader to go out and win an aristocratic marriage partner (Bettelheim, 146).

This is so unlike what happens to Eleanor Vance, that it is a helpful exercise to look at the other characters in Jackson's narrative and question how they survived while she perished. Put simply, all of the characters know their place within Hill House. Dudley the caretaker guards (I use the word advisedly) the gates to the house. His wife pays it homage by replacing all items to a particular cupboard or shelf (HH, 101). Dr Montague finds his place soon following his arrival, objectively measuring and making notes. Following an initial reckoning, Theodora enters into a disarming, humorous relationship with the house (HH, 199). And Luke is simply Luke Sanderson, pondering upon how one day, the house will come into his possession (HH, 211). But why does imagination always supersede reality?

Irving Malin explores the role that the image of the castle plays in gothic literature, citing it as a metaphor of *social disorder* (Malin, 145). This part of the pattern is fairly apparent. In fiction, a neat and tidy, well-ordered dwelling is indicative of a family or group of people who keep their lives in order. When Jane Eyre looks through the window of Moor House, she sees: 'a room with a sanded floor, clean scoured; a dresser of walnut, with pewter plate ranged in rows, reflecting the redness and radiance of the glowing peat fire' (JE, 331). This warmth, cleanliness and order is not only an indication of the personal state of the Rivers family, it is also a metaphor of how Jane is soon to emerge from the disorder of the natural world and return to society. According to servant Hannah, the name of Jane's new home is metaphorical: 'Some calls it Marsh End, and some calls it Moor House' (JE, 341). To the reader, 'Marsh End' suggests the volatility and constant change of marshland while 'Moor House' suggests a dwelling pegged in place. In the gothic sub-genre, the castle is a focus for the yearnings of the protagonist and a vehicle in which attitudes and weakness emerge.

In her Introduction to *Northanger Abbey*, Marilyn Butler explores Ann Radcliffe's use of architectural imagery, describing it as 'the landscape of Unconscious' where all the traumas of the past are replayed in a certain way (NA, xxix). In *Romance of the Forest*, the Abbey represents the personal ruin of the La Motte family and their attempts to regenerate order in their lives. In literature, an ordered castle can reflect the inner state of its owner.

Safe within the boundary of the well-ordered Woodston, Henry Tilney is aware of the privacy that he is aiming for when he scratches his head over 'voluntary spies'. By contrast, the inner turmoil of Paula Power is metaphorized by her wanting to place a Greek peristyle within the walls of the medieval Castle Stancy. She espouses an admiration for democracy: 'I am a Greek' (AL, 108) She opens the castle to visitors, but all of her intentions are blind-sided by the prospect of marrying an aristocratic name.

The theme of order and chaos runs right through *Bleak House*. Tom-all-alones collapses because of lack of structural investment and because of its status in Chancery. The unfortunate brickmaker longs for a life of order, but he has not the means to do it: 'Look at the water. Smell it. That's wot we drinks' (BH, 158). By contrast is the orderliness and neatness of the Jarndyce dwelling. Esther is responsible for keeping Bleak House clean and tidy: 'Little old woman, and whither so high/To sweep the cobwebs out of the sky' (BH, 89). In her way, Esther is not so different from Pip, who wishes to remove the cobwebs from Satis House: '(Miss Havisham) reserved it for me to restore the desolate house' (GE, 197). But the reader must wonder: why *does* Esther assume so much responsibility? Could it be her innate talent for tidiness in combination with her gratitude to Jarndyce for saving her from a life of poverty and ignominy? Or could it be the Victorian desire to make everything clean? The text of *Bleak House* is filled with episcopalian characters who are seemingly determined to create a type of order in other peoples' lives, such as Mrs Pardiggle looking with disdain upon the squalor of the brickmakers' family. Mr Chadband seems almost trying to exorcise the devil out of Jo, the poor crossing sweeper. Mrs Jellyby is trying to organise a colony of British families to go to live in West Africa. Mrs Rouncewell is hereditary housekeeper to the Dedlocks, Rosa the willing lady's maid, Charley Neckett laundering for the disordered Smallweeds, and Caddy Jellyby learning to clean the already spick and span lodging of poor Miss Flite. Mr Chadband is the odd one out among the pack; the majority of these orderlies are female and all trying to bring indoor cleanliness and order to other peoples' dwellings. The reader must ask: why women and why cleanliness?

For 'women' substitute the underdog here, to include all disenfranchised characters that populate the texts. Although Pip has come into his fortune by the time he experiences his Satis House-cleansing fantasies, he still has not made the magic connection with his princess that will enable the love-match to progress. In his book, *The Meaning of Enchantment*, Bruno Bettelheim explains how that most famous of all fairy-tale characters, Cinderella, must undergo a long period of what might be called penance for the sin of having a father who loved her more than he loved his new wife. Thus she spends her formative years among the dust and ashes, cleansing away her notional transgression, actually committed by someone else. As Esther industriously works, is she unconsciously atoning for her illegitimacy? As ever, it is the underdog who feels obliged to put houses and lives in a notional order. Harold Skimpole is financially inept but he is Jarndyce's friend and is possessed of an easy tongue and enough talent to comment wryly on Esther's seeming obsession with the housekeeping: 'When I see you, my dear Miss Summerson, intent upon the perfect working of the whole little orderly system of which you are the centre, I feel inclined to say to myself – in fact, I do say to myself, very often – that's responsibility!' (BH, 587).

Is Pip hoping that by wishing order upon Satis House, his own dreams will come true? And if cleaning, dusting, polishing, scrubbing and so forth does cathartically cleanse the guilty soul, what of the *lady*, e.g., Lady Dedlock, who does not have the 'privilege' of getting down and dirty with the housekeeping? Could this inaction be one source of her affected *ennui* and insouciance? And does Berthe Mason's madness spring from a similar inaction, confined as she is in an attic all day by her jailer, Grace Poole? And what of the practically redundant Mrs Danvers, with her beloved mistress deceased and a new Mrs de Winter with which to play cat and mouse? In her article, 'Marking her Territory: Feline Behaviour in The Yellow Wall-Paper', Catherine Golden quotes Charlotte Perkins Gilman: 'The absolutely stationary female and the wide-ranging male are distinctly human institutions.'[45] My question: could this obligation to remain 'stationary' be why 'imprisoned' women contemplate burning their dwellings: Berthe Mason, Mrs Danvers? And assuming underdog William Dare *did* burn down Castle Stancy, could this be a form of ritual cleansing to rid the ancestral piles of interlopers, dirt and guilt?

Does Eleanor Vance make her journey in order to find a new home to put *in order*, hoping that it will erase the past? Her fantasies on the journey to Hill

---

[45] Catherine J. Golden, *Marking her Territory: Feline Behaviour in The Yellow Wall-Paper*, (Essays) pp16-31, p21. Subsequent references will be to this edition and will be inserted parenthetically into the text, for example "(Golden, 21)".

House betray as much: 'Journeys end in lovers meeting.' One of the more remarkable things about the progression of Jackson's text is Eleanor's *ennui* onset once she has 'escaped' the family home. Initially, at least, the journey fills her with delight (HH, 15). Her new friends fill her with a similar glee and a sense of belonging (HH, 60). And with her childlike response to her new surroundings, to the first-time reader of Hill House, her future seems bright, imagining herself about to meet her 'prince in disguise' (HH, 52). According to Michael Wilson, this flight of imagination demonstrates that Eleanor has the makings of an artist, but her misfortune is she never becomes one, unlike Theodora whose has already exercised that talent that defines her life (Michael Wilson, 121). The broader point is that Eleanor arrives in Hill House, charged with a type of creative energy – and she fails completely to channel that creatively. So, it has to go somewhere and she channels her fantasy into the house. Eleanor's mistake lies in her belief that, because she senses the energy of the house, that it must somehow want *her*. In one, comical description, Hill House comes across not so much as a phallic male but as a Victorian matron in tight corsets (HH, 112). But the leg-pulling in Hill House succeeds in playing a game with her. In one scene Theodora discourages Eleanor from clearing away cutlery following a meal. Theodora's prohibition may be well-meant: she doesn't want her roommate reduced to the status of a cleaner. But not she nor any of Eleanor's new family realise that Eleanor needs something to do. Because Eleanor has been an active though hampered person all of her adult life, caring for her invalid mother in her imperfect way, she cannot cope with her new leisure. And Eleanor, like every gothic heroine before her is seeking a project upon which to expend her energy: what else is her is frantic, notional escape in the car she half owns but a bid for a better life? On the way to Hill House, her head is full of plans of things to do: marry a prince, tell fortunes, whatever. On arrival, the enforced idleness is almost as insidious as the house itself. Theodora has already channelled her nervous energy, a trait she shares with Eleanor, into becoming an artist. Dr Montague is in command of his academic career, while Luke Sanderson simply is so assured of his own future that he does not need an occupation. But even he redeems himself morally by rescuing Eleanor from the staircase. Indeed, the writing on the wall telling her to 'come home' could be an impassioned plea from one of the more benign spirits of the house, exhorting its inmates to find Eleanor something meaningful to do, find her rightful place in her life, her spiritual estate, her 'cup of stars'. One by one, each inmate of the house fails Eleanor in this matter at least as crushingly as her birth family has done. In the Robert Wise movie of the novel, the viewer sees Eleanor pleading with Luke Sanderson to be allowed to stay and help Mrs Dudley with the housework, a plea that is spurned more subtly in Jackson's original text.

Poignantly, she fails to find the kinship that she sought, even following her death, the author stressing at the close of the narrative that spirit in the house was yet alone (HH, 246). This being the case, it is evident that Eleanor's attempts to project her dreams onto its upright walls and sturdy floors are in vain. And the reader may wonder if Hugh Crain had also felt its pernicious effects, that his book filled with hellish images and signed in his own blood is his attempt to pacify whatever is causing havoc with lives and personalities? As Michael Wilson argues, Hill House is not a place to realise dreams but to face reality. However, the characters create their own subjective rationale, for this encounter with 'absolute reality' (Wilson, 114, 115, 116, 117, 118, 119, 122).

But reality has many definitions, often defined by the people who occupy the physical space that is the castle. And as stated at the outset of this chapter, the role of the castle has changed in conjunction with the changing nature of the family, which is why the next chapter explores this all-engaging institution.

Danger in the Family

Why the family? ♦ The aristocracy fixation ♦ Orphans and children ♦ The matriarch and the patriarch ♦ Siblings: warring and benevolent ♦ The individual, individualism and Eleanor's rampage

Why the family?

Donald J. Olsen wrote of the family as a benign entity that served the church, state and individual, while posing no threat to the liberty of anyone.[46] His ideas, however, concerned the nineteenth-century *perception* of the family, a time when illustrators and journalists collaborated with royal aides to regale the public with images and sketches of Queen Victoria and her family enjoying grouse hunting or Christmas, whatever the season. But the family hadn't always 'represented uncontroversial good' and from its beginning, the gothic sub-genre has served as a literary arena for dissecting and exploring a wide variety of family situations, as assuredly as the newly-fledged eighteenth-century surgeon class began to wield their scalpels on diseased anatomies and pathologized their findings. Contrast the ideas of Olsen with those of J. Hillis Miller who states that a person who is born into a family or 'system' loses hope of ever having a 'present self' or a 'present satisfaction', loses hope of respite from his 'present restless state', and has no end in front of him, except death (BH, 27).

These ideas of Hillis Miller have been written as part of his Introduction to *Bleak House*; presently, I will explore the many troubling implications of the matter of 'family' in that text. But an overview of fictional families in general will present the reader with a line-up of the situations that underline the

---

[46]Donald J. Olsen, *The City as a Work of Art: London, Paris, Vienna* (Yale: Yale University, 1986), p89. Subsequent references will be to this edition and will be inserted parenthetically into the text, for example "Olsen, 89".

quotation. In *The Castle of Otranto*, Manfred seeks to divorce his wife of twenty years and to marry a bride who is about the same age as his daughter. In Ann Radcliffe's text, Adeline learns that her uncle has had her father murdered and has the same fate lined up for her, all following his earlier sexual designs. That scion of a happy family, Catherine Morland, is thrust suddenly under the roof of the tyrannical General Tilney, a prototype of the emerging Victorian *pater familias*, and finds much to question there. *Bleak House* itself abounds with abandoned, neglected and pyschologically-abused children, and strongly features a patriarchal figure who desires to morph into the husband of one of his young charges. In the same text, the uber-fanciful Harold Skimpole does not treat his wife with any serenity, leaving her to the mercy of unpaid trades' people and debt collectors. Writes the author: 'It seemed to escape (Skimpole's) consideration that Mrs Skimpole and the daughters remained behind to encounter the baker; but this was so old a story to all of them that it had become a matter of course' (BH, 656). In *Jane Eyre*, characters like Mr Brocklehurst, Edward Rochester and St John Rivers all show aspects of the controlling male. *Great Expectations* espouses the darker aspects of femininity in the form of a tyrannical mother/sister to Pip and a warped foster mother for Estella. In *Hard Times*, the invalid Mrs Gradgrind continually echoes her husband's credo to 'follow only facts', a quest that saps her health and vitality so much that she dies prematurely. Henry James's Governess hints at 'disturbing letters from home, where things were not going well' early in the narrative, making the reader wonder if her act of accepting such a curious position as a first job may not have been an attempt to escape – whatever afflicts *them*? (TOTS, 141).

In *Rebecca*, Maxim de Winter refuses to let the new Mrs de Winter assume the same sartorial elegance of his late wife, lest it remind him of *her*, he disdains intimacy – they sleep in separate rooms – and he forces her into a series of uncomfortable social encounters that he insists are her duty (R, 162). The beginning of the novel is actually the end of the story, and we first encounter Mrs de Winter in a position of servility similar to what she endured with her former employer, Mrs Van Hopper. In summary, the mousy young companion to Mrs Van Hopper reverts to a mousy young companion to her wretched husband. In *The Haunting of Hill House*, Eleanor Vance fails entirely to forge a satisfying love union, despite her constant mantra 'Journeys end in lovers meeting', her life ending in car-crash ignominy. In *The Woman in Black*, it is the bitterness effected by the loss of the son of the ghostly Jennet Humphries, the titular woman in black, that causes Arthur Kipp's family tragedy in the novel. Of the contemporary heroines, only Lyra is triumphant at the conclusion, having trounced her inadequate biological parents, and effected her reunion with her 'true' family, the band of academics, scholars and elevated servants at Jordan College. But Lyra is the heroine of a fantasy: as the centuries have progressed, why do so few of the heroines of realist novels fail to forge the happy endings of Adeline, Catherine and Jane Eyre, the latter who can proudly declare: 'Reader, I married him'? (JE, 448).

Of course, the notions of 'family' and 'happiness' have changed through the centuries and decades. When *Romance of the Forest* was written, a 'family' meant everyone, servants included, living under the same roof (ROTF, 3). By the nineteenth century, the family had dwindled to filial groups and persons attached by marriage. John Jarndyce opens his house to a group of obscure cousins, as does Sir Leicester Dedlock in the larger Chesney Wold. A century later, matters had changed once more: Eleanor Vance growing up with her mother and sister underneath the one roof typify the twentieth-century nuclear family. But no one model of the family seems to guarantee happiness. When her mother dies, Eleanor is not wanted by her sister and brother-in-law: but she is needed for chores, babysitting and comically, the use of the half of the car that she owns (HH, 209). Once more, this chapter will raise more questions than it provides answers as it attempts to dissect the conundrums surrounding the literary family, both ancient and modern.

The aristocracy fixation

> In Aristophanes there is usually a central figure who constructs his (or her) own society in the teeth of strong opposition, driving off one after another all of the people who come to prevent or exploit him, and eventually achieving a heroic triumph, complete with mistresses, in which he is sometimes assigned the honour of a reborn god (Frye, 43).

From this quotation of Northrop Frye, the reader can quite easily discern the origin of the word 'aristocratic' and see that despite its origin in ancient Greece, fixation with aristocracy has never ceased to run through literature. I take 'aristocracy' to mean the highest social class in the context of all of the narratives, comprising people and animals of noble birth. By 'noble', I mean rarefied and out of the ordinary, in social and political contexts. In *Great Expectations,* Mrs Pocket leafs constantly through *Burke's Peerage,* longing for the title that has bypassed her in life. In *Bleak House,* the narrator describes the relatives of Sir Leicester Dedlock as 'cousins ... amiable and sensible ... likely to have done well enough in life if they could have overcome their cousinship' (BH, 447). And this fixation extends to the peculiar social and personal regard that seems to surround the Byronic hero.

In the **Introduction**, I described the Byronic hero: 'Whatever his attainments, whether rich or poor, he must possess an air, an attitude of being his own person, of a disinclination to conform to social convention ... Never comfortable in society, the hero likes to wander in remote places, usually to brood upon whatever has blighted his life either in reality or in perception. Whatever his condition, the hero carries with him a perpetual air of mystery ... Much of whatever narrative consists of the heroine trying to pierce this fog of mystery, to get to his heart, in every sense of the word.'

The parallels between the exclusivity of aristocracy and the rarefied world of the Byronic hero are apparent here. Of course, the description 'hero' is ironic because very few Byronic heroes are *heroic* in the accepted sense of the word. David Wright points out that Don Juan is not the hero of *Don Juan,* Lord Byron's extended poem (Wright, xxi). In *Pride and Prejudice,* Mr Darcy is hardly heroic, much less Heathcliff or even Henry Tilney. Edward Rochester does try to save Berthe Mason from the flames, but it is difficult not to gain the impression that his act is one of atonement rather than sincerity. And Pip's attempt to save Miss Havisham from her conflagration marks only the beginning of his better nature, not the culmination of it.

It is not difficult then to discern that the prose version of the Byronic hero has never taken wings because in the realist school of literature, the Byronic character is simply too existential to go out and slay dragons. On the other hand, the old-fashioned, swashbuckling and very romantic hero of *The Castle of Otranto,* Theodore, is an active and ebullient peasant. And yet, the female protagonist of a narrative is invariably drawn to the Byronic male in the same way that the female subject of the fairy tale is drawn to the prince. Regarding more allegorical literature, the reader might ponder upon Bettelheim's exhorting that the typical ending of the narrative 'the prince and princess lived happily together always' is simply a metaphor of the integration of the male and female aspects of the personality, rather than an encouragement to the listener to go out and win an aristocratic marriage partner (Bettelheim, 146).

Because it straddles both sides of the allegorical/realist modes, the gothic sub-genre is populated with fairy-tale situations that sour in the light of rationality. The theme of aristocracy permeates *A Laodicean* and defines all of the relations that the characters have with one another and towards themselves. It is the centuries of noble tradition that have endowed the narrative with Castle Stancy, providing Paula with her home and her friendship with Charlotte de Stancy. And it is the notion of living in grandeur that spurs William Dare to commit the number of acts, bordering on the criminal, that might nudge his father into making the manoeuvres he does, that may secure Paula as a bride. At the conclusion, when Paula and George Somerset have forged a love union and seem all set to sail into happiness, Paula suddenly says: 'I wish my castle wasn't burned and I wish that you were a de Stancy' (AI, 437).

Though her statement is half – only half – humorous, it is a chilling reminder to the reader that all of the trouble in the narrative stems from her fixation on gaining an aristocratic identity.

A similar fixation with antiquity permeates *Rebecca*. At the opening of the text, the narrator is struck by Maxim de Winter's 'arresting' and 'medieval' face (R, 15). A few pages later, the narrator is eager to place a 'presence medieval' in her drawing (R, 20). And as the narrative progresses, the reader learns that this 'arresting' hero may be in thrall to the aristocracy of others, namely, that of the female narrator, shortly to be Mrs de Winter. The reader never learns her name, either her personal or family name. All we learn, through the voice of Maxim, is that Mrs de Winter's name is 'lovely and unusual' (R, 25). Here, the reader must wonder if this rarity of the name is one of the qualities that attracts Maxim to his new bride? And again, I use the word 'hero' ironically; Maxim is no more a hero than Mr Darcy or Edward Rochester. The beginning of the novel is actually the end of the tale, and the de Winter pair have already been through the grotesque discovery of the regurgitating by the sea of the titular heroine's body. And it is Maxim's horror of a lineage that does *not* carry the de Winter blood that no doubt causes him to pull the trigger of the weapon that kills Rebecca and their notional unborn child. It is Maxim's aristocracy that saves him from the hangman's noose, the magistrate closing the case when he finds grounds that Rebecca *may* have committed suicide. But Maxim has seen his ancestral home burn down. With his *raison d'etre* gone, that is, an ancestral pile to provide heirs for, Maxim has lost both manhood and motivation. Another puzzle: why did Rebecca marry him – or need to marry at all? Erotic and beautiful, she has intelligence to match her looks and runs Manderley with chilling, clerical efficiency. At the same time, like Paula Power, she is under-educated and simply cannot visualise life without a man at her side plus the enhanced social status of having married into a county family. It is also a sign of the times; even in the early twentieth century, female socialites simply did not engage in paid labour. Rebecca no doubt longed to preside over a residence, the luxury and social status of which matched her own perceived pedigree and physical loveliness.

Realist literature is filled with themes of aristocratic yearnings gone sour. In *Great Expectations*, Pip's notional princess never brings him happiness. In *Bleak House*, Caddy Jellyby marries Prince, quite literally, in her longing to escape her parents' chaotic household. But her dreams of a happy family life and domestic bliss are not to be realised. Her only child and daughter is born deaf and her husband becomes lame, a strange transposing of the assumed abuse of his late mother onto the son. Caddy herself is obliged to step into the role of her impaired husband, to constantly teach dance. Indeed, this tragicomic outcome is reminiscent of the Wicked Queen in Snow White, obliged to dance forever in red-hot slippers. And in Jackson's text, Eleanor has constant visions of marrying *her* Prince Charming, an identity that she transposes, with unfortunate consequences, onto the titular house. In the Robert Wise movie of the novel, the viewer sees Eleanor pleading with Luke Sanderson to be allowed stay and help Mrs Dudley with the housework, a plea that is spurned just as readily as in Jackson's original text.

Aristocracy underpins the entire plot of *His Dark Materials*. It is represented by social hierarchy, family ties, power grabs and eventually, underwrites the individual fates of the characters. In Chapter 3, the reader learns the Parslow family has 'for five generations' been undertaking the College masonry and that Mr Parslow is now engaged in teaching his son the craft (HDM, 34). The admission that the Parslow family is preparing another generation for work in scaffolding and masonry indicates that aristocracy in Lyra's world is not set to change any time soon. In a later chapter, Ma Costa tells Lyra that she might assiduously master everything that the race of gyptians do, but that as a fire person, as opposed to water, she never will truly be one of them (HDM, 34). And strong family and tribal ties hold the gyptian society together, which is another type of aristocracy.

Orphans and children

Literature is filled with orphans, from actual familial orphans such as Oliver Twist, and Pip from *Great Expectations*, to notional orphans such as Esther and Lyra, whose parents cannot bring them up or do not want to care for them, for whatever reasons. The body of literary orphans could also be constituted of young people whose legal guardians fall short of the mark, Jane Eyre being an example, or whose natural parents are less than caring, such as Eleanor Vance, and young people who have become separated from their parents, either because they want to be or feel that they have no choice but to be, such as Will Parry's father, who deserted his son and his wife.

Just as the separation and/or alienation from a parent or two is one of life's more profound experiences, it is no wonder that the theme permeates literature to the point where it haunts modernism, making it difficult for a reader to find a character whose psyche hasn't been formed by this experience. Paradoxically, the very absence of a solid family is a presence that never ceases to announce itself, shaping the life and the eventual fate of the character in the most profound ways.

This theme runs throughout the gothic form, the gothic heroine being prone in a number of ways. Her youth implies a mixture of innocence and naiveity, qualities that render her vulnerable to certain forces. And almost always, she is away from other family members or separated from them for a variety of reasons. It is with shock that Adeline – and the reader – learns towards the end of Radcliffe's narrative that Adeline's life has been in danger right from the time that she left the convent, and all because of the family that she was born in to.

At the outset of *Northanger Abbey*, to strengthen the burlesque element of the narrative, Jane Austen stresses that Catherine has grown up within a happy family. Yet, Catherine is soon to meet the lonely Eleanor Tilney, mourning her mother, a situation that has a profound effect upon the events at Northanger. *Bleak House* is teeming with subplots about orphans, families and their often disaffected children. Early in the narrative, the reader meets Caddy Jellyby in her parents' house, with a mother determined to found a coffee plantation on the banks of an African river. The author pours his disapproval on the situation by describing in detail the domestic chaos that has resulted from Mrs Jellyby's venture. Forced to function as her mother's secretary, Caddy is perpetually miserable and to express this, she says to Esther, concerning the blonde and accomplished Ada: 'An orphan ... She knows a quantity, I suppose? Can dance, and play music, and sing?' In the outburst that follows she says: 'The whole house is disgraceful. The children are disgraceful. I'm disgraceful' (BH, 93). The irony is, of course, that Ada is a fully-fledged orphan, though not a neglected one. Caddy's solution to her problem is to 'improve' herself. When the reader meets her again, she has taken dancing lessons and become engaged to the dancing master, Prince Turveydrop. A delighted Caddy invites Esther and the reader to the dancing studio, which seems hardly less squalid than her own parent's home. According to Esther: 'I found the Academy established in a sufficiently dingy house at the corner of an archway ... it was a bare, resounding room, smelling of stables' (BH, 241). Caddy's future father-in-law is a selfish and sensual middle-aged man who, although socially polite and charming, insists upon a constant supply of creature comforts which he expects his son to provide through the constant grind of teaching dance. Caddy's eventual fate is so bizarre that her leaving her birth family for a happier life elsewhere seems a grotesque and absurd move.

In literature, even the children of the well-to-do are vulnerable to neglect. According to Joseph Firebaugh, young Flora and Miles of *The Turn of the Screw* are neglected by everyone concerned, most notably their uncle who refuses to visit them, leaving them under the care of a constantly-changing raft of underqualified tutors and servants. It is this situation that leads indirectly to Miles's death (Firebaugh, 57). Throughout the narrative of Jackson's text, Eleanor is haunted by the unhappy years that she spent nursing her invalid mother. And even well-cared for protagonists seemed destined to suffer for the sins of others. In Susan Hill's text, Arthur Kipps constantly refers to his comfort-filled younger years: 'I can recall it still, that sensation of slipping down, down into the welcoming arms of sleep, surrounded by warmth and softness, happy and secure as a small child in the nursery' (Hill, 49). In the chapter, 'In the Nursery', Arthur hears a sound coming from the locked-up nursery of Eel Marsh House, the sound of rocking chair runners moving to and fro. It is a sound that reminds him of his childhood and he says: 'I felt that nothing could come near to harm or afright me, and I had a protector or guardian close at hand' (Hill, 157-158). Arthur's perception proves incorrect; in a later episode, he and his little dog almost die in the marsh and later again, he finds the nursery door open with all of the toys and furniture inside of it smashed up. His gentle and happy upbringing by his loving parents is powerless, it seems, in the face of relentless evil. Arthur does eventually find a calm and beneficent life, but only following much suffering.

But in Pullman's rarefied world, *His Dark Materials* ends with Lyra listening to nightingales and calmly contemplating her bright future. Again, the reader is reminded of Deborah Russell's exhortation that, only in fantasy does the family and indeed, the individual, end up happy (Russell, 780).

The matriarch and the patriarch

In his book Bruno Bettelheim comments much on the phenonemon of the weak father, the absent fathers of heroines like Cinderella, and the abnegating father of Hansel and Gretel who allows his wife to talk him into abandoning the children in a forest. In gothic literature, parental figures are so varied in character and contradictory even within their own category, that it's almost impossible to pin them into types or archetypes. The good-hearted John Jarndyce is actually a sinister force in Esther's life, providing her with financial security yet scheming to make her his bride. The seemingly twisted Miss Havisham rescues Estella from poverty and introduces her to Pip, who becomes the moderating force in Estella's indulged and warping life. And even Estella's birth mother eventually emerges from the shadows. Yet, one theme emerges again and again in the sub-genre: as the narratives progress, the apparently 'wicked' maternal characters grow more responsible towards their charges, while the patriarchs give way to indulgences, their behaviour towards others growing harsher – or they leave the scene altogether.

An odd symmetry imbues *Romance of the Forest*. At the opening of her story, the only parental figures known to Adeline are the nuns in the convent where she has spent her young life. When she rejects this cold and clerical fate, circumstances thrust her into company with Madame La Motte. Initially, the older woman treats her tenderly but eventually, jealousy intervenes and Adeline finds herself at risk of the designs of the Marquis. In the later episodes of the novel, Adeline finds herself nursed by the elderly sister of Arnaud La Luc, a woman which, the text more than broadly hints, becomes Adeline's surrogate mother, this even before she is bound to the La Luc family by marriage. The paternal characters, Monsieur La Motte and the Marquis, who *should* have acted with responsibility towards the young woman, are convicted and exiled, or die an ignominious death. The happily-married Adeline, now a mother herself, has become the maternal figure that she lost as an infant.

His Dark Materials grants heroine Lyra a similarly bright outcome. We see her at the end of the narrative, comfortably reconciled to her fate as an academic and in the company of scholar Dame Hannah Relf. The academic woman now seems a much more interesting subject than the 'dim and frumpy person' that Lyra remembered (HDM, 1081). It could, of course, simply be Lyra's changed perspective, having been through adolescence since leaving Jordan College. But that does not matter; what is significant is that the author gives the reader the impression that the Master of Jordan College – a foster father of sorts – is going to play a less significant role in her future life than he did in her past. Yet, ineffectual though she has been, it is worth mentioning Lyra's natural mother. Mrs Coulter is indeed the powerful *tour de force* in the novel, the power behind the General Oblation Board or 'gobblers' that are kidnapping the children. At the same time, she is at constant loggerheads with the more orthodox Magisterium. She is the girlfriend of the socially lissom Sir Charles Latrom, that is, until she murders him. All the while, she continues to pursue Lyra, actually in pursuit of the powerful – she thinks – alethiometer. At the end of Book 2, Mrs Coulter finally succeeds in finding her daughter. But the only way to keep Lyra with her is maintain her in a drugged sleep, under the guise of 'enchantment'. At this point in the narrative, the reader may wonder if Mrs Coulter is truly devoid of affection for her daughter, doing what she is doing simply not to want to appear weak in her own eyes or is she secretly hoping to bond with the daughter that she abandoned earlier in life? Mrs Coulson is such a complex and contradictory character, by turns killing a friend and later, showing this display of tenderness towards Lyra, that her premature death leaves this question unanswered.

The above texts are but the bookends of my selected sagas; the pattern of advancing maternity and receding paternity is evident in the majority of the primary narratives. In *Northanger Abbey*, Catherine has the dubious benefit of three 'fathers', before breaking ties with all of them. Her natural father hardly features in the narrative, and Mr Allen is as ineffectual with guiding the young girl as he is with controlling the shopping exigencies of his wife. That leaves the tyrannical General Tilney, who simply expels Catherine from his household when he learns the truth of her financial status. But on her return to Fullerton, Mrs Morland welcomes Catherine back, and offers her counsel until she is reunited with Henry. In *The Snow Queen*, Kay rejects his gentle grandparent in favour of the icy glamour of the mysterious woman from the north – not unlike the allure of Mrs Coulter. In going out to rescue Kay, Gerda pulls him from his frosty fate and back to the warmer climes of the south – and they are reunited with the notional grandmother.

In spite of the troubled families all about them, moderation seems to dwell permanently in *Bleak House*, both the novel and the titular dwelling; order in the place of confusion, consideration instead of selfishness, and benignity in the place of passion. Yet, this domestic order is apparently underpinned by a darker undercurrent. J. Hillis Miller writes of John Jarndyce as Dickens's 'most successful version' of the benevolent father figures that recur in his fiction. 'But with the exception of Mr Pickwick, such characters in the hands of Dickens were never very successful.'

Here, I cast doubt on Hillis Miller's interpretation of 'benevolent'. Early on in the event of the orphans' arrival at Bleak House, Esther describes a scene in which she speaks to John Jarndyce in private. By now, Richard and Ada have declared their love for one another, and Esther is beset by pangs of loneliness so intense, that the contentment that she had earlier expressed at her lot: 'quite lost in the magnitude of my trust' has been blown away (BH, 118). She confronts Jarndyce directly, asking him what he knows about her parentage, if anything. Jarndyce answers in the negative, and a regretful – though not ungrateful – Esther replies: 'she (Esther) blesses the Guardian who is a Father to her' (BH, 291). Esther explains: 'At the word Father, I saw his former trouble come into his face. He subdued it as before, and it was gone in an instant; but it had been there'. But it eventually becomes apparent to the reader that Jarndyce's marital designs upon Esther were not the result of an ever-growing personal closeness, but a design of his from the beginning of his summoning her to work in his household, possibly even from her encounter with him in the carriage that she experienced when she was still a child. He has, in modern terminology, been stalking her since her youth. Of course, the meaning of 'benevolent' has shifted throughout time; Esther may have been left destitute if it hadn't been for Jarndyce. But the serious age-gap between Esther and Jarndyce is bound to leave the modern reader unsettled. And this is why his handing over of Esther to Allan Woodcourt is so unconvincing; that the young couple are going to live in an eerie replica of Bleak House points to

Jarndyce's sexual authority over her being not yet concluded. Even more disquieting is that Jarndyce is about to acquire a new 'bride'.

Throughout, he has refused to support Richard Carstone financially. When Richard dies, probably from TB due to poverty, though dressed in the book as a result of the passion of the unfulfilled yearning for a Chancery settlement, Ada and her son return to Jarndyce to live in Bleak House. Although the reader does not see Jarndyce actively woo the young widow, it is not difficult to perceive the symbolism of the younger woman taking Esther's place in the house: 'my guardian ... asked Ada when she would come home?' (BH, 932) Jarndyce has accomplished what he apparently set out to do at the outset of the narrative: install a surrogate spouse in the house. He effectively does this, and acquires her son, into the bargain – when Richard has undergone the final emasculation – death.

But maternity – or assumed maternity – is not all beneficent, or even benign. Much of Esther's plight is brought about by the lack of a loving maternal character. Early in the text, her heartless foster mother, Miss Barbary, dies, leaving her to the care of the legal system and a raft of tutors. Eventually, kindlier female figures emerge, including Esther's own mother: though illegitimate Esther still has to stave off the harsher designs of Mrs Woodcourt, her lover's mother, who is determined to find an equal match for her son in terms of family pedigree. At the outset of *Jane Eyre*, harsh guardian Mrs Reed hands her young charge to the harsher Mr Brocklehurst. When Jane eventually encounters Mrs Reed on her deathbed, her aunt seems to have softened towards her. But Jane has yet to experience the ignominy of being jilted at an altar, and to fight off the exhortations of the deranged – it would seem to the modern reader – St John Rivers. Jane spurns St John's offer of, or rather, insistence, upon marriage with the words: 'If I were to marry you, you would kill me. You are killing me now' (JE, 412).

In *Great Expectations*, the narrative is shot with the familiar thread of the mother or mother figure being benevolent and malevolent by turns. Pip has been 'brought up by hand' by a resentful sister who had been obliged to marry the local blacksmith in order to provide for two orphans, herself and her young brother, with a home. Much of Pip's youth is boxed-ear misery at the hands of this sister. But Pip is more than compensated by the warm, loving bond between him and his foster father, Joe Gargery – the exception to the many absent/weak fictional fathers, it seems - which gradually weaves through the events in Dickens's narrative: 'You mustn't go on a-overdoing it, but you must have your supper and your wine-and-water, and you must be put betwixt the sheets' (GE, 399). Joe says these words to Pip when the familial bond between them – Pip's sister – has died. Curiously, Joe has seemingly morphed into a maternal character: he has taken on Pip's debt *and* nursed him back to health following the protagonist's near-fatal fever. Lovely Estella is both nurtured and mentally poisoned by the twisted Miss Havisham, who has brought her ward up to take revenge upon all mankind. Even before she succumbs to the conflagration that kills her, Miss Havisham is repenting of what Estella has become 'I stole her heart away and put ice in its place' and apologises to Pip: 'Until you spoke to her the other day, and until I saw in you a looking-glass that showed me what I once felt myself, I did not know what I had done. What have I done! What have I done!' (GE, 338). Here, Miss Havisham seems to have taken on the role of Andersen's Snow Queen, transforming her young charge to ice. To complete the symmetry of Dickens's narrative, the good Joe marries the gentle Biddy, and the reader sees the couple in the role of loving parents as the tale ends.

Perhaps the most grisly image of the parental relations appears in *Rebecca*, when Mrs de Winter declares to Maxim that he is all her male relatives, father, brother, son, all at once (R, 163). This overt Oedipal yearning perhaps shocks the modern reader, seeming as it is not unlike one of those disquieting Dickensian child-bride alliances, such as David Copperfield and Dora Spenlow, and indeed the engagement of Esther and John Jarndyce. Even more grisly is Mrs de Winter's assertion that she regards Maxim as a son, a yearning that she reiterates later in the narrative when she expresses a yearning to be his mother, and to be old (R, 220). The irony is that Mrs de Winter does indeed end up as his 'mother', caring for Maxim in his shattered mental state. It might be of significance that she was without a mother's love herself, at the opening of the narrative.

Fatherhood is, of course, the flip side of motherhood. The man whom Adeline believes to be her father tries to persuade her into a life in the convent and when he fails, he delivers her into the hands of brigands. Her rescuer, La Motte, though kindly at the beginning of their acquaintance, abandons her to the designs of the Marquis de Montalt when it proves advantageous for him to do so. On discovering that he is Adeline's uncle – a surrogate father – the Marquis plots for Adeline's death. But could it be that all of this wickedness is actually a deflection from the ineffectuality of Adeline's real father? Conveniently dead by the time the action in the narrative begins, and subsequently proved to have been murdered by his brother, Adeline finally has the luxury of loving him from afar. I say 'luxury' because she never considers that he and the Marquis are of the same blood. Every possibility exists that if she had grown up under her father's curation, he may have been as ineffective in life as in death, and been prepared to barter her in an injudicious marriage, or use her for his own end in another way. In *A Laodicean*, this situation is mirrored in a most sinister way when Paula's Uncle Abner – an eerie reincarnation of her father – schemes in collusion with William de Stancy and William Dare to bring about de Stancy's desired marriage with Paula. By making him a fugitive from a European secret and political society, Hardy produces a lumbering and improbable situation to invest Abner Power as the 'bad' living uncle in contrast to the 'good' dead father.

Almost a century later, another protagonist tries to fight the malign influence of a father, though not her own. When Eleanor Vance arrives at Hill House, she is still experiencing what the modern writer might deem 'mother issues'. Her experience as a daughter has not been a happy one; her father died when she was but twelve and her adult life has been one of caring for her invalid, maternal figure. This could explain why much of the journey on the way to Hill House is spent romanticising about marrying a prince and longing: 'Journeys end in lovers meeting' (Pascal, 478).

But instead of finding herself in a haven of male gallantry, aside from Dr Montague and initially, Luke Sanderson, Eleanor finds herself at the maelstrom of opposing forces. As pointed out in **The Allegorical Castle**, the tension in the house may be caused by Hugh Crain's attempts to establish a patriarchy, as demonstrated by his hand-written morality books, at war with the female forces that reign within. Critic Richard Pascal suggests that the ornamental heads in the hall over the door of the nursery represent opposing parental forces (Pascal, 473). Of course, the sub-genre fields other family relations, one in particular being that of the bonds between siblings.

Siblings: warring and benevolent

In their elucidation of sibling relationship, Sandra Gilbert and Susan Gubar write of *Goblin Market* by Christina Rossetti: 'For there is no friend like a sister/In calm or stormy weather', as a demonstration of the power of sisterly love, the theme of the sister or surrogate-sister bonding running through the gothic sub-genre (G&G, 577).

In *The Castle of Otranto*, cousins Matilda and Isabella join forces against Matilda's scheming father, Manfred. In *Romance of the Forest*, Adeline's wanderings come to a halt when the La Luc family adopt her, and Clara becomes her surrogate sister in advance of her marriage to Theodore, thus making Clara her 'sister in law'. In *Northanger Abbey*, Catherine Morland gains two sisters, first, the false Isabella Thorpe and then, the more authentic Eleanor Tilney, a relationship that is legally sealed when Catherine marries Eleanor's brother, Henry. In *Bleak House*, the sisterhood of Esther Summerson and Ada Clare falls apart when the two women cease to confide in one another, albeit in circumstances beyond their control. However, Esther has managed to forge other female friendships that ensure her happiness by the end of the narrative.

The *most* unfavourable fates await those heroines who fail to forge meaningful and lasting bonds with the other women of their narratives. The Governess of *The Turn of the Screw* has left her home (and sisters) to live a life of isolated splendour in Bly, where her 'literacy' places her above the longer-standing household members. On at least one occasion, she snubs housekeeper Mrs Grose, and the disintegration of her friendship with young Flora heralds the tragic end of the narrative. In *Rebecca*, Mrs de Winter is 'haunted' by her dead counterpart, while the icy Mrs Danvers despises and hoodwinks her. Maxim's sister does reach out to her, but too many chasms, in the form of class distinction and age, exist for the two women to forge a true and lasting friendship. Consequently, Mrs de Winter's fate, revealed at the beginning of the novel, is no surprise to the reader. The opening of *The Haunting of Hill House* shows protagonist Eleanor Vance warring with her sister Carrie over the car that they own in tandem. The text reveals that the pair have never, as adults, been friends. Eventually, female companion Theodora rejects her which is gall and wormwood to the needy Eleanor, as is Luke Sanderson's expelling her from Hill House (HH, 208, 238). Spurned by all about her, Eleanor's only recourse – she believes – is into the embrace of death, offered by the house.

Much of Jane Eyre's loneliness at Gateshead stems from her Aunt Reed's hatred and her *female* cousins' spurning of her. Here, I stress 'female' because it seems evident to the reader that enjoined with Georgiana and Eliza, the three young women could have construed a credible faction against the tyranny of the spoilt John Reed. It is the cousins' failure to recognise the good qualities inherent in Jane that brings about the demise of their mother – and their separation from each other in later life – one to a convent and the other into a life of dissipated and fashionable idleness. And there is more than an echo of Eliza's fate in the eventual condition of Charlotte de Stancy. Born into the reduced-in-fortune de Stancy family, Charlotte forges a friendship with the wealthy and elegant young Paula Power, mistress and owner of Castle Stancy, which her late father bequeathed to her. The significance of Paula's family name is not lost here, of course, and Paula becomes engaged to Charlotte's brother, William. Eventually, revelations about William's personal life halt the impending marriage – on the morning of the wedding, in fact. But Paula is no embittered Miss Havisham: and embarks on a quest to reclaim her true love, George Somerset. The misfortune falls instead, on to Charlotte.

Denied either the dignity of becoming a widow (her fiancé died before they could marry) or the status of becoming Paula's legal sister, Charlotte falls into a series of the unidentified illnesses that Victorian heroines seem prone to when misfortune besets them. Paula gallantly nurses her friend who, providentially, accompanies her on the quest to find George Somerset. Upon recovery, Charlotte announces that she is entering a convent to take the veil. Again, echoes of Eliza Reed, but Charlotte is not the energetic, self-determining Eliza. Unlike the earlier Victorian character, whom the reader can envisage throwing herself into religious life with a relish, the reader suspects that Charlotte's shrinking from society has more than a little to do with the discovery that her brother has fathered a 'natural' son. But however much Paula rails against her friend's choice of life: 'I had been expecting her to live with us always ... and to think she should have decided to do this', Charlotte – to her credit – stands firm and is defended by George Somerset: 'She was genuine, if anybody ever was, and as simple as she was true' (AL, 433). And this stance 'de Stancy', this feisty woman of aristocratic blood, stands in contrast to the rather ambivalent ending of the narrative, with Paula's declaration to husband George: 'I wish my castle wasn't burned and I wish that you were a de Stancy' (AL, 437). This ambivalence runs parallel to Jane Eyre's hinting that she more than a little envies the life of passionate energy that St John Rivers is leading in contrast with the rather tame, domestic sphere that she has chosen. But Jane has also forged firm friendships with cousins Diana and Mary Rivers, whom together, represent the sisterly affection that she failed to find in the Reed household. This relationship, forged in Moor

House, together with the love of her husband and son, are more than enough to firmly 'anchor' Jane to domestic life.

Non-familial sister-brother relations that transform into lover-pairs are less usual in realist fiction, but in folk tales and fantasy, they thrive. Of the selected texts, in Pullman's fantasy, they are represented by Will Parry and Lyra Belacqua becoming lovers before they finally part company. In *The Snow Queen*, Kay and Gerda emerge from the icy palace of the titular character as the friends they had been in childhood but when they return to their home town, the author informs us that they are grown up, a hint at the adult love that is to blossom between them. That is why I dislike film versions of *The Snow Queen* in which the scriptwriters render Gerda and Kay a pair of siblings rather than childhood friends. This compromises the narrative symbolism because a romantic relationship can never happen between them, thus preventing the completion of the child-adolescent-adult cycle of the original Andersen tale. Because the majority of gothic heroines are female, many of the protagonists, as described above, have acquired sisters, whether step or surrogate, or a close female relative who takes on the role of sister. Young women in close tandem often 'mirror' each others' values and actions, a matter discussed more in depth in the chapter, **Deceptions, the Doppelganger and the Dark Dis**. Whatever, 'sisters' in literature generally take on the role of friends, companions, confidantes and counsellors. Brothers are another matter. Generally, three types of male populate the gothic narrative:

1. The tyrant/parent figure, typified by Manfred, the Marquis de Montalt, General Tilney and John Jarndyce.

2. The hero/lover, typified by Theodore (Walpole), Theodore (Radcliffe), Henry Tilney and Allan Woodcourt. Above, I have described the Byronic character, the nineteenth-century descendant of the swashbuckling and very romantic heroes, such as both eighteenth-century Theodores. Indeed, so sociopathic does the nineteenth-century Byronic hero become, that characters such as Edward Rochester and Maxim de Winter seemed to blend with the tyrannical parent.

3. The ineffective father/brother figure: Adeline's father (deceased), Monsieur La Motte, Louis De la Motte, James Moreland, Captain Tilney, Rowland Rochester (deceased), Mr Power, the Governess's Master, the Governess's Master's brother (deceased) and Dr Montague.

As I explained earlier, Adeline's father is conveniently dead by the time the action in the narrative begins. Because he is of the same blood as the Marquis de Montalt, every possibility exists that if she had grown up under her natural father's curation, he may have been prepared to barter her in an injudicious marriage, or use her for his own end in another way. In *A Laodicean*, this dead-good-brother and bad-live-brother is reflected in the Mr Power and Abner Power brother pairing. The reader may ask: if Mr Power had been around in Uncle Abner's stead, would he have been any *less* likely to pressure Paula into a marriage with William de Stancy?

These questions, of course, remain arguable. What is evident is that in the gothic sub-genre, it is difficult to find a benevolent brother-brother or even, a brother-sister pairing. In *Northanger Abbey*, Captain Tilney seems not so much the brother of Henry, but an off-shoot of his vicious father, General Tilney. And Catherine has to stand up to the pressures that brother James places her under to become further involved with the odious Thorpe siblings. Edward Rochester reveals to Jane Eyre that his injudicious marriage to Berthe Mason was brought about by his avaricious and grasping father, while his elder brother, Rowland, organized the affair: 'My father, and my brother Rowland ... thought only of the thirty thousand pounds, and joined in the plot against me' (JE, 306).

The reader may then wonder if any successful brother relations exist in the sub-genre, and yes, there is one glorious exception to the aforementioned line-up of casualties. The friendship between Pip and Herbert Pocket is one of the most successful of all the explored texts. From their very first meeting, that is, the fisticuffs' fight in the grounds of Satis House to the underpinning of Herbert's career by Pip, the young men understand one another. Without patronising his less-socialised companion or envying his fortune, Herbert takes his new room-mate under his wing and tutors him in the ways of society with the same level of professionalism that father Matthew Pocket instructs Pip in more academic matters. Eventually, Pip repays his friend by clandestinely setting him up in business and in turn, Pip is repaid by Herbert's very great understanding of Pip's background, from the awkward presence of Joe Gargery to the *very* awkward presence of Magwitch the convict. If this sequence of events is unlikely, the human emotion is not. Pip, of course, had learned successful male-to-male relations early in life by his communion with gentle foster father, Joe. From this point of view, it is more than a little significant that Joe Gargery never, in any area of the text, shows a tendency that has haunted and still haunts literature and public life, since the Industrial

Revolution.

The individual, individualism and Eleanor's rampage

Above, I explained how the meaning of *the family* has changed and how its size has dwindled throughout the centuries, slowly deflating from a community of household members and servants, through the extended family, through to the nuclear family of the twentieth and twenty-first centuries and eventually, to the individual. In gothic literature, the individual is not so much a source of conflict as *individualism*.

Across eighteenth and nineteenth-century literature, the individual arose in the spectre of the Byronic hero. To recap the description provided earlier in this text: 'Another trait is his solitariness. Never comfortable in society, the hero likes to wander in remote places, usually to brood upon whatever has blighted his life either in reality or in perception. Whatever his condition, the hero carries with him a perpetual air of mystery, and the reader – and the heroine – gain the impression that he has been hurt psychologically by an incident in his life.'

Earlier heroes, Don Quixote and Robinson Crusoe, had sought to join society, but the later Byronic hero demonstrated a penchant for solitariness. As David Wright points out, this penchant for wandering, this lack of inclination for mainstream society, brought about the near-extinction of the literary trope in the earlier decades of the nineteenth century. St John Rivers sails off into an Indian sunset, but what Dionysian havoc would he have wreaked in the life of Jane Eyre, if she had chosen him as a spouse? William de Stancy returns to soldiering and Victor Frankenstein ends his days improbably wandering Arctic wastelands. However, another breed of Byronic hero was born in the later 1800s. According to Michael Szollosy, Romanticism saw the unleash of the unconscious, the revelation of the more basic aspects of the self, and this critic could have been talking of Stevenson's Mr Hyde.[47]

In his article, 'Walking Alone Together: Family Monsters in the Haunting of Hill House', Richard Pascal describes how, by the twentieth century, the average American family was not so much a nuclear family but a group of individuals living in the same household whose disparate needs and desires

---

[47]Michael Szollosy, 'Freud, Frankenstein and our fear of robots: projection in our cultural perception of technology' in *AI & Society*, 3 (2017), 433-439, p435. Subsequent references will be to this edition and will be inserted parenthetically into the text, for example "Szollosy, 435".

were a source of much or indeed, all of the tension and conflict that reigned within. And Pascal cites Jackson's text as a parable that details what this tension leads to, ultimately Eleanor's childish rampage, before the conclusion of the narrative. When regarded in the light of twentieth-century child-centred psychology – much of it post-war – his theory carries much weight (Pascal, 481). But the individualist individual had been lurking in popular literature for a much longer period: what else is the Victorian *pater familias* but an individual insisting upon having everything his way? Pascal asserts that Hugh Crain's three wives made only the barest impression on Hill House, in addition to leaving little trace on the narrative (Pascal, 470). I have to disagree with Pascal in this assertion – because in Jackson's narrative and other texts, dead wives are present by their very absence. Indeed, the sub-genre is filled with male characters trying to either negate their living female relatives or shrug off the influence of deceased ones.

Manfred is married but thinks little of divorcing his wife of twenty years' standing and taking the young Isabella as a bride. General Tilney's wife died of natural causes, but he has effectively banished her memory by forbidding even members of the household from entering her chamber. William Dare's mother died before his father, William de Stancy, could marry her.

It is unclear why John Jarndyce never married: perhaps he waited for the young Esther to grow up because he felt that a helpmeet, much less his equal in years, would be more compliant when he laid out plans and schemes? But Jarndyce has that much self-awareness, at least. Not so lucky is the wife of his friend, the supremely selfish, narcissistic and self-indulgent Harold Skimpole. This individual is quite simply Romanticism run riot, given to enjoyment of nature, relishing gourmet foods and fine wine, music and poetry, all bought at the price of his long-suffering spouse and their impoverished family. Another of the narrative's self-absorbed characters is Prince Turveydrop's father. When Caddy meets her future father-in-law, the author hints that Mr Turveydrop has bullied his late wife (Prince's mother) and describes Prince as: 'a little blue-eyed fair man of youthful appearance ... I received the impression that he was like his mother, and that his mother had not been considered or well used' (BH, 242).

Jane Eyre judiciously declines to marry St John Rivers, a man who shows almost the same marital reserve as John Jarndyce does in matters of the heart, except when religious zeal infuses him, Rivers. And John Reed, bullying his mother and sisters and humiliating Jane, shows the same *enfant terrible* tendencies as Eleanor Vance before the conclusion of Jackson's text. And the modern reader must wonder on the extent to which a measure of conjugal affection and tenderness from her husband would have helped Berthe Mason Rochester lead a more normal, less confined life? John Reed's own excesses finish him off before he can wed, but Estella of *Great Expectations* is not so lucky. The author does not reveal Bentley Drummle's background but he shows a similar bullying instinct and disaffection to John Reed – and he too dies as a result of his own behaviour. But this fairy-tale tidiness, that is, the punishing of the baddie, does not extend to realist fiction. In *Hard Times*, Mrs Gradgrind, who has constantly echoed her husband's edict to 'stick to facts' literally fades away. In Daphne du Maurier's text, Rebecca perishes at the hand of her husband, while the new Mrs de Winter, in contrast to the banished Berthe Mason, is *obliged* to shadow her husband, to literally sit at his side for the remainder of *his* life.

As stated above, in the sub-genre, the lover and tyrannical parent sometimes seem to blend, which is why I use a combination of parent figures and lovers to state the case. And as I have stressed through much of this text, the behaviour of the Byronic hero is ironic rather than heroic, evident from this summation. To psycho analyse all of the 'cases', in the post-Freudian sense, to try to pin down the reasons for the odious behaviour of subjects such as Bentley Drummle, is not only beyond the reach of this text, it would be utterly futile. The narratives were written as fables, not as studies in psychiatry. And this is why I would commend Shirley Jackson, if she were around today, in *not* attempting to 'analyse' that Victorian martinet, Hugh Crain, whose idea of saving his daughters' souls was filling scrap books with the most terrifying images of an imagined hell that he could find, in the hope of subduing them into good behaviour. And all signed lovingly with his own blood.

Hugh Crain simply *is* – or was: like many a Byronic hero, bound to remain single or become a widower or to die, in order to maintain his authoritarian status. The overweening personality in Jackson's narrative is that of Hill House, a female presence that wars with extraneous elements, other women and disregarding males, such as the male person who, eighteen years previous to Dr Montague telling the assembly of inmates his story, had tried to leave Hill House late at night (HH, 67). Hill House seems to dislike females intruding from outside, because it is itself female, despite the phallic references, such as the tower that houses the library. The house only tolerated the female offspring of Hugh Crain, probably because their father built it. Mrs Dudley senses this when she places Eleanor in a blue room and Theodora in a green room, the 'male' colours, while she places the doctor and Luke each in a 'female' lemon room and a pink room, respectively (HH, 92).

Inevitably, the Byronic hero appears in the family, living either already within its walls as the cause of existing dysfunction or as an intruder arriving to turn harmony into discord. Here, the reader might think of Henry Crawford causing havoc at Mansfield Park. The Byronic hero was not needed in eighteenth-century narratives; both Manfred of *Otranto* and Marquis de Montalt of Radcliffe's narrative supplied the Dioysian element essential to disrupt Apollonian harmony within the texts. With the advent of realism in literature, this dying-out of the old pantomimic villain left narratives with a deficit. The chapter **Maid in the Mirror** explores how the addition of the later archetype adds conflict to what would otherwise be bland morality fables. Without Henry Crawford, *Mansfield Park* would be little more than a 'good girl wins good boy' fable, as Fanny Price so crushingly renders it. But Henry Tilney's proto- Byronic hero is reborn and lives on in Mr Darcy of *Pride and Prejudice*. If a wealthy Byronic hero is insidious, a poor one is disastrous.

Here, we may juxtapose Edward Rochester of *Jane Eyre* and Harold Skimpole of *Bleak House*. One is wealthy enough to never have to worry about the flow of this life's goods, while the other is continually fleeing creditors. One is eminently calm and in control of his life, while the other dwells in a fantasy of poetry and music as his family falls into ruin and misery. Although Rochester's illusion of control is blown away by the conclusion of the narrative, the reader may argue that he took care of wife Berthe Mason, at least. A number of critics have cited Berthe as being the titular Jane's alter ego. But there is grounds for belief that the archetypal *madwoman in the attic* might represent the psyche of the outwardly-controlled and controlling Byronic hero.

In *A Laodicean*, Thomas Hardy's treatment of the theme is more subtle. An obvious contender for the role of Byronic hero is soldier William de Stancy. Although he tries to join society, represented by Paula Power, his efforts are half-hearted and only at the behest of his son, William Dare. However, Dare plays the same role in the narrative as does Berthe Mason in *Jane Eyre*, his relation to his father aborting the society marriage at the penultimate stage. Here, the reader might argue that Dare is another manifestation of de Stancy's personality, its nature hinted at by his surname. As Dare observes his father, when he, de Stancy, has taken steps to make him more marriagable, he (Dare) notes: '(de Stancy's) voice was firmer, his cheeks were less pallid; and he was above all authoritative towards his present companion, whose ingenuity in vamping up a being for his ambitious experiments seemed about to be rewarded, like Frankenstein's, at the hands of his own creature' (AL, 214). This allusion to Mary Shelley's novel is little short of genius on the part of Hardy, even more so when the reader considers that the roles between creator and creature have been reversed, that it is the younger, socially weaker man who attempts to engineer the life of his parent, not the other way around. Only five years following the publication of Hardy's novel, Robert Louis Stevenson created what might be called an allegory on this earlier plot, namely, the tale of a man who brings forth the monster inside of himself, and then finds that monster taking over his life and identity. And I use the phrase 'bring forth' advisedly; just as de Stancy fathers a son, and Dr Jekyll discovers his inner Mr Hyde, Victor Frankenstein, in the words of Gilbert and Gubar 'has a baby' (G&G, 232). By the twentieth century, many writers had eschewed these almost pantomimic expressions of duality for more subtle effects. Advances in psychology enabled authors to create characters so complex that 'good' and 'bad' could reside side by side without the need for extraneous relatives or fleshly creations running amok. Witness the 'good' Lyra Belaqua spinning untrue tales to her hosts in the land of the dead – and see the dutiful Eleanor Vance transforming into a rampaging, entitled version of her former, docile self, her inner Byron, indeed.

In our times, the Byronic hero has been reborn as James Bond, squashing Soviet spies but never showing a tendency towards monogamy. And in another strand of literature, the wife has been replaced with a robot by a husband who wants to maintain firm control of his household. The case that Eleanor's death is the result of, as Richard Pascal puts it, her failure to 'construct a unified adult personality' is compelling (Pascal, 469). Yet surely, Eleanor's rampage is metaphorical of the frustration of adult women everywhere, who know that their plans for professional fulfilment – if they ever travel that far in life - are in any case going to be torn apart by the exigencies of marriage and motherhood? (Bailey, 26). The event of 'ghosting' of women by dominant male partners does lead on naturally to another, unavoidable strand of the gothic sub-genre.

The Lexicon of Haunting

Why the supernatural ♦ The lexicon of haunting ♦ Haunted people ♦
The sleep of reason ♦ Projections and perceptions ♦ The Ghosts
of Things to Come

Why the supernatural?

Delia Da Sousa Correa cites Andrew Bennett and Nicholas Royle as defining the uncanny as being related to a 'disturbance of the familiar' (DDSC, 109). In the **Introduction**, I define a satirical novel as one that takes place in a familiar setting, but with modifications to familiarity that make the reader uneasy. From this point of view, the definition of the uncanny by Bennett and Royle 'a disturbance of the familiar' could, in fact, refer to the satirical literary form. In the eighteenth century, with the transferring of popularity from the satire to romantic and social realist literature, the reader may discern that the presence of the uncanny or supernatural in a narrative has become almost a surrogate for satire, the sensing by the reader and the novel's protagonist(s) that something in the environment is out of synch with reality.

The major difference between literary satire and the uncanny and/or supernatural is that the former is experienced on social and political planes, whereas disturbances by a sense of the uncanny is a more personal experience. This makes sense: the rise of individualism around the time of the Industrial Revolution paved the need for a more introspective literature, and the supernatural was at hand to externalise the discomfort felt by the individual. The paradox is that the Industrial Revolution arose from the same advances in scientific knowledge that promulgated Enlightenment, a time when, theoretically, at least, belief in supernatural entities ought to have been waning. But this paradox does bear deeper thought. According to Northrop Frye: 'in high mimetic, where we are within the order of nature, a ghost is relatively easy to introduce because the plane of experience is above our own, but when he appears he is an awful and mysterious being from what is perceptibly another world' (Frye, 50). To remind the reader, in the high mimetic mode, the heroes are flesh-and-blood humans who create their own fates, but are often pitted against supernatural forces that surprise, scare and confound them.

And the reader will not find obscurity in Frye's argument; the night-ghasts with 'bleeding stumps where their heads should have been' that – in Pullman's fantasy trilogy – appear in Lyra's room at night may unsettle the reader but they have no more effect upon the young girl than rodents straying into the living space of a modern family and, the author assures the reader, are as readily chased away (HDM, 48). But the ghost that appears in the recognisable world of Susan Hill's text petrify all of the characters, not least the hapless property agent Mr Jerome. Ghosts in literature flourish because the literary forms since Enlightenment have veered towards realism and because writers need metaphors of, and externalisations of personal, environmental and political disturbances. The ghost stories that emerged in the eighteenth century do not fall into the mode of high mimetic because the protagonists were neither pitted against nor allied with supernatural forces. The ghosts that appear in the low mimetic – and the gothic sub-genre – express truths about the natural world and the mentality of the protagonist(s).

To complete Frye's argument: 'In low mimetic, ghosts have been ever since Defoe, almost entirely confined to a separate category of 'ghost stories' ... In some forms of ironic fiction, such as the later works of Henry James, the ghost begins to come back as a fragment of a disintegrating personality' (Frye, 50). On the question of this, the 'psychological' ghost, Banquo's full-bodied apparition that appears to the titular character of Shakespeare's play, is a possible sign that Macbeth's guilty conscience is interfering with his perception because the other present characters cannot see it. This aspect of the supernatural is explored in a later section of this chapter.

Sandra Gilbert and Susan Gubar provide another, plausible explanation for the idea – although not always the actual instance – of the ghost in the gothic sub-genre. According to the pair it is the person who fails, either through choice or helplessness, to determine what they want in life who is at risk of being undermined by circumstance or 'haunted by everybody' (G&G, 176).

Gothic literature is filled with references to the deceased parents that pervade their children's lives: Mrs Tilney, whose absence in *Northanger Abbey* haunts the life of her daughter and eventually, protagonist Catherine Moreland, Jane Eyre's deceased relatives who will not let go of her imagination, and the dead Rebecca who pervades every aspect of Daphne du Maurier's narrative. And the ghost need not even be dead. Mrs Danvers seen through Mrs de Winter's eyes, takes on the ghastly appearance of a skelton, with her 'skull's face' (R, 74). The use of 'dead' imagery reminds us that while Rebecca is no more, her former servant lingers about Manderley but both Mrs de Winter and Mrs Danvers are complicit in this danse macabre, Mrs de Winter through helplessness and Mrs Danvers through choice.

In trying to find her place in society, the gothic heroine is in a state of *becoming* and remains vapid and insubstantial until her full personality manifests – or not – at the end of the narrative, when she takes on a robust effectiveness. Sally Shuttleworth states that it is Jane's 'sense of powerlessness' that is contributing to her terror (JE, x). In her days as a disaffected young orphan, Jane Eyre is terrified by the notion of a ghost appearing in the Red Room of Gateshead, in which she is imprisoned. But later on, as a self-realised young woman, she simply dismisses the very idea of supernatural happenings, even when she has good reason to believe that something unnatural might be afoot, such as hearing the voice that notionally summoned her to Rochester's fireside: 'Down superstition!' I commented' (JE, 420).

Here, I point out the distinction between the ghosts of the gothic sub-genre and the short fictions of M.R. James, the English author and Cambridge don who excelled in composing narratives surrounding the haunted object. These fictions are not included in this text, not least because the short form is inappropriate for the *bildungsroman* element of much gothic fiction. But more profoundly, the typical M.R. James protagonist is a self-assured professor or archaeologist or researcher, often with no small degree of arrogance, and the shock of the narrative is generated when a protagonist is caught in the teeth of whatever frightening and unexplained manifestation he – always he – encounters. This shock would simply not take place if an uncertain, disaffected protagonist were to be introduced to a haunted engraving or whistle, a dancing bed-sheet or slime creeping underneath a door. In a typical gothic narrative, suspense mounts up over several pages (or happenings or chapters), until the heroine finally obtains release through information and insight, rather than the short, sharp and shocking climax of the M.R. James' narrative. But the suspenseful form does not *exclude* an assured protagonist.

In *Romance of the Forest*, this suspense is enunciated over a number of pages. Alone in Madame La Motte's dressing room, Adeline sees the arras moving (ROTF, 114). She overcomes her apprehension to explore the area and finds herself opening a door that leads to a cellar, where she discovers a rolled and tied parchment (ROTF, 116). Adeline's attempts to read the parchment are confounded by both events in the Abbey and the poor condition of the pages. But read it she does: one night, and while engrossed in it, she hears a voice whispering 'here' (ROTF, 132). A little later, she sees – or fancies she sees – a shadow roving about an obscure part of the room (ROTF, 134). Following several events, she is still struggling to decipher the parchment, which she can only do by lamplight at night, in the privacy of her room, when she imagines she hears a voice calling her name. Subsequent events reveal that it was actually Peter the servant attempting to communicate with her, an improbable scenario since the chamber is one of the few private areas of the Abbey, and Peter had been attempting to communicate with her all of that day and could easily and naturally have spoken to her within the confines of her chamber (ROTF, 144).

But the scene serves its purpose expertly, to build the type of suspense that Edmund Burke laid out in his *Philosophical Enquiry*: 'it is our ignorance of things that ... chiefly excite our passions' (Burke, 50-51). And in a sense, Peter *is* a ghost, a serving man whose employer reminds him that he, Peter, often does not have the right to speak. In an earlier episode, Monsieur La Motte had said to Peter: 'Your opinion was not asked ... learn to be silent' (ROTF, 69). Together with women, the disenfranchised male is another of the group that struggle and seek to be heard and understood. In doing thus, they often behave like what we *think* ghosts are, thus making sense of the words of T.J. Lustig: 'to see a ghost is potentially to become what one thinks ghosts are' (TOTS, xxv). In Henry James's text, the Governess stalks the pair of children whom she believes are stalked by the pair of dead servants. In Shirley Jackson's text, Eleanor Vance cannot shrug off the memory of her recently-dead mother. Finally, her efforts to become a rounded adult fail and she reverts to rampaging through Hill House, behaving like the poltergeist that has held the inmates in thrall since their arrival (HH, 229). At the outset of the narrative, she is a meek, supplicating wraith, not unlike the nineteenth-century heroine until the insidious influence of the house turns her into a wilful, self-seeking individual (Bailey, 34). In Emily Bronte's narrative, *Wuthering Heights*, Heathcliff is an outsider, an adoptee reduced to the status of stable-boy when his foster father dies. This poisonous treatment, together with his rage at losing lover Catherine Earnshaw to another suitor, provides him with the potency to change his fortune and return to Wuthering Heights as an improbably rich man, a fairy-tale element in the novel. For a while, he wreaks revenge upon all those he *perceives* to have wronged him. But reality slowly replaces the fantasy narrative and with it, Heathcliff's potency slowly dwindles. As the young couple Catherine Linton and Hareton insist upon their love match, Heathcliff succumbs to anorexia, growing more and more vapid until he dies. This strand of narrative is not unlike that of Caroline Helstone of Charlotte Brontë's other narrative, except that the titular heroine, Shirley, rescues Caroline.

In *Bleak House*, Esther Summerson becomes *the* flesh-and-blood ghost that is about to rock the house of Dedlock: 'My echoing footsteps brought it suddenly into my mind that there was a dreadful truth in the legend of the Ghost's Walk, that it was I; who was to bring calamity upon the stately house and that my warning feet were haunting it even then' (BH, 571). The difference between the self-aware Esther and the hapless Eleanor is that the former protagonist is caught in circumstances of other peoples' making, whereas Eleanor has a modicum of choice over her behaviour, and refuses even the possibility of leaving Hill House. In Susan Hill's narrative, *The Woman In Black*, the ghost of Jennet Humphrye represents the dreadful flip-side of *not* becoming, wreaking revenge upon an agent of the law who happens to be blessed with the happy family life that had ever evaded her. And the two ghosts that occupy Daphne du Maurier's narrative are the dead titular character and the barely-alive Mrs de Winter. Housekeeper Mrs Danvers is arguably another. Other allegories for the supernatural include the *ineffable*, defined by Michael Wilson as an entity that 'cannot be described' entangled with our world, and that trying to face it is 'more than mortals can bear' (Wilson, 114). Wilson explains that the word 'ineffable' was formerly applied to experiences that were perceived as religious, but can be applied to certain, confounded states of mind of fictional characters that are encountering the unknown.

By the time that Jane Eyre perceives Rochester's summoning voice, she has matured enough to disentangle the experience from the terror of her belief in ghosts that manifested at the opening of the narrative: "Down superstition!' I commented, as that spectre rose up black by the black yew at the gate ... This is not thy deception, nor thy witchcraft; it is the work of nature' (JE, 420). Jane's refusal to acknowledge the supernatural could be a symptom of her having grown up, a consideration in all works of fiction in which a character perceives – or not – the supernatural.

Earlier in the text, she has declared that: 'Sympathies I believe exist (for instance, between far-distant, long-absent, wholly estranged relatives; asserting, notwithstanding their alienation, the unity of the source to which each traces his origin): whose workings baffle mortal comprehension' (JE, 220). But in her declaration that 'it is the work of nature' the reader may wonder if the protagonist isn't drawing back from stating a more frightening case, a case that unnatural forces *may* be at work in the universe? Sally Shuttleworth explains that it is likely to be the voice of the author working through Jane, preparing the reader for that untenable strand that is inextricably bound with the majority of gothic novels: that is, the 'breaking down' ... of the boundaries between the natural and the supernatural' (JE, xii). One characteristic of Jane's attitude to the instance of hearing the voice: she does not try to name what has happened. A century following Brontë's narrative, Shirley Jackson's Dr Montague states a more philosophical case for the follies of trying to pin a name on every esoteric experience. He declares that no-one who has ever stayed in Hill House has been able to define their experiences. And at the end of the narrative, the author frustrates the reader by *not* revealing what the surviving characters even imagined happened to Eleanor.

In certain cases, authors use *the ghost* (ghoul, vampire) to metaphorise the return of an old idea or archetype. The late nineteenth century saw the resurrection of the vampire, a creature of medieval legend, yet re-born as the utterly uncivilized – but outwardly civilized – pale-skinned gentleman, paradoxically drinking the blood of the young maidens whose hearts he could never, in the romantic sense, win. Vampires had ever existed in folk literature and, it must be said, the success of Bram Stoker's novel was due in part to the coinciding of its publication with the birth of the movie industry. But only in part. In Thomas Hardy's text, William Dare says to William de Stancy: 'Our days as an independent division of society, which holds aloof from other sections, are past' (AL, 326). The time was ripe for resurrecting this folkloric creature and his counterpart, the almost extinct aristocrat, and Stoker understood the connection between them. Just compare the following description of Stoker's Transylvanian Count with that of Brontë's Edward Rochester: 'His face was a strong – a very strong aquiline – with high bridge of the thin nose and peculiarly arched nostrils; with lofty domed forehead and hair growing scantily round the temples, but profusely elsewhere. *His eyebrows were very massive, almost meeting over the nose and with bushy hair that seemed to curl in its own profusion.* The mouth, so far as I could see it under the heavy moustache, was fixed and rather cruel-looking ... The general effect was one of extraordinary pallor'[48] with 'the moon was waxing bright. I could see him plainly. His figure was enveloped in a riding cloak, fur collared and steel clasped; its details were not apparent, but I traced the general points of middle height and considerable breadth of chest. *He had a dark face with stern features and a heavy brow; his eyes and gathered eyebrows looked ireful and thwarted just now;* he was past youth but had not yet reached middle age' (JE, 113).

The authors' intentions are made clear in the text that I have italicised. When it comes to the hero/unsocialised male, the eyes have it; Jane Eyre responds to Rochester's sexual magnetism while Jonathan Harker is struck by his host's sheer force of personality. Since Bram Stoker's day, a myriad vampires have been born; teenagers, paupers, children, but *his* vampire endures, the aristocrat living in his own castle – Manfred, Marquis de Montalt, General Tilney, John Jarndyce, Edward Rochester – exercising authority over a coterie of humans, extracting whatever he wants from whomever he chooses in order to nurture himself, quasi-aristocrats with a brace of mad or, at least, isolated women in his thrall. But the reader should be aware that vampirism is but an off-shoot of the gothic sub-genre. Stoker took one motif of gothic, that of the powerful, unsocialised male – the Byronic hero? – alone in his castle, exaggerated it greatly and formed it into the familiar narrative. More than one hundred years following publication, it makes for a superb supernatural motif. Many other accepted tropes for the representation of the supernatural have long been in place. What are these and how do they serve literature?

---

[48] Bram Stoker, *Dracula*, (London, Orion Books Ltd, 1992), p14. Subsequent references will be to this edition and will be inserted parenthetically into the text, for example '(Dracula, 14)'

The Lexicon of Haunting

The quotation 'Whose hand was I holding?' derives from Shirley Jackson's text, *The Haunting of Hill House*, in which the disaffected Eleanor Vance imagines, as she is lying in bed that she is squeezing a human hand (HH, 162). Initially she belives it that of her room mate Theodora (HH, 163). Unable to bear it any longer, Eleanor shouts 'STOP IT', the lights are suddenly on and she discovers that Theodora is lying in a bed on the other side of the room. And the phantom hand is no longer there. Eleanor's reaction has since become a cultural meme, used in likely and unlikely humorous situations. But what is striking about the situation is the sheer materiality of whatever assails Eleanor, the absence of vapidity and uncertainty. Eleanor just knows that she was clutching a flesh-and-blood hand.

The reaction of the reader might be to conclude that this was not a 'real' ghost, that it was too material. And this begs that question: where has the accepted lexicon of haunting come from, the fleeting shadows and white shapes, the mists and blasts of icy air, the soft whisperings and loud bumps in the night? An ancient Babylonian clay tablet, 3,500 years old bears the image of a dead man being led to the afterlife by a female figure. She is leading him with the rope that ties his wrists. A glum expression is just about discernible upon his bearded face. His muscular feet walk stolidly on the ground and his leg muscles are as flexed and firm on the floor as those of any living human. Dr Irving Finkel, curator of the Middle Eastern department of the British Museum has featured the tablet as an illustration in his book, *The First Ghosts: Most Ancient of Legacies*. In summary, this ancient ghost is solid and recognisable as human, bearing muscle and bone and walking upon the same ground as living entities. Why then, the vapidity of fictional spooks, the pale mists and screeching voices, the skeleton faces and clanking chains? Where does our notion of 'the ghost' derive from?

One of the most famous literary ghosts is Hamlet's father. In Act One, Scene One of Shakespeare's play, the ghost appears just after one o'clock in the morning to characters who *expect* it to appear, because Bernardo has already seen it. He now comments to guards Marcellus and Horatio: 'Looks a' not like the king.' When the spectre leaves, Bernardo describes it: 'For it is as the air, invulnerable' (Act 1, Scene 2). In the three thousand years between the engraving of the Babylonian clay tablet and Shakespeare's pen and ink, the spirit had dwindled from flesh on bone to a vapid form that could not be injured in any way by sword. Granted, the expression of the Shakespearean ghost is literary rather than graphic, but burgeoning literacy had played a part in this. And as the centuries have rolled, the literary ghost has become even more vapid. One particular quality is that they often appear in the night. In Scene Five of *Hamlet*, the ghost appears to the titular character, and father and son hold a cogent conversation. The scene concludes with ghost telling his son that he only appears in darkness and must vanish when the sun rises. This darkness-only mandate was possibly a device instigated by the stage people to help spectators suspend disbelief when, for example, the supernatural character might be painted white and draped in pale clothing.

In Charles Dickens's watershed ghost story, *A Christmas Carol*, protagonist Ebenezer Scrooge endures the sight of no fewer than four full-bodied apparitions in the space of a few hours, one Christmas Eve night. Through Scrooge's eyes, we see his dead friend: 'Marley in his pigtail, usual waistcoat, tights, and boots; the tassels on the latter bristling, like his pigtail, and his coat-skirts, and the hair upon his head.' In addition, Marley bears a chain made of a concatenation of: 'cash-boxes, keys, padlocks, ledgers, deeds and heavy purses wrought in steel'.[49] So far, so material and yet this ghost is transparent enough for Scrooge to look through his friend's waistcoat and see: 'the two buttons on his coat behind'. It was well within this author's power to have created such a strange and contradictory entity. He had spent much of his life absorbing the grotesque and macabre, possibly through the channel of one of his nurses who told him bedtime ghost stories when he was a young boy. But his imagination did not merely collect old ideas and fashion them together into a new body, like Frankenstein creating his monster: he created a new *idea*, the idea of a ghost as the essence of a person's life, deriving from particular times.

No modern writer, by which I mean from the mid-eighteenth century onwards, had ever done that. *A Christmas Carol* is such a piece of seminal writing that Dickens' ghosts still haunt us today. In addition, Dickens pulled yet another haunting device into his narrative. Today, we all accept that ghosts float around rather than being connected to a physical body. But from where did Dickens derive the idea of ghosts flying across the rooftops and over

---

[49]Charles Dickens, *A Christmas Carol* (Hertfordshire: Wordsworth Editions Limited, 1993), p19. Subsequent references will be to this edition and will be inserted parenthetically into the text, for example '(Carol, 19)'

countryside? The Victorians were very fond of fairies. One of their favourite plays was *A Midsummer Night's Dream*, facilitated by that wonderful theatrical invention, aptly named the *flies*. In most sophisticated nineteenth-century theatres, fairies and other fantasy figures flew across the stage on this wire suspension apparatus and sometimes, across the heads of the patrons in the auditorium. Dickens was no stranger to the theatre and his creativity didn't have to travel far to endow his spirits with flying abilities. But, perhaps his imagination received a boost from another direction?

In October of 1837, a young servant was walking from her parents' home in Battersea to her employer's house in nearby Lavender Hill. While walking through a dark alley, a man leapt at her. Only her screams saved her, drawing people to the scene and causing the attacker to flee. Following this incident, the press filled rapidly with reports of ladies fainting and indeed, dying of fright at either seeing or being attacked by a sinister man who had the ability to escape by vaulting over high walls and running across rooftops. Eventually, this man was dubbed 'Spring-heeled Jack'. No-one was immune from Jack, it seemed. Gardeners were attacked while working in the confines of their plots, and servants and residents attacked on their doorsteps. Writers had a field day, especially the hacks who filled the cheap periodicals known as 'penny dreadfuls' with tales designed to inspire shock and awe. And in 1843, just as the Jack hysteria was at its height, Dickens, who had worked as a reporter and newspaper columnist, penned *A Christmas Carol*. He may just have imagined the flying element, of course. But if readers accept that writers' ideas derive from their environment, then the media of the day most likely inspired the Inimitable. And about a century before Dickens's day, another mode of ghost representation had arrived in literature.

In his excellent book, *The Cock Lane Ghost,* Paul Chambers, recalls a 'genuine' eighteenth-century haunting, genuine in the sense that the incident concerned actual people, and was not simply a work of fiction. The incident concerned unexplained activity in the Clerkenwell area of London, in the 1760s. During its time, this activity sparked enormous public interest, a media frenzy and a landmark court case, which resulted in a number of jailings. To sum up, a number of people heard tapping and scratching in a room of a public house lodging whenever a particular young woman happened to be present. Because it received copious coverage from the media of the time, the population of the City and indeed, Greater London, went ghost crazy. And hoaxers had a field day. In one of the earlier incidents, a publican went into the notionally haunted house and fled in terror when he saw a figure covered in a sheet, beckoning to him. Today, we would just roll our eyes and laugh - but be aware that this event took place long before the advent of television and movies. And by the nineteenth century, ghosts had gained the ability to make amorphous sounds.

In his description of Chesney Wold, Dickens writes: 'If there be a little (fancy) at any odd moment, it goes, like a little noise in that old, echoing place, a long way, and leads off to ghosts and mystery' (BH, 133). Later, the reader learns the legend of the Dedlock ghost, concerning a traitorous incident during the Civil War, The narrative finishes by stating that whenever a misfortune concerning sickness or death is about to take place in the house of Dedlock, an echoing sound, like that of dripping rain, is heard upon the ghost walk or terrace of Chesney Wold (BH, 141). Of course, the telegraph was in place by Dickens's day and it would not have been difficult for the Victorian reader to imagine a denizen of the past communicating to the present through the medium of sound. But it is most likely that the author had read avidly of the tappings and scratchings of the eighteenth-century spectre, particularly when the writers of *that* day, notably Samuel Johnson and Horace Walpole, became enmeshed in the controversy. And the reader should note that the Cock Lane ghost manifested between 1758 and 1760, a few short years before Walpole published *The Castle of Otranto*.

In the last decade of the nineteenth century, Henry James published his novella, *The Turn of the Screw*, and the ghosts that the Governess sees are silent. But on her first night in Bly, she imagines that she hears – or indeed does hear – the sound of a child crying (TOTS, 125). Oddly, she fails to try to discover its source, an insouciance in contrast to the zeal with which she pursues 'ghosts' later on. In *The Haunting of Hill House*, Eleanor and Theodora hear a child or children laughing on the night that the poltergeist begins to manifest, a subtle foil to the overweening sense of menace created by the terrifying, crashing noises heard late at night in the house. Other devices used by Jackson are the writings upon walls and the vile imagery of spilt blood in Theodora's bedroom, a situation that causes Eleanor to temporarily loathe her new friend (HH, 158). Jackson could have taken this reference from Oscar Wilde's short story *The Canterville Ghost*, in which bloodstains cannot be removed permanently from the flooring of an old house. But it is also likely that Jackson was interested in the increasing research into the paranormal in the early twentieth century, and displacement of matter and disruption to everyday life has indeed been reported in relation to many instances of unexplained happenings.

Since the days of the Sumerian engravings, it is as if the wheel has rolled around and the vapid ghost of Shakespeare's spectre has solidified into material manifestations, such as Shirley Jackson's hand, a situation that lends itself to satire. I have already referred to the link between the satire and the haunting, of how satire works at a political level while a haunting involves an individual. Once again, it was Dickens who created the most metaphorically haunted character of all time.

Haunted people

Today, in the wake of M Night Shyamalan's movie, *The Sixth Sense*, the phrase: 'I see dead people' has become a cultural meme. We always think of hauntings as happening collectively, the jolly phantom appearing in the midst of a number of people who share, more or less, the same experience. But as English literature matured and ripened, a new phenomenon arrived, that is, the person haunted by spectres, whether real or imagined, unperceived by anyone else. J Sheridan le Fanu was one of the earliest writers to introduce a psychological element into tales of the supernatural, thus rendering the narrative as much about the person haunted, as the actual phantom.

Renowned for his ghost stories, le Fanu lived between 1814 and 1872 and from these dates, we can see that his life was concurrent with that of Charles Dickens, the two writers being practically born and dying within a few years of one another. Here, it would be futile to try to unravel which one of these writers influenced the other, and how. In 1848, Dickens published a short story, *The Haunted Man and the Ghost's Bargain*, another one of his so-called Christmas stories. The subject of the narrative is the chemistry teacher, Redlaw, who has had an unhappy past. He broods and broods until a phantom: 'an awful likeness of himself' appears and proposes to Redlaw that he can allow him to: 'forget the sorrow, wrong, and trouble you have known ... ' In short, the phantom will help him to forget all of his memories. Redlaw agrees to this strange proposal, but without memories, Redlaw has trouble explaining all of the emotion he feels. Eventually, Redlaw reverts to his normal, emotional self. The subject has learned his lesson from the ghost: without memories, even bad ones, we cannot be the complex people that we are.

In 1861, Dickens published *Great Expectations*, the subject of the story being a disaffected youth who struggles to come to terms with his place in society. In the hands of the Inimitable, the novel has become almost the anatomy of a human being: Pip being by turns sad, funny, unpredictable, capricious, snobbish, compassionate, passionate, arrogant, humble, guilty, contrite. From its beginning to its end, the galaxy of spectres that Pip encounters renders him one of the most haunted characters in the entire body of English literature. Paradoxically, the novel is all but devoid of supernatural happenings. Near the beginning of the narrative, Pip tells the reader: 'I was in mortal terror of myself' (GE, 14). At the end, Pip is presented with a miniature of himself: 'sitting on my own little stool looking at the fire, was – I again' (GE, 408). The child that he sees is the son of Joe, his foster father, who is now happily married to the down-to-earth Biddy, the author's way of indicating that the cyclical nature of life but is, in itself, the essence of an existential haunting.

Mention of the supernatural takes place early in the novel.

When he is still a young child working in his foster father's forge, the unpleasant journeyman, Dolge Orlick, tells Pip of a devil that 'lived in a black corner of the forge, and that he knew the fiend very well; also that it was necessary to make up the fire, once in seven years, with a live boy, and that I might consider myself fuel' (GE, 95). Pip's discomfiture here is akin to that felt by a petrified Jane Eyre in the Red Room. In the words of Sally Shuttleworth the 'sense of powerlessness' to which an unformed personality is prone (JE, x). Terrifying indeed, for a credible young child – but Pip had nothing to fear from a devil. The perils he encounters arrive from the human plane. At the opening of the narrative, an escaped convict, Abel Magwitch, happens upon the very young Pip in a graveyard, on Christmas Eve. The starving man grabs the child, turns him upside down and will not put him down until Pip has answered his questions. Presently, the convict terrorises the young boy to try to extract food from him: 'There's a young man hid with me ... That young man has a secret way pecooliar to himself, of getting at a boy, and at his heart, and at his liver. It is in wain for a boy to attempt to hide himself from that young man. A boy may lock his door, may be warm in bed, may tuck himself up, may draw the clothes over his head, may think himself comfortable and safe, but that young man will softly creep and creep his way to him and tear him open' (GE, 6).

The joke is upon Magwitch when presently, Pip *does* see the actual 'young man' dressed like Magwitch in a convict's outfit. When Pip innocuously recounts the occurrence to Magwitch, the older convict reacts with such agitation that Pip fears for his life once more: 'He held me by the collar and stared at me so, that I began to think his first idea about cutting my throat had revived' (GE, 18). Much later in the narrative, the other convict does indeed stalk Pip: 'the special and peculiar terror I felt at Compeyson's having been behind me like a ghost' (GE, 328). Pip, of course, had complied with the convict's original request for food, stealing it from his sister, and suffering agonies of guilt about it for years afterwards. Worse than the guilt is the fact of the convict that he once helped is practically stalking him from a distance, following the events of his life and indeed, sending Pip the fortune that rescues him from life as a blacksmith. Eventually, he turns up on Pip's doorstep. Magwitch says to him later: 'Look'ee here, Pip. I'm your second father. You're my son – more to me nor any son' (GE, 273). Pip is only released from this obligation when he – Magwitch – dies.

From the beginning to end, the novel is filled with strange and eccentric characters, including Miss Havisham, a woman who insists upon dressing in the gown that she was wearing many years earlier upon her wedding day, only to be jilted at the last minute. Even when out of her company, Pip fancies that he sees: 'A figure all in yellow white, with but one shoe to the feet, and it hung so, that I could see that the faded trimmings of the dress were like earthy paper, and that the face was Miss Havisham's, with a movement going over the whole countenance, as if she were trying to call me' (GE, 54). Before the end of the narrative, Miss Havisham is beset by terrible injury when the dress catches fire, and Pip saves her life. Even so, when recovering from his own injuries, he is unable to rest: 'If I dozed for a minute, I was awakened by Miss Havisham's cries, and by her running at me with all that height of fire above her head' (GE, 342). In the same manner, Pip is haunted by the notion of his injured and dying sister, probably because he senses that the person with whom she was arguing immediately before her attack caused her harm, and it was an action of Pip that began the argument. But all the guilt and wonderment that the young boy and man experience have not the power, either alone or together, to evoke in him the emotion at even the thought of the lovely Estella. From the moment that he encounters the blossoming young girl in Miss Havisham's house, Pip falls in love with her. As he grows from a boy to a young man, his love turns to passion, an unrequited passion that amounts to a haunting. Eventually, Pip says to Estella: 'You have been in every prospect I have ever seen – on the river, on the sails of the ships, on the marshes, in the clouds, in the light, in the darkness' (GE, 309). In one event, Estella has gone to live in a house in Richmond, at Miss Havisham's behest, to take society by storm. And Pip now living in London follows Estella to dinners and parties, house gatherings and balls. Gradually, he becomes, in his own words: 'the unquiet spirit in me haunted that house when Estella lived there' (GE, 256).

In spite of all of Pip's personal dilemmas, there is a strong undertone of satire in Dickens's narrative. Because of the realist nature of the text, the reader is ever aware that no devil, as described by Dolge Orlick, dwells in the forge. From our comfortable stand-point, we share the joke with the journeyman and the author. Eventually, the real 'devil' proves to be in Pip's own psyche and indeed, the danger to Pip and his family that Orlick himself eventually provides. One century following Dickens, Shirley Jackson uses a similar, teasing device to brilliant effect.

The sleep of reason

Long before Orlick tried to spook Pip, mischievous characters and supernatural pranksters had been present in literature. Shakespeare's play, *Macbeth*, was written in 1606 when King James, nephew of the deceased Elizabeth 1, had succeeded the throne. Throughout, the play presents a troubled landscape, opening with a scene that the author describes as 'a desert place' (Act 1, Scene 1). From the beginning of the scene to the end, the words of the three weird sisters evoke the natural world: 'When shall we three meet again/In thunder, lightning, or in rain?' In Act 1, Scene 3, the sisters discuss how they have the power to actually manipulate the weather, and they boast of doing it so successfully that they force a ship to endure a tempest that lasts for eighty one or 'nine times nine' weary weeks, while the people on board pine away. The idea of the malicious spirit was born and this is what the sisters achieve when they fill the titular character's mind with the idea that he will be monarch one day. For the remainder of the narrative, havoc ensues. Of course, the play could have served as a warning to King James, who actually believed in the supernatural, to not give way to superstition. His death in 1626 was followed by a 100-year period of scientific discovery and technological advance that gave rise to the number of social, economic and political conditions, among them the Industrial Revolution, and the Agricultural Revolution, and the American War of Independence, and the philosophical mode we call Enlightenment. In paradoxical parallel, the hunting and execution of 'witches' continued into the eighteenth century.

In her flight to Switzerland, Adeline sought to escape the influence of dogma and aristocracy, to cast off the old, autocratic world dictated by family mores and birth status, and embrace the new. She did, in fact, become part of a new and enlightened – in the learning sense – family. And in theory, *Northanger Abbey* and Jane Austen's other books marked the end of the earlier series of 'enlightened' novels of the Enlightenment. In spite of the subject of the supernatural, this epoch of Enlightenment echoes in Shirley Jackson's narrative. Dr Montague expresses anger about Hugh Crain's handwritten book filled with reproductions of the artist Goya's work, which he hoped would fill his daughters with the terror of hell, and that the inmates of Hill House pour over with horror (HH, 168). Assuming that this was Hugh Crain's intention, he seemingly misunderstood the intent of artist Francisco de Goya. Born in Spain, in 1746, Goya became court painter to the Spanish monarch, Charles III. This progressive monarch had effected many agricultural and economic reforms, and had no doubt been guided by the Enlightenment. In 1788, Charles III died and his son, Charles IV became monarch, but the new king was not the progressive monarch that his father had been. On succeeding the Spanish throne, Charles IV dismissed his father's equally progressive prime minister and began to hand more power to the Inquisition, the secret police who imprisoned, tortured and executed persons who were even suspected of being heretical, whether religious or political.

Spain risked being thrust back into the dark and superstitious age from which it had just emerged and Goya was not slow to recognize this. Jackson never reveals the title of the reproduced work of the prodigious Goya that the Hill House group gazes upon, and trying to discern it is beyond the scope of this text. But here I explore one of his most typical and recognisable images to further interpret the intention of the author. In 1799, an advertisement appeared in a Madrid newspaper offering a set of eighty prints 'The Caprichos' or caprices, for sale, images that censured political mores and human vices. Pictorial satire was then being used to brilliant effect by the English artist, James Gillray, and there is no doubt that Goya had seen much of his prolific output. Satire differs from fine art in that it only thrives in a context of social and political turmoil – and Spain of the 1790s was the perfect environment. The preface to the set of drawings was titled: '*Sleep of Reason Produces Monsters: the artist dreaming. His only purpose was to banish harmful vulgar beliefs and to perpetuate in this work of caprices the solid testimony of truth.*' In the image, an artist is sleeping, slumped over his desk, while bats fly about his head and an owl-type creature holds his chalks. Despite the title, there are no monsters or even grotesque creatures to be seen. The satire works at one level as a warning to the viewer against relying on imaginings of dark and superstitious forces? Later on, Goya retitled the image 'Imagination abandoned by reason produces impossible monsters; united with her, she is the mother of the arts.' Again, the reader cannot know what image that Hugh Crain placed in his book, but referring to Goya was no doubt the author's joke, the artist having warned the denizens of the late eighteenth and early nineteenth centuries on the dangers of giving way to irrational fears. But knowing what Jackson heretofore revealed of Crain's character, it was likely that he was simply using one of Goya's more frightening images to terrify his daughter. In trying to do this, Crain was hoist by his own petard, not understanding what Goya was really trying to convey – or did Crain work in the expectation that Sophia would not have understood the eighteenth-century artist?

From a fictional point of view, the answer to this question hardly matters; the damage done to the child most likely heightened the tensions that manifested as poltergeist activity to its twentieth-century occupants. Most often, the pranking spirit simply evokes all that is worst in human nature. If Macbeth had not been so suggestible, he would have simply dismissed the claims of the weird sister that spoke to him and Banquo: 'All hail Macbeth, that shalt be king hereafter' (Act 1, Scene 3). It is his greed and ambition that causes the ensuing havoc, not any supernatural element. The spilt blood in Theodora's chamber simply highlights the tension between herself and Eleanor; it does not cause it. And it is Eleanor's choice to destroy herself, not any alien force. Indeed, only one entity in the array of primary texts shows any true malice, and that is one of the more recently published. In one of the final scenes of *The Woman in Black*, Arthur Kipps is happily married to his erstwhile fiancée, Stella, and they are proud parents of a young son, Joseph, whom they take for a walk in the grounds surrounding a grand house: 'There was a festive, holiday air about the place, a lake on which small boats were being rowed, a bandstand with a band playing jolly tunes' (Hill, 213).

The woman in black appears, the horse that is pulling the carriage that Stella and Joseph are seated in, rears in terror and soon, Arthur's little family is a thing of the past. Significantly, this most evil of all literary ghosts operates within a late-twentieth century text, and its event may be a postmodern, post-feminist comment on the virtues or otherwise of family life?

Projections and perceptions

Before the nineteenth century ended, an emerging science, that of psychology, opened the door to many shades in the palette of human emotion. Scholars and psychologists alike agree that Macbeth's sighting of Banquo at the feast was at least as likely to be Macbeth's psychological projection, the fallout of his conscience over the murder of his friend, as much as an actual spectre.

Guilt, fear, puzzlement, passion and love are emotions that are likely to conjure the type of ghost that writers seek to involve us with. In Walpole's text, the scheming Manfred sees the spectre of his grandfather Alfonso, while the almost equally guilty Frederic imagines that he encounters the ghost of the hermit who originally directed him to the gigantic sceptre. According to Michael Szollosy, one element of psychological fantasy is a process whereby we project thoughts, feelings and fantasies into notional containers, persons, objects and ideas. The better parts of us are projected onto attractive containers, while the more negative and less socially acceptable, sexualised and even violent aspects of ourselves are projected into the monsters, demons and zombies of fiction (Szollosy, 436).

Shoshana Felman points out that the tension in Bly, the country house of Henry James's text, *The Turn of the Screw*, is caused by the absence of the instigator of the situation, that is, the Governess's employer. Citing Sigmund Freud, she states that what the Governess is perceiving could be a step from 'a conflict between two forces (Felman, 110). Felman presents the debates that surround the cause of the Governess seeing the assumed ghosts. Today, critics still argue over the meaning of James's text, over the nature of the phantoms that the unnamed Governess sees – if indeed, she *does* see any. Robert Heilman vigorously refutes Edmund Wilson's Freudian theory 'repressed passion', Wilson stating that the supernatural sightings are fantasies projected by the Governess's own, sexually-repressed self (Heilman, 436). Heilman states that her emotion is not 'repressed' but well out in the open, that in Chapter 1 of the text, she emphatically declares her love for her employer: 'I was carried away in London'. Objectively, this is clear to the reader – but does this mean that she is not 'haunted'?

Henry James's Governess comes from a troubled, clergyman's family. In her eagerness to escape the strictures of her ecclesiastical upbringing, she accepts a job teaching children for an employer who tells her that he is never going to communicate with her. And unused to men to whom she is not related, she immediately conceives a passion for this very man. Her mind a-sizzle with the Victorian potboilers she reads every night, the Governess begins to see a man – or men – about Bly, who very definitely do not live in the house. A man gazes at her from the house's tower, one summer's evening. She sees a man staring in through the library window at her. She encounters the same man on the stairs, late one night. But is he a 'real' man, or the real ghost of a man, or is her passion causing her to imagine either man or ghost?

Around the same time, she sees women – or a woman. The Governess imagines the man and the woman to have been lovers, although she never sees them together. On information given her by the housekeeper, Mrs Grose, the Governess persists in believing that she is seeing the ghostly manifestation of former valet Peter Quint and a former governess, the deceased Miss Jessel, aflame for one another. The Governess becomes suffused with a type of missionary zeal – she *is* a clergyman's daughter – to save the children. From what, we never quite find out. The Governess may have been inadvertently projecting her repressed desires onto Bly's very receptive atmosphere, or the haunting may indeed have been 'genuine', in the sense that she was not psychologically involved in any way with the phantoms that provoked her. Or there may be another explanation entirely.

The ghosts of things to come

In contrast to noisy and disruptive haunting is the silent ghost, and one characteristic of the phantoms experienced by Henry James's Governess is the silence expressed to the reader whenever one of the ghosts appears: '(He goes into the) 'silence', she declares, when the notional Peter Quint appears on the staircase of Bly (TOTS, 171). And when she perceives him for the first time, the Governess declares: 'I can hear again ... the intense hush in which the sounds of the evening dropped. The rooks stopped cawing in the golden sky' (TOTS, 136). This is in contrast to the sensations she perceived when she first arrived at Bly: 'the broad clean front, its open windows and fresh curtains ... the lawn and the fresh flowers ... the clustered tree-tops over which the rooks circled and cawed in the golden sky' (TOTS, 123).

This constant, menacing silence is very different from the noisy poltergeist of Jackson's text, but is no less unsettling to the reader. And this same silence is evoked by Susan Hill when she describes the discomfiture experienced by protagonist Arthur Kipps of *The Woman in Black*, when he encounters the titular entity: 'her expression began to fill me with fear ... I had never in my life been so possessed by it, never known my knees to tremble and my flesh to creep ... I was as certain as I had ever been ... I would drop dead on the wretched patch of ground' (Hill, 81-82). In addition, Arthur's earlier sighting of the spectre renders her not unlike the living avatar of Du Maurier's narrative, Mrs Danvers. Writes Arthur: 'not only was she extremely pale, even more than the blackness of her garments could account for, but the skin and, it seemed, only the thinnest layer of flesh was tautly stretched and strained across her bones, so that it gleamed with a curious blue-white sheen, and her eyes seemed sunken back into her head' (Hill, 57). This description is comparable with that of Mrs de Winter's reaction to Mrs Danvers in Du Maurier's narrative, that of a tall, white-faced woman dressed in black (R, 74). Neither Susan Hill's dead woman in black nor the living Mrs Danvers gained the opportunity to partake of family life nor that of wider society. Behind Du Maurier's caricature, the reader might sometime ask: who really was Mrs Danvers? What personal dreams did she renounce to invest emotionally in a beautiful and pampered young socialite? And why did she fail to find another investment when her flesh-and-blood future, died?

Essentially, in the two hundred years since the zenith of the gothic subgenre, the ghost has morphed from the sense of unease in the landscape of the environment to that same sense within the psyche of the protagonist. And this unease has moved from being an entity external to the protagonist – Byronic character or monster – to a demonstration of disturbed behaviour on the part of the protagonist. Before finishing this chapter, I explore one more trait of the literary ghost.

Overall, its nature does have a habit of being in keeping with the technological developments of the time. Witness the banging and rapping of Victorian parlour seances aping the tapping telegraph and the screeching steam whistles of the times. In the later nineteenth century, a number of optical devices were invented, including the so-called magic lantern and the moving picture camera. Henry James wrote *The Turn of the Screw* when the silent movie had just been launched on the public, flickering images that ran across screens in movie theatres, just like the man – or men – and woman, that the Governess sees. The ruder variety of film footage 'what the butler saw' could be viewed by turning a handle – *the turn of the screw*? – in private viewing machines. And Hill's ghostly 'woman in black' is not unlike the complex, virtual or CGI images reminiscent of the film technology of today. Have James and Hill superseded the technologists, projecting their own imaginings of our future which has become the present, a world of interactive images flickering onto cinema and television screens, smartphones and computers?

Once more, I mention that paradox of the ghost in literature, namely, that the more we succumb to materiality, the greater the number of literary ghosts. The technology that enables us to hear disembodied voices and see moving images of people who are simply *not there*, is enabling us to suspend our disbelief in ever more creative ways. You could say that the more machines we invent, the more literary ghosts emerge. In Shirley Jackson's text, the poltergeist manifestations appear linked to what is materially inside the Hill House. The ghostly rabbit and dog appear to ape the painted animals in the nursery – animation? The bangs and raps that sound in the house tease Eleanor with the memory of the knocks that her mother used to summon her with. The blood that appears on Theodora's clothing is reminiscent of the red nail polish that she insists upon painting Eleanor's toenails with. The chalk scribbling upon the wall appears to mock Dr Montague's habit of measuring areas of the house and marking them out with chalk. But by the end of the narrative, the house – or the ghost or ghosts – are focussing entirely upon Eleanor. And the sound that only she can hear, ghostly singing, is reminiscent of the bright and breezy jangle of popular music played over and over on radios and the jukeboxes of the time (HH, 225-6). And this instantly-available entertainment highlights another tenet of the time. I remind the reader once again of that edict of Dale Bailey, that the way we behave is often a simple reflection of the culture that produces us. It stands to reason then that if literary ghosts are manifestations of extreme human behaviour, then the action of a ghost is bound to say something about the times in which it manifests. (Bailey, 34)

Dickens penned *A Christmas Carol* in the nineteenth century, a tale that shows how Scrooge's personality changes for the better following the visitations of the four ghosts, thus creating the 'improving' ghost, extending the Victorian tradition of seeking a personal improvement in every experience – and thus with the supernatural. But by the twentieth century, this notion of moral improvement had somewhat modified. Prevailing social conditions often require the individual to become selfish and go-getting and it is interesting that soon after Jackson published her narrative, the *zombie* movie was born. George A. Romero's *Night of the Living Dead* (1968) is a seminal movie, one that has spawned countless tales, it seems, of uncaring, unfeeling quasi-humans, infected with the desire to eat human flesh and ride roughshod over other peoples' needs and sensibilities. According to Dale Bailey, in tales of modern hauntings, the protagonist often bears an image of herself that reflects what her environment made her (Bailey, 34). In one instance, Eleanor and Theodora go out of doors late at night and see a ghostly picnic taking place, which as I explain in the chapter **The New Alchemists: Text, Travel and Time**, is strongly reminiscent of the techni-coloured advertising world of the 1950s, with the author's use of words like 'blue', 'gold' and 'scarlet' (HH, 177).

Interestingly, the scene does reveal in a measure the women's states of mind. Theodora is a nonconformist who has avoided conventional marriage and motherhood. No doubt, this tableau of happy family life does indeed fill her with terror. But Eleanor is imbued with curiosity rather than fear, and almost resents Theodora as she pulls her away from the scene (HH, 177). But this phantom show of *what she wants* does *not* make Eleanor a better person: her midnight rampage and expulsion from Hill House are not far away.

Ultimately, the literary ghost is there to tell us what we are – and what we are *not*. The ghost, the phantom, the unexplained phenomenon puzzles us, scares, tests character, teases, taunts, jeers, mocks, mirrors, entertains and sometimes, works in collusion with – the protagonist. Indeed, you could say that as many types of phantom exist as story plots and characters. And as long as technology extends our faculties and capabilities, and as long as we *continue* to be human, writers will continue to invent new types of phantom to scare, amuse and challenge us.

The Journey

Statis and movement ♦ Moving away from authority ♦
Bildungsroman: the fairy tale journey ♦ The unfinished journey

Stasis and movement

In a narrative, movement provides a riposte to stasis. Movement and the journey provide occasion to move the plot along and entertain the reader. It punctuates the narrative with variation in action and tone. In a number of genres, the journey is metaphorical, a sub-textual way of highlighting the protagonist's self-awareness and growing maturity, at the same time as learning about the wider world. So metaphorical has the journey in literature become, that the journey is the major thread of many classic famous texts: *The Odyssey*, *The Canterbury Tales* and *The Pilgrims' Progress*.

The eighteenth-century picaresque tale, for example, *Tom Jones* by Henry Fielding, is a direct descendant of these narratives. And the work that pitched Charles Dickens from freelance columnist to best-selling author, *The Pickwick Papers*, is a descendant of this form. It is quite likely that the name 'Pickwick' is a sly reference to the picaresque form, being as it is the journal of four, well-to-do males wandering at will in England. Dickens's tales grew darker as the nineteenth century progressed, though several of his narratives do retain an element of the picaresque: the titular Oliver Twist and David Copperfield, and Pip of *Great Expectations*, commit to a fair amount of journeying. Journeys can be allegorical as well as actual and in *Jane Eyre*, Charlotte Brontë seems to blend the two. Brontë's use of names for the places Jane journeys between – Gateshead, Lowood, Thornfield, Marsh End – echoes Bunyan's allegorical style' (DDSC, 95).

Why did the gothic sub-genre assume – and transform – this trope of the journey? According to Irving Malin, the journey in a narrative was in contrast to the authority represented by the castle, that the journeying protagonist went on his or her journey to escape 'authoritanian confines' (Malin, 151). The chapter, **The Allegorical Castle**, explores how tension in a narrative is built by the conflicting forces within the walls of a dwelling or other building. One function of the journey is that of release, that is, 'to move away from authoritarian confines' of that tension. In the chapter **The Lexicon of Haunting**, this building of tension by the addition of suspense is explored and the journey facilitates, at least in part, that suspense, which is often associated with comedy. Northrop Frye defines comedy as: 'the movement from *pistis* to *gnosis*, from a society controlled by habit, ritual bondage, arbitrary law and the older characters to a society controlled by youth and pragmatic freedom' (Frye, 169-170). Immediately, the reader can recognise the trope of the young person in thrall by the dictates and customs of older, supposedly wiser people, the younger and more realistic person wishing for a release from that bondage. Just think of Jane Eyre leaving Gateshead and indeed, Thornfield, to discover her own psyche, the Governess leaving her family home for the freedom of Bly and Eleanor Vance escaping the strangle-hold that her relatives have upon her life.

In addition to these pragmatic motives, comedy facilitates, as Frye puts it, 'a movement from illusion to reality. Illusion is whatever is fixed or definable, and reality is best understood as its negation; whatever reality is, it's not that.' Hence the importance of creating and dispelling illusion in comedy: the illusion caused by disguise, obsession, hypocrisy, or unknown parentage' (Frye, 169-170). Frye is, of course, referring to metaphorical movement as much as actual. But his definition puts me in mind of two characters from *Northanger Abbey*, coming from different social classes yet being very alike in intent and motivation. When disputing the distance he has travelled, John Thorpe cries: '*Three*-and-twenty ... five-and-twenty if it is an inch' (NA, 44). This boast, of course, leaves Catherine Moreland unperturbed about such fine measurement, and even the quality of the carriage: 'Curricle-hung ... seat, trunk, sword-case, splashing-board, lamps, silver moulding, all you see complete; the iron-work as good as new, or better leaves her quite unimpressed' (NA, 45). Such a boast is Thorpe's pre-empting of General Tilney's later showcasing of the Staffordshire tea-service in Northanger Abbey (NA, 165-166). And Thorpe and Tilney are not unalike in other ways. On the outward journey to the Abbey, Catherine becomes aware of the General's obsession with time and time-keeping: 'The bustle of going was not pleasant – The clock struck ten while the trunks were carrying down, and the General had fixed to be out of Milsom-street by that hour' (NA, 147).

In the chapter **The New Alchemists: Text, Travel and Time,** I explore in more depth modernity's increasing obsession with time and time-keeping. With help from the staging post system that marked the stirrings of the industrialization of travel, journeys are timed almost to the minute. The morning following Catherine's arrival at Northanger Abby, the General takes Catherine on a tour of the kitchen grounds, where she is surprised to see amid the growing spaces: 'a village of hot-houses seemed to arise among them, and a whole parish to be at work within the inclosure' (NA, 168). This regimentation is inherent within the private life of the Abbey, the split-second timing of the meals, the hot-house vegetables and fruit cultivation in the kitchen garden. By the end of the narrative, the warring characters of General Tilney and John Thorpe prove to be the forces that are pulling Catherine's fate in contradicting directions, jostling one another in notional contests, in attempt to prove that *he* is the stronger/better/faster man. Ultimately, her various journeys provide Catherine with the truth about either man and, as Frye puts it, shifts her consciousness from 'illusion to reality', the reality being the love bond that she is building with Henry Tilney.

Because of this comedy element and because General Tilney is a military man, he and Thorpe are just one shade away from the role of *miles gloriosus* or military braggart, a Falstaffian character boasting of notional victories (Frye, 163). In General Tilney's attitude and status, he is not unlike Lawrence Boythorn of *Bleak House*, when Esther, Richard and Ada arrive notionally late on the journey from Bleak House, to pay him a visit: 'Twenty-five minutes! Twenty-six minutes!' replied Mr Boythorn, referring to his watch. With two ladies in the coach, this scoundrel has delayed his arrival six and twenty minutes. Deliberately! It is impossible that it can be accidental!' (BH, 298).

The twentieth-century novel, *Rebecca*, is filled with contrasts of stillness and movement, the enforced travelling of the companion by the loathsome (and allegorically-named) Mrs Van Hopper, the rounds of social visiting that Mrs de Winter is forced into when she arrives at Manderley, and the fancy dress party that Maxim sets out for his friends. This activity is in contrast to the stagnant and poisonous Mrs Danvers, and the tedium of life abroad for the de Winter pair following the destruction of the mansion. Ultimately, the journey provides the protagonist of the gothic sub-genre narrative with a vehicle in which to sift concrete reality from the illusion of others. And, as Irving Malin puts it: 'a quest away from authoritarian confines.'

Moving away from authority

Before she leaves Lowood for Thornfield, Jane Eyre ruminates on her environment and expresses a longing for 'liberty', or, failing that, 'a new servitude' (JE, 85). Once she has secured her position and arrived at Thornfield, Jane yet feels an existential restlessness. From the battlements of Thornfield, she surmises: 'It is in vain to say human beings ought to be satisfied with tranquillity: they must have action and they will make it if they cannot find it. Millions are condemned to a stiller doom than mine, and millions are in silent revolt against their lot' (JE, 109). Jane continues her ruminations, twinning her existential restlessness with the political landscape of the time, namely the condition of women: 'Women are supposed to be very calm generally: but women feel just as men feel' (JE, 109). Brontë's novel provides the watershed in which the nineteenth-century heroine questions the role of domesticity or passivity, in which the protagonist questions if domestic bliss equates with finding a place in society. In their essay 'The Queen's Looking Glass', Sandra Gilbert and Susan Gubar outline the condition of *the angel of the house*, drawing parallels, in particular, with Coventry Patmore's poem, *The Angel in the House*, an epic poem in which the poet outlines the 'ideal' woman: 'by her gentleness made great' (G&G, 376).

In their chapter, the critics explore icons of femininity, such as Snow White, the Sleeping Beauty, Florence Dombey and Agnes Wickfield, all of whom, despite obvious virtue, are given to meekness and passivity. In the persons of Little Nell and Beth March, they liken meekness with death, and explain how these passive and/or dying females are but the lighter foils of Circe and Lady Macbeth (G&G, 34-35). In her restlessness, Jane provides an energetic foil for this notional angel, from Gateshead to Lowood, from thence to Thornfield and from there to a wilderness in which she barely survives until finally finding shelter in the aptly-named Moor House. It is here that she staves off the entreaties of St John Rivers, to marry him and to travel to India as his assistant missionary. But another kind of restlessness, more profound than a mere desire for travel prompts Jane to continue her personal journey and she is finally reunited with her lover at Ferndean.

In spite of her opting for domestic bliss, Jane cannot hide her admiration and indeed, envy of, the physical freedom of St John Rivers. But given Jane's moral fibre throughout the narrative, a morality that leaves the reader in no doubt of Jane's attitude to marriage and duty, the reader is more certain that Jane is *not* going to leave her husband and family to embark upon yet another quest for love and personal happiness. Instead, her words 'Surely I come quickly;' and 'hourly I more eagerly respond' at the conclusion of the narrative is more a spiritual response than a physical call to which to rally. It is as if she is longing for the spiritual glory and freedom that physical death will bring. This is arguable but what is evident here is that, in spite of her settled status, Jane will never espouse *stillness* as a means of survival. Her constant journeying throughout the narrative – I count no fewer than four journeys, five, if you split her final journey to Edward Rochester in two, one stage to Thornfield and the second to Ferndean – are essential to the betterment of her physical and moral condition, and not just as a response to caprice and trivial inner urgings. Jane has, by turns, escaped the tyranny of the Reeds, the vocational strictures of Lowood, the moral danger represented by Thornfield and the yet-married Rochester, and the emotional sterility of a life with St John Rivers and stagnation with his sisters, loving as they are towards Jane. Here, Brontë plays beautifully with words, bestowing two names on the Rivers' family home, and offering the reader a verbal paradigm of what the future might have in store for Jane: 'Some calls it Marsh End and some calls it Moor House' (JE, 241).

Jane indeed could have 'moored' herself to the emotional stability offered by her female cousins. But Jane's nature undoubtedly interprets this stability as stagnation. Jane's real dilemma, her vacillation almost, is that faced by many gothic protagonists: that of wanting to belong to a wider society yet being unwilling to accept authority. In her book *Romantics, Rebels and Reactionaries* Marilyn Butler wrote of how restless, eighteenth-century characters often sought a fine mode of existence in remote areas, a fashion that continued well into the nineteenth century (RRR, 16). I suggest here that Jane's flight from Thornfield is not at the prompting of mere moral scruple but a search for a more profound way of life, one of almost existentialism. On her journey Jane encounters a number of natural landscapes, among them Whitcross: 'there are great moors behind and on each side of me; there are waves of mountains far beyond that deep valley at my feet' (JE, 322). But the bucolic paradise of Whitcross is as unremitting as the glittering artifice of Thornfield. Before hunger overcomes her entirely, Jane begins the struggle back to the hamlet. While doing so, she has another revelation, a more pastoral and cultivated perception of nature than earlier. Jane sees agricultural labourers at work, and has renewed hopes of finding a place in this society 'I must struggle on: strive to live and bend to toil like the rest' (JE, 325). The protagonist does indeed struggle to regain her place in society; in fact, she almost loses her life in the narrative's progress. But regain it she does and slowly progresses towards a life balanced between self-fulfilment and submission to authority.

The voyages of Radcliffe's Adeline read in part in the manner of a catalogue of journeys throughout Europe. With help from other people or through personal compunction, Adeline leaves the convent that she has been brought up in. She escapes, by turns, the house of brigands, the chateau of the Marquis de Montalt and the Abbey, for the safety of Leloncourt. She journeys south with the La Luc family in a quest for a 'cure' for Arnaud, and then travels to Paris to provide evidence against the Marquis to secure Theodore's life and finally, returns to Switzerland. Each of the earlier journeys mark an escape from a condition that Adeline does not want to espouse, From the absolute dogma of the convent where she was brought up, to the absolute danger of the brigand's house, the Abbey presents a middle ground for Adeline. In spite of the realist nature of the novel, it has an almost fairy-tale ending.

The Bildungsroman: the fairy tale journey

> 'Of all fictions, the marvellous journey is the one that is never exhausted, and it is this fiction that is employed as a parable in the definitive encyclopaedic mode of the poem, Dante's Commedia' (Frye, 57).

Here, I refer to the fairy tale, because in many folk tales, the literal journey is almost always a trip from childhood to growing up; just think of *Jack and the Beanstalk, Hansel and Gretel, Little Red Riding Hood*. The protagonist of a traditional fairytale is usually an ordinary person beset by extraordinary circumstances, a challenge or set of challenges that the subject must overcome. In the animistic world, every rock, tree, mountain and talking animal is a symbol of an inner quality or yearning that he or she must overcome in order to arrive at whatever they are seeking. Jane Eyre is both subtly and overtly filled with fairy-tale elements; the young girl locked away by her relatives who proves to be a true princess – or heiress; the prince who must be purged of his Bluebeard element before she can marry him (DDSC, 109). The workings of nature in the story, from the Whitcross episode onwards, concur with Bruno Bettelheim's description of the animistic world, one in which every entity that the fairytale protagonist encounters is symbolic of his or her inner yearnings and take on the roles of actual characters (Bettelheim, 25). The natural elements that Jane encounters from this part of the story onwards serve to symbolise the struggle that she will face in her journey back to society.

The La Mottes befriend Adeline and provide her with food and shelter, but they betray her in an episode in which she ends up a prisoner in the chateau. There, Adeline witnesses the Marquis enjoying a series of sensual delights – and she determines that she is not going to be one of them. She makes her escape and embarks on her second perilous journey where she meets her lover Theodore again, and is presented with an opportunity to save his life. Subsequently, Adeline is compelled to make a third perilous journey, one that rewards her with a lengthy period of safety – and the companionship and friendship of people who cherish her finer qualities. Overall, in rejecting high society and luxury in favour of true love and friendship, Adeline has uncovered the personal reserves of courage and skill that enable her to grow to maturity, and lays down the social ties that last her a lifetime. What Ann Radcliffe has written is, in effect, a *bildingsroman*, the novel that charts the central character's progress from youth to maturity.

Hans Andersen's *Snow Queen* is the apotheosis of the journey as *blidungsroman*. The text is not only the most eminently readable fairy tale for children and adults, it is an astonishing triumph of feminist writing produced anywhere in the nineteenth century. The young Gerda leaves the comfort and safety of home and hearth to go in search of her young friend Kay, who has left town in the company of the titular character. Why Kay should prefer this other woman in preference to his more homespun friend Gerda matters not here. The fact is, Gerda conducts her search with no help other than from a clutch of talking animals, and using nothing other than her own eloquence and intelligence to escape the grasp of a witch, and abduction by a band of robbers. Presently, Gerda marches boldly into the icy castle, fighting off treacherous snowflakes as she does so, and pulls Kay out of his trance and brings him home to where it is 'summer, glorious summer'. In addition, the children emerge from the uncertainty of adolescence and are now ready for young love. Potent imagery abounds in the text. When the Snow Queen pulls Kay into her carriage, she wraps her fur cloak around him and kisses his forehead. Later on, the red shoes that Gerda offers in sacrifice by throwing them into the flow of the river might represent the onset of menstruation. The animated flowers in the witch's garden could be aspects of Gerda's blossoming personality. And the text is simply threaded with references to the changing seasons, snow and winter as undeveloped childhood, the storm as adolescence, 'summer, glorious summer' as fulfilled, romantic adulthood.

In Shirley Jackson's narrative, the earlier part of the story presents a paradigm of choice for Eleanor. On her journey to Hill House, she encounters three females, corresponding to the three wishes of the fairy tale, what Bettelheim deems the 'rule of three' (Bettelheim, 71-72). Though the encounters are brief, we learn a little about each female through words and actions. First, Eleanor collides with an old lady and to her – Eleanor's – distress, destroys a packet of food that the lady carries. The lady reveals the food to have been 'left over' (HH,13). This reference to leftovers indicates that the old lady may be in reduced circumstances. Eleanor mollifies the lady by paying for her taxi home and the woman offers to pray for her. The incident provokes a number of questions: who is the old lady and what drives her to eat leftovers? Why is she intent on praying for a young woman who has just destroyed her breakfast? Does she sense that Eleanor is in turmoil over life-changes and is in need of spiritual help? These questions, like many others that the book raises, are left unanswered. The trajectory of the journey to Hill House continues, evoking a sense of freedom in Eleanor, who fantasises about getting out of her car and exploring the landscapes and buildings she sees about her (HH, 20). From there onward, Eleanor's inner monologue is filled with references to 'stone lions' that she has seen and longed for, awakening in her a desire to live in a place of old-time grandeur. About mid-way to Hill House, Eleanor stops for lunch at a restaurant and here she witnesses a young girl who refuses to drink her milk because it has not been served in her favourite cup 'with stars in the bottom' (HH, 21). Mentally, Eleanor supports the girl, willing her not to give in to pressure from her parents. For the remainder of the story, Eleanor repeats the phrase 'cup of stars' when she is trying to define what she wants, for instance, when she is notionally furnishing her imagined apartment (HH, 213).

The third female is a young waitress, overweight and unattractive, working in a run-down diner (HH, 24). The story shows the waitress as devoid of autonomy, of freedom of movement or of social prospects. Her only way out of her restricting job is apparently to marry the young man with whom she converses. The surroundings are so downbeat that the reader senses the dismay that fills Eleanor. Like the old lady with the leftover food, the waitress does not serve as a model for Eleanor's future. By the end of the narrative, the identity that Eleanor seems to assume is that of the wilful child, refusing to drink her milk because it is not from her 'cup of stars'. In addition to daydreaming about living a fairy-tale life many other metaphors and symbols abound: the rushing water of the mill where Eleanor meets the child is a metaphor of freedom (HH, 23). The poisonous oleander reminds Eleanor of where her future might end, while the meaning of the sign 'DARE EVIL', which she eventually surmises to be a broken sign declaring 'daredevil' is one of the more overt incidents (HH, 19). In expressing Eleanor's journey as a fairy-tale quest, Shirley Jackson has used a traditional form of writing. But her protagonist's eventual fate is post-modern, fatal and without desert or precedent. It is not Eleanor's 'fault' that she is destined to be the least-developed personality of the Hill House gathering any more than Luke or Theodora or even Dr Montague are morally deserving of their better fortunes. Jackson's text embodies a twentieth-century conundrum: things just happen to be that way and it's too bad about Eleanor. This progression from eighteenth-century morality tale with the protagonist triumphing over the unfortunate influences surrounding him or her to the plight of protagonists such as Eleanor was gradual, and its roots were decidedly in the nineteenth century.

The unfinished Journey

Jay Griffith writes about 'modernity' as an eternal dance, one that involves making the same journey over and over again at the expense of failing to gain any connection with the environment, the lack of continuity depriving the individual to put down root and enjoy the present (JG, 219). But a hundred and fifty years earlier, a character from Dickens's *Bleak House* declared: 'Now?' asks Richard. 'There's no now for us suitors' (BH, 580). Here, Richard Carstone could be alluding to the 'present restless state' outlined by J. Hillis Miller and discussed in the chapter, **Why the family?** Richard is in a particularly harsh and irony-strewn situation. Though he 'belongs' legally to the Jarndyce, he is without the priviledges that might have accrued to a biological son of his guardian. Forced to 'prove' himself worthy of marriage to Ada Clare, he enters into an almost ritual dance as he tries his hand at a number of well-worn professions. Unable to settle to any of these, he latches on to the chimera of a win in the long-running Chancery dispute. Frustration, despair and death are not far in the offing.

It is ironic that a book named after a building should be so filled with characters who are forced to keep moving in order to survive. Jo, the poor crossing sweeper, is always 'moving on', while the brick makers and their wretched families are forced to keep traipsing between St Albans and London. In addition to the restless dance of Richard Carstone as he tries one occupation after another in search of a suitable life, an impoverished Allan Woodcourt is obliged to travel on a ship to practise his profession while George Rouncewell gives up his steady home to become that perpetual wanderer, the soldier. He has been a friend of Nemo, Lady Dedlock's disenfranchised lover while 'my Lady' herself is in a perpetual state of restlessness. At least once, the scapegrace Harold Skimpole's likens himself to a butterfly (BH, 296). In spite of being archetypal Victorian women, confined to the 'home', Esther and Ada are perpetually moving between London, Gloucester and St Albans. But Esther's most profound journey of all takes place when she lies desperately ill, that is, a journey expressed in the dreams of her troubled psyche, where she 'laboured up colossal staircases, ever striving to reach the top, and ever turned ... by some obstruction, labouring again' (BH, 544). Her words may put the reader in mind of the illustrations by the seventeenth-century artist, Giovanni Battista Piranesi, whose set of fourteen engravings '*Imaginary Prisons*' represent the interiors of ruined, classical castles, skylit staircases that seem to lead nowhere emerging from and disappearing again into gloom. In Esther's life, the old, classical order is soon about to die, in the demise of the Dedlock family. But Esther will continue to be part of the society in which she reluctantly plays a part: 'Dare I hint at a worse time when, strung together somewhere in great black space, there was a flaming necklace, or ring, or starry circle of some kind, of which I was one of the beads. And when my only prayer was to be taken off from the rest, and when it was such inexplicable agony and misery to be a part of the dreadful thing?' (BH, 544). Most grotesque of all is the fate of Caddy Jellyby, destined to spend her better years, dancing in order to keep her family in necessities. Caddy's eventual fate is so bizarre that it seems to parallel that of Snow White's wicked stepmother, destined to dance forever in red-hot slippers (Bettelheim, 115, 196). Like Eleanor, none of these characters seem to deserve their fates, except maybe George Rouncewell, who left his family by choice. But even he cannot find a place in which to settle, and he and henchman Phil Squod stand ever in the threat of homelessness.

Another heroine who does not seem to merit her suffering is Mrs de Winter. In the chapter, **The Lexicon of Haunting**, I posed the question: 'Behind Du Maurier's caricature, the reader will sometime ask: who really was Mrs Danvers? What personal dreams did she renounce to invest emotionally in a beautiful and pampered young socialite? And why did she fail to find another investment when her flesh-and-blood future, died?' This fate seems apt for the obsessive housekeeper, yet that of Mrs de Winter is not too far removed from it. At the end of the story, actually the beginning of the narrative, the author affords us a glimpse of Mrs de Winter's lifestyle, days spent sitting about with little more to anticipate except for mealtimes. Yet, she declares it to be the better alternative to fear (R, 6-8). Mrs de Winter's stagnant fate is no less tedious nor crushing than the life of constant movement that she endured with Mrs Van Hopper. And even more dreadful is the realisation that Mrs de Winter has become, in her way, a yet-living person who invested in and is still bound to another person who, if not quite dead, is but a shadow of his former self (R, 5). In other words, she has become another Mrs Danvers, caring for a person who is 'dead' to the world.

The Governess of Henry James's text embodies another type of stagnation, the trap. It is curious that on arrival at Bly, her journey is only beginning. She describes the journey there in the: 'bumping, swinging coach' (TOTS, 123). This language continues on throughout the text. She is, by turns: 'carried triumphantly', 'swept away', and 'lifted aloft' (TOTS, 123, 132, 133). In one instance, she says to Mrs Grose: 'I'm rather easily carried away. I was carried away in London' (TOTS, 126). These expressions, which she uses to communicate her combination of passivity and personal agitation, add rhythm to the text, conveying a sense of swaying back and forth in the manner of a pendulum clock. The way in which she expresses the growing menace of events: 'that hush in which something gathers or crouches' reinforces this expression (TOTS, 134). She further states: 'The change was actually like the spring of a beast', the significant word is 'spring', giving the narrative the sense of a mechanism grinding on to an inevitable end (TOTS, 134). Because the narrative was written in retrospect of events, the Governess writes of the events of the time: 'oh it was a trap' (TOTS, 134). This may have been true from her point of view, but the wider question is: whose trap? There is much evidence that the Governess was complicit in creating her own trap. Following many instances where the Governess believes that she has seen phantoms, and that these entities are in pursuit of the children – for what end is never quite revealed – Mrs Grose tells the Governess that she must induce the children's uncle to arrive and intervene (TOTS, 182). The Governess refuses on every ground; her agreement, her reputation, her responsibility absconded, all because of the possibility of relinquishing romance: 'his derision, his amusement, his contempt for the breakdown of my resignation at being left alone' (TOTS, 183). And she warns Mrs Grose – on pain of her leaving the household – not to interfere (TOTS, 183). Consequently, a game ensues between the Governess and the children: 'It was as if, at moments, we were perpetually coming into sight of subjects before which we must stop short, turning suddenly out of alleys that we perceived to be blind, closing with a little bang that made us look for each other' (TOTS, 184). The Governess avoids all instances of teaching that would involve discussion of dead people, presumably lest she be forced to confront the reality of what is happening in the house and be obliged to leave. Instead, Flora and Miles listen avidly to tales of her home life in the vicarage and village. However, she imagines that their questions do not spring from natural child-like curiosity but rather, the children are throwing a blind: 'They pulled with an art of their own the strings of my invention and my memory' (TOTS, 184). The antics that follow, the Governess perpetually marking the whereabouts of the children, echoes Caddy Jellyby's permanent dancing.

But the journey of the Governess does eventually and suddenly end: in the death of Miles. The question for the reader here must be: what was James's purpose? In order to survive, whether in quest of physical safety, fortune or love, freedom of movement must be tempered with fixity of purpose. Henry James's Governess seems unable to complete a project, for instance, the letter that she writes to her master and that she fails to post, and that Miles puts his hands upon: 'He gave the most mournful, thoughtful little headshake. Nothing' (TOTS, 233). It is not that the Governess does not want to find another, better self – all gothic heroines do – but that her affirmed self-determination is infused with an equal, if not stronger degree of passivity. Indeed, the Governess is not unlike the present-day employee who has set him or herself a goal, but refuses to make any move that will violate whatever employment terms and conditions. The Governess will not even write the master a letter detailing the strange – from her point of view – happenings in the house, in case it compromises her promise not to bother him about any matter, not even concerning the condition of his nephew and niece. Unlike so many gothic heroines, she is not interested in escaping authority but submitting to it. Here, Miles's name is allegorical, suggesting that her interaction with the child becomes but another tally upon which to notch the progress of her own, personal conquests.

From Adeline to Lyra, it seems clear that *judgementally* moving on is the key to mental, moral and physical survival. At the opening of *The Haunting of Hill House*, twentieth-century Eleanor Vance is young-ish and healthy. She has, at least, had a basic education and is alive in an era when feminine careers outside of the tradition of the companion and the governess, are more than accepted. She has displayed the initiative to take the car that she part-owns, in defiance of her family, in response to the invitation from Dr Montague, the academic conducting the experiment in Hill House. Above all, she has the wit to recognize the quality of her new companions, when she finally arrives there (HH, 60). In addition, Eleanor expresses a sound opinion of the fate of a young woman, a companion to Abigail Crain, who lived the house following her inheritance of it, and who had eventually jumped to her destruction, namely, that she should have gone away and left it. The words not only echo Eleanor's actions with respect to her family, but point ominously towards her own end. So, why – when it seemed like she should have taken action – was Eleanor unable to enact her own advice and finish her journey? Eleanor – despite her shortcomings – is a denizen of the twentieth century, with the use of a motor vehicle and a basic education, at least, which would have assisted her into rudimentary employment: why could she not have built upon these basic amenities?

Dr Montague's letter set up, in part, a dream for the psychologically-damaged Eleanor, one that she expressed mentally throughout her journey to Hill House: 'Journeys end in lovers meeting'. Michael Wilson suggests that the majority of the characters in Jackson's narrative survive by throwing a blanket of non-reality between them and the events that take place in Hill House, reducing them to a series of cliches and symbols (Wilson, 114). For example, Dr Montague persists in making notes and taking measurements, all as fodder for his forthcoming book. Theodora shields herself with her constant flashes of humour (HH, 130). Luke Sanderson enters into play with Eleanor flirting aimlessly with this woman with whom he is never going to be romantically involved (HH, 209). To summarise Wilson's argument, the inmates insist on indulging in flights of 'ignorance, rationalisation and blindness' (Wilson, 120).

But it is Eleanor whose state of mind exposes her to the actual danger posed by the heightened energy of the house. She is at risk because she *believes* in the fantasies that she spins almost immediately upon leaving her family home. Eleanor takes delight in the quality of her new friends, and immediately imagines a connection with them, so much that she tells Theodora that she, Eleanor, wants to go and live with her. Theodora's rebuff is what pitches Eleanor from mere daydreaming into a dangerous insistence that the house wants *her* (HH, 204). Remaining in Hill House is strategically impossible, of course; even Dr Montague, who has leased the house for a mere six weeks, is unable to stay there. As Dale Bailey notes, Eleanor's primary coping mechanism is to constantly slip in and out of reality and into fantasy (Bailey, 35). Eleanor is a peculiar mixture of pretension and servility. Beaten down by her family and scorned by her peers, her longing to stay in the grand house is suspect of her believing herself to be a misplaced princess, so much that she will clean and scrub for her place there. Yet upon the journey to Hill House, she looks askance at the condition of the overweight waitress in the diner at which she, Eleanor, has stopped to buy coffee. Eleanor does not fear work, but exposure to the world, and is lost in a fantasy that the house has become her special companion. In summary, Eleanor has moved from illusion, to delusion to the perception of the reality that Michael Wilson writes of. And because she hasn't processed it through the veil of the non-reality of the others, it destroys her. At one level, Jackson's novel is a parable to young women on the dangers of reverting to fantasy when unable to face reality. By now, it is apparent that failure to finish a journey is a tenet of self-deception.

Deceptions, Doppelgangers and Dark Dis

Deception: Shakespearean, refusal to deceive, self-deception ♦ Deception and *The Turn of the Screw* ♦ The Doppelganger: comedy and fantasy ♦ Perception of reality ♦ Mirroring, projecting likeness and changing places ♦ Dichotomies and duality ♦ Uncovering the truth ♦ Modernity, surreality and the doppelganger today ♦ The nebulous dis ♦ The servant/housekeeper ♦ The Governess, the Lawyer and the Detective

Deception: Shakespearean, refusal to deceive, self-deception

Marilyn Butler asserts that Isabella Thorpe is *the* deceiver of *Northanger Abbey* when she, Butler, explains that this anti-heroine's agenda is to forge a marital alliance between at least one member of her, Isabella's, family and that of the Morland family: James and Isabella? Catherine and John? Or both? (NA, xxxi). However, Isabella is not alone in enacting deception. Unknown to Catherine, John Thorpe has misrepresented her, Catherine, to General Tilney, the man whom she hopes will be her father-in-law. When the General discovers the truth, his reaction is to expel Catherine from Northanger Abbey, an action that leaves her in shock because she sees it as a judgement upon her character: 'If aware of her having viewed him as a murderer, she could not wonder at his even turning her from his house' (NA, 216). But Catherine has grounds for *her* mistaken belief as to why the General has expelled her from the Abbey, namely, that she had mistaken beliefs about *his* character and the fate of his family. Eventually, the author reveals that the General's behaviour stems from beliefs about Catherine's family situation, not her character, and that he is *not* aware of his son Henry's discernment of *her* character. This almost comedic layering of deception is an old device in literature, one that digs into the roots of the literary form itself.

In literature, a deception by a character is often a form of the masquerade, a showing of an assumed self to others to hide the reality of a situation. Yet, the literary form is inherently deceptive; the very attempt by the writer to create a verisimilitude by the simple occasion of placing words on a page is a form of sham, as is the artist working with his brush or actors in a play upon the stage. The audience member knows that what he sees is unreal, thus giving the dramatist further licence to expand his illusion, the actors playing in the context of their dramas and letting the audience in on the jokes. For example, to heighten the irony of a situation (or to escape an enemy) an actor in character masquerades as another character, possibly changing gender, social status or racial identity.

William Shakespeare makes much use of this dramatic device; *Twelfth Night* and *As You Like It* are plays that act as metaphors of themselves, the duplicitous actors both entertaining and stretching the credibility of the audience. Because of the realist nature of her writing, Jane Austen's characters never assume the guise of another person. The attempt at drama in *Mansfield Park* is the exception, one that is further discussed below. Disguise and mummery are archaic forms of entertainment, exported from the past by later writers. Mid-nineteenth century, mummery had another wheeze in Edward Rochester's attempt at disguise in *Jane Eyre*. His masquerading as a gypsy woman is unbelievable in real terms, but it has a place in the context of the narrative. Here, the reader is asked to collude in the notion that a wealthy, well-bred man could, with a few turns of dress and voice distortion, take on the semblance of a semi-feral, nomadic woman and fool a group of well-educated young society ladies. But governess Jane is not deceived: 'You did not act the character of a gipsy with me' (JE, 202).

But a more profound deceit lies in the text: can the reader credit Jane when, on discovering the actual identity of the gypsy woman, says: 'I had never thought of Mr Rochester' (JE, 203). What is Charlotte Brontë doing here? To begin with, the character of Rochester is inherently deceitful, making Jane believe that he is about to marry Blanche Ingram: 'Adele must go to school and you, Miss Eyre, must get a new situation', just before he proposes to her (JE, 250). But the greatest deception of all is enacted by Jane on herself. Does she really not wish to probe the true source of the strange voice in the attic? Or question the reason for the mysterious fire that engulfs Rochester's bedchamber? Or the bizarre attack upon the visitor, Mr Mason? Or try to find out who Mason really is? Or question the identity of the extraordinary apparition that appears in Jane's bedroom and rents her wedding veil in two, a few nights before the marriage? Most profound of all, does Jane not wish to probe beneath the surface of Rochester's constant and cryptic verbal meanderings into the happenings of his own life?: 'The results of what you have done become in time to you utterly insupportable, you take measures to obtain relief; unusual measures, but neither unlawful or culpable' (JE, 218).

On consideration of Jane's state of mind, the reader must wonder on that exhortation of Pip, from *Great Expectations*: 'All other swindlers on earth are nothing to the self-swindlers, and with such pretences did I cheat myself' (GE, 192). Irving Malin defines self-deception from the context of the American hero 'who cannot distinguish what is before his eyes' (Malin, 161). For 'American', of course, read British or French or Italian. It stands to reason that when a person 'cannot clearly see reality', he has the capacity of being fooled by anyone, including himself. Aside from the addition of a little Shakespearean clowning about, what purpose does deception serve in a narrative? One is pure drama, for example, in Radcliffe's eighteenth-century text, the narrative is enlivened by the semi-comic episode where Adeline believes that she is being taken from danger by La Motte's servant, Peter, but finds that she has been carried off to the château by a servant of the Marquis. Another purpose of deception is paradoxically, to reach the truth about a character. In their dishonesty, John and Isabella Thorpe betray their characters to readers and Catherine Morland, alike. In *Bleak House*, the proprietor of the rag-and-bottle shop, Krook is so afraid of being deceived that he won't allow a literate person to teach him to read: 'but they might teach me wrong', that he spends much time copying single letters from manuscripts on the walls of his dwelling (BH, 254). Later in the century, the same paranoia is demonstrated in Henry James's narrative, when the Governess – following her first sighting of the man on the tower – speculates upon whether the servants may have 'practised upon' her (TOTS, 139). And of course, there is the mere fact of facilitating the story line. In *A Laodicean*, if William Dare had not exercised the series of deceptions that set in motion the engagement of William de Stancy to Paula Power, she and George Somerset would have gravitated romantically together, and much sooner. But while earlier writers expounded the more pantomimic deception by others, self-swindling became the realm of later writers. Not long after Radcliffe's day, the inaccurate posturing of information to oneself had begun to flourish. In *Northanger Abbey*, in spite of all evidence to the contrary, in spite of Catherine's uneasiness about

John Thorpe and his contradictory behaviour, and no less that of Isabella in her undue concern over James Morland's eventual financial means when he and she marry, Catherine continues to believe that she has found good friends: 'her conviction of being favoured beyond every other human creature, in friends and fortune, circumstance and chance' (NA, 133).

Another profound form of deception is that of refusing to accept the world of fantasy. This statement might seem contradictory but the inability to imagine, to step outside of oneself and accept possibilities other than what is manifest in the immediate and material environment, is a severe personal limitation. According to Bruno Bettelheim, developing one's 'inner resources' is the certain way to cope with life's crises, so that one's emotions, imagination and intellect are in accord with one another (Bettelheim, 4). We see this behaviour in the character of Sir Thomas Bertram in *Mansfield Park*, when he will not accept that his grown-up children need the fun and fantasy of make-believe. He believes, as Marilyn Butler states it, that his private abode has been somehow 'violated' (Butler, 107). But the 'violation' is only from *his* point of view. A personality capable of evaluating matters from various points of view would feel amusement rather than perturbation. In her introduction to *Northanger Abbey*, Marilyn Butler states that the way to gain understanding of a matter is to see it from various points of view, and she could have been stating truths over a number of literary instances (NA, xxi). In the later nineteenth century, Sir Thomas Bertram is reincarnated in the person of Dickens's Thomas Gradgrind, a man who continually exhorts his children to 'stick to facts', followed by events that show the resulting alienation of his family. In the twentieth century, Maxim de Winter is unable to put on fancy dress, even on the occasion of his own costume ball. It is 'powerful' characters such as these who stand at risk of being mentally and emotionally crushed when the behaviour of family members does not run in accordance with whatever notional course the patriarch has mapped out for them at birth, or in the teeth of an unexpected and profound loss, such as that of the ancestral home. (See **The Allegorical Castle**)

Just as a storm can destroy the mightiest palace while a pebble will simply roll about unscathed in the same turbulence, it is the powerful, in the worldly sense, who are at risk of destruction when failing to exercise imagination. But the powerless and dream-filled Eleanor of Jackson's text perishes also: so, what is at work here? As Dale Bailey put it. Eleanor is trapped in a mode that she is unable to escape from (Bailey, 33). The difference between Eleanor and the afore-mentioned characters is that she does in fact possess a power, not that of authority, but *a power to act*. She is not in possession of a title or lands, a fine house or a thriving business. But the key to her future is, quite literally, in her own hands, in the form of the car she has driven to Hill House. Unlike Adeline, who flees from peril whenever opportunity presents itself, or Jane Eyre with her well-developed instinct for preservation, Eleanor simply refuses to take a decisive step once she has reached Hill House, having fallen under its malign influence. As argued in **The Allegorical Castle**, she so identifies with the place and believes that it 'wants' her, she cannot leave it. And unlike Sir Thomas Bertram or Thomas Gradgrind, Eleanor possesses imagination in plenty, demonstrated at the outset of the narrative by her constant reference to fairy tale motifs. It is her failure to act on her desires that destroys her, possibly Jackson's message to all women?

And Eleanor's failure to move out of danger and towards a more fulfilling future is a reference to another, earlier narrative, 'the psychological ghost story' as Bailey describes it (Bailey, 25). In her destructive behaviour, Eleanor is not unlike James's Governess, refusing to act on opportunity either of informing her master of the trouble at Bly or leaving the house altogether. In attempt to probe why, I quote: 'How can I retrace today the strange steps of my obsession?' (TOTS, 186). I have selected this sentence as the key to the meaning of James's novella, but I could have chosen many other phrases. For example 'There are directions in which I mustn't for the present let myself go' (TOTS, 165). Or 'They can have but one meaning' (TOTS, 129). Or 'They had nothing but me and I – well, I had them' (TOTS, 153). And there are many other such cryptic quotations. Because James's text is so filled with puzzling allusions and phrases, it is as if the author is practising an enormous joke on his readers, as if he wrote the text, in his own words: 'it is a piece of ingenuity pure and simple, of cold artistic calculation, an amusette to catch those not easily caught (the 'fun' of the capture of the witless being ever but small, the jaded, the disillusioned, the fastidious)' (TOTS, 1). And 'cold artistic calculation' there is in plenty. I remind the reader again of Marilyn Butler who stresses that the way to gain understanding of a matter is to see it from various points of view (NA, xxi). And it is in direct contradiction to her, the Governess's, own attitude throughout the novella: 'They can have but one meaning' (TOTS, 129).

Events in the narrative can have *many* meanings, and this applies to the Governess's own behaviours and assumptions. When she said: 'oh it was a trap' it was indeed, the trap is not one set by the people she fears are deceiving her, rather one that has been set by her own imagination. It is the 'obsession' mentioned earlier, one that she could have climbed out of if she had engaged with the notion of Miles's expulsion from school having multiple meanings. It is my belief that this is the game that the author is playing with the reader, that the text is open to several interpretations, and that the obduracy of the Governess throws a blind over what these might be. Later, I will offer a couple of alternative meanings. First, I want to explore actual deceptions by the characters in the text, because these are many and lend it its theme and multiple interpretations.

Deception and *The Turn of the Screw*

Here, I cite Dale Bailey's assertion, that the psychological novel began in the late nineteenth century (Bailey, 25). But psychology *per se* in literature had earlier stirrings. To grasp this, the reader need only consider the differences between Adeline and later heroines. Not once in Radcliffe's narrative does Adeline consider putting forward an untruth to others. Her story about her obscure origins, the man she knew as her father, her sojourn in the convent and how she came to be in the brigands' house, turn out to be transparently true. She is steadfastly moral and never masquerades as compliant, not even when it might have assisted her escape, for instance, from the machinations of the Marquis. But Adeline becomes so enmeshed in the duplicity of others that the time comes when she can barely trust Peter, La Motte's servant. Two thirds' of the way through *Romance of the Forest*, Adeline has no choice but to flee with him. Her 'reward' for trusting the good Peter to convey her safely to Leloncourt – a matter that La Motte could have organised much earlier in the narrative, if he had wanted to – is to be thrust into the bosom of a new family, thus placing Radcliffe's narrative in the category of fairy tale. But even in Radcliffe's day, the taste for realism and the moral ambivalences that it brings, was burgeoning. It was no longer enough to – in the words of Northrop Frye – to organise the narrative like a chessboard, to place moral opposites against one another, 'good', 'bad', 'honest', 'deceitful', and so on (Frye, 195). It was the blurring at the edges of these dichotomies that showed that even the best of people are capable of trumpery and trickery, both to the self and to others.

A century following Radcliffe, words such as 'fluttered', 'anxious', 'nervous' and 'agitation' fill out Henry James's text, all used by a person who is in no peril whatsoever (unlike Adeline), except in facing a new situation. In *Bleak House*, Esther Summerson's amoral blindness to the duplicity around her is expressed by Dickens in the harrowing episode where she lies ill with smallpox and becomes literally blind. In *Great Expectations*, Pip adds a dimension of fun to the narrative by spinning stories to Joe Gargery about what he has seen in Satis House: 'a black velvet coach' (GE, 57).

Henry James's text is arguably the apotheosis of literary psychological manipulation, i.e. deception, in all of its possibilities. One, significant characteristic of *The Turn of the Screw* is that it is written from the first-person viewpoint of the Governess, the narrator showing us her state of mind as the events unfold. As I will show, it is not a good state of mind: 'oh I was grand!', being a combination of egoism, self-servitude and delusion (TOTS, 226). And from *this* point of view, the narrative is one of unmitigated honesty. It is, of course, a strange type of honesty that showcases its attempts to deceive. In the narrative, these are legion and to attempt to discuss them all here would not only be futile, but would obscure what the author – *not* the narrator – was trying to achieve. From start to finish, the characters of James's text enact a set of deceptions upon themselves and upon one another. Certain of the deceptions are facile and easily debunked, for example, the children's playing at charades (TOTS, 168). And this play-acting, this masquerading, is inherent to the theme of the text. Initially, the love-lorn Governess imagines that the master was going to arrive any day and 'would stand before me and smile and approve' (TOTS, 135). This is the mind-set by which certain critics have claimed that her seeing of the ghosts is the result of her own turbulent emotion. A.J.A. Waldock cites from Edmund Wilson's article on James's text, stating that it might not be a ghost story at all, 'but a study in the pyschology of a frustrated Anglo-Saxon spinster.'[50]

In the earlier part of the narrative, the Governess continually tries to impress on the housekeeper that she is telling the truth: 'I found that to keep her

---

[50] A.J.A. Waldock 'Mr Edmund Wilson and the Turn of the Screw Author(s)' in The Johns Hopkins University Press: Modern Language Notes, Vol. 62, No. 5 (May, 1947), pp331-334. Subsequent references will be to this edition and will be inserted parenthetically into the text, for example "(Waldock, 332)"

thoroughly in the grip of this I had only to ask her how, if I had 'made it up', I came to be able to give, of each of the persons appearing to me, a picture disclosing, to the last detail, their special marks – a portrait on the exhibition of which she had instantly recognise and named them' (TOTS, 160-1). Certainly, in her sightings of the unknown people, the Governess has good reason to have faith in her powers of discernment. But by Chapter Eleven, her attitude and words border upon the egotistical and by now, she refers to an 'odd recognition of my own superiority' (TOTS, 177). This is because Mrs Grose seems slow to take up her hints that Bly may be haunted: 'But she was a magnificent monument to the blessing of a want of imagination' (TOTS, 176). This is the Governess's way of saying, of course, that *she* is blessed with imagination in the extreme. To the reader accepting James's narrative as a realist text, perhaps the most unsettling form of the self-deception by the Governess is her insistence that the eagerness with which the children respond to her is a charade on their part, a facade hiding their relationship with the notional ghosts. This leads to the Governess being imbued with a sense of mission (TOTS, 152-3). She believes that she has by some providence become 'a screen. I was to stand before them. The more I saw, the less they would' (TOTS, 153). The word 'screen' is significant, because there is indeed a point where the Governess is unable to take anything in the house at face value: 'Their more than earthly beauty, their unnatural goodness. It's a game, I went on. 'It's a policy and a fraud' (TOTS, 181).

The Governess is equally self-convinced in the meaning of Miles's consideration for his sister: 'I came across traces of little understandings between them by which one of them should keep me occupied while the other slipped away' (TOTS, 168). Good manners in children, when they exist, tend to stem from the example of the adults that they spend or have spent time with, but the Governess disregards this – or in her youth and inexperience, she is unaware of it. Eventually, this disregard of the work of the people who came before her is channelled into blatant virtue-signalling, and it is here that her egoism mounts to: 'odd recognition of my superiority' (TOTS, 177). One of the Governess's more direful self-deceptions is her conviction that Flora is trying to deceive *her*: 'At that moment, in the state of my nerves, I absolutely believed that she lied' (TOTS, 172). And this conviction is accompanied by the type of paranoia referred to earlier. When Miles and Flora eagerly lap up the details of the Governess's home life, instead of accepting it as proof of their youthful eagerness for knowledge and new experience, the Governess feels: 'They pulled with an art of their own the strings of my invention and my memory; and nothing else perhaps, when I thought of such occasions afterwards, gave me so the suspicion of being watched from under cover' (TOTS, 185).

At Bly, summer turns into autumn and the Governess does not see any more phantoms – but she is still filled with: 'this conviction of the secret of my pupils' (TOTS, 186). And she continues in her conviction that the children are seeing: 'things terrible and unguessable' (TOTS, 188). Being unable to guess what the children are about, she actually deceives *them*. The children are begging to see their uncle: 'When do you think he will come?' (TOTS, 188). They write a series of letters to him and soon after, the Governess reveals to the reader the shocking knowledge that she never passed on the children's beseeching letters to their uncle: 'I have them all to this hour' (TOTS, 188). It is one matter to be aware of oneself or at least, know what posture one is trying to convey to others; what is most strange about the Governess is that she claims to know the hearts and minds of other people, even those whom she has never met, and to misrepresent these occasions to other people. Of the unknown man whom she has encountered, she says: "He was looking for little Miles.' A portentous clearness now possessed me. '*That's* whom he was looking for" (TOTS, 149). When the Governess goes unexpectedly into the schoolroom and sees – or thinks she sees – Miss Jessel, she writes: 'I had seen the spectre of the most horrible of women' (TOTS, 196). Yet, she never offers any justification of *why* she believes that Miss Jessel is 'most horrible'. Later, she lies to Mrs Grose about having spoken to Miss Jessel, another deception enacted upon the housekeeper (TOTS, 197). Yet all the while, the Governess justifies her behaviour to the reader and to herself: 'I was justified' (TOTS, 212). This is a matter that the reader might dispute, a perception that lasts almost to the end of the text: 'It so justifies me' (TOTS, 221). And in the final shocking scene, by now shocking to the reader, she says: 'Oh I was grand' (TOTS, 226). Overall is the Governess's conviction that the focus of the children's behaviour is upon her own self. 'I think he wants to give me an opening', she says of Miles, on the morning that Mrs Grose is going away with Flora (TOTS, 219). In **The Allegorical Castle**, I explored the notion of Bly as

---

[51] Mazella, Anthony, *Henry James Goes to the Movies*, ed. Susan M. Griffin, University Press of Kentucky, 2015 (11-124), p124. http://ebookcentral.proquest.com/lib/open/detail.action?docID=1915197. Subsequent references will be to this edition and will be inserted parenthetically into the text, for example '(Mazella, 12)'

a framework or solid bastion for spinning fantasies upon and I repeat it here: in her imagined duty to the master, and her infatuation with him, the Governess spins a web of self-deceptions, a notion, a mission to save the children (what from, she never expresses), a web that ties her to Bly as surely as a spider's web traps a fly.

But being aware of what the Governess imagines just invites other questions: were other deceptions at work? Anthony Mazella presents the following interpretation of events. This critic claims that Peter Quint never existed at all because, unlike the cook, housemaid, dairywoman, old pony, old groom, old gardener and a 'young lady' referred to in the Prologue, the valet is never mentioned.[51] The critic asserts that if Quint had been 'real', then the Governess would have discovered his identity when she 'made sure' that he was 'nobody about the place' (TOTS, 145).

Mazella claims that the clue to what is going on is all tied up in Mrs Grose's statement to Flora: 'We know, don't we love? ... It's all a mere mistake and a worry and a joke.' The 'we know' phrase implies conspiracy. The 'mere mistake' might apply to what the Governess is convinced of – or what Mrs Grose did. The 'worry' might indicate how Mrs Grose is now feeling, that it has all gone too far. And the 'joke' refers to the funnier aspect of the matter, to the obsessive behaviour – the Governess's own assertion – of how her own self has behaved. But what did Mrs Grose do? When the Governess describes the man she has seen to Mrs Grose, she sees in the housekeeper's eye: 'the delayed dawn of an idea' (TOTS, 145). This idea, Mazella asserts, is to let on that another young man once lived in Bly. Mazella justifies Mrs Grose's masquerading to the younger woman on the grounds of her jealousy, being given the 'state room' to live in, by presuming Mrs Grose couldn't read, by shutting her out, and so on. If Mazella is correct, then the Governess really was 'justified' when she feared that she was being practised upon. And it also lends a massive irony to her notion that Mrs Grose was lacking in imagination. Many weaknesses exist in Mazella's theory: who was the man that the Governess saw? And who was the woman in the schoolroom (on the stairs, by the lake)? Were there other servants colluding in the joke? Were they hallucinations? Were they 'real' ghosts?

Maybe Mrs Grose *has* seen them, and knew them as phantoms of people who had lived in the house, and saw in their appearance an opportunity to throw a screen over what really happened? I offer the following interpretation, not to insist on its being the 'right' one, but to show how easy it is to misinterpret a situation when one is not, like the Governess, in possession of the full facts. Whatever is really taking place in the house, it is apparent that Mrs Grose is hiding something from the disingenuous Governess. In an early scene, the housekeeper speaks of a person whom she will only refer to as 'he', thus arousing the interest of the Governess, who says: 'But of whom did you speak first? (Mrs Grose) looked blank, but she coloured. 'Why, of *him*'' (TOTS, 131). The ensuing, stinted conversation is filled with pointers to deception on the part of Mrs Grose. In spite of her character flaws, could the Governess really be 'innocent', possibly as innocent as the children that she minds, thus justifying the title of Jack Clayton's 1961 movie of James's text? Shoshana Felman asserts that the reader is just as likely to try to derive 'but one meaning' from the text as that which the Governess seeks to impose upon the events in the house (Felman, 151). I concur with Felman: the Governess is never in possession of the full facts about the house, and neither are we. As T.J. Lustig asserts, the plot is filled with blanks; for example, the Governess never tries to find out why the *master* does not want to come to Bly? (TOTS, xvii). And I agree with Felman in her statement that the novel is ultimately about 'the act of seeing' (Felman, 132). I take this as admonition to question what we are seeing, and who, and how, and why. If the novel is 'an act of seeing', and open to many interpretations and assumptions, then what we assume about the narrative's events bespeaks the character of the reader as much as it does that of the Governess (Felman, 132). If we do not question our interpretations, then we are just like the Governess when she spuriously jumps to conclusions over the expulsion of Miles from school (TOTS, 129).

Suppose that there really had been a valet in the house, and that the philandering master had an affair with Miss Jessel? Consequently, the woman gave birth to a baby that died at Bly. This is why the Governess hears a crying child – a 'real' ghost – on her first night in the house (TOTS, 125). In the absence of the master, who dare not come to Bly again because of his susceptibility to the charms of 'young and pretty women', valet Peter Quint takes charge of the household (TOTS, 130). He befriends the bereft Miss Jessel, and the young boy who longs for male company, Miles. This protosocialism fills the conservative Mrs Grose with horror. '*She* was a lady', the housekeeper says, in relation to Miss Jessel (TOTS, 159). One winter's night,

Quint dies in an accident (TOTS, 52). Miss Jessel leaves Bly and dies at home, possibly of TB. Miles is sent to a school where he talks of his great friend, Peter Quint, to 'Those I liked' (TOTS, 234). On learning that Quint is a valet, the head-master – as class-conscious as Mrs Grose – expels him from school (TOTS, 128). Thrust back into feminine company, the loneliness of Miles draws to him the phantom of his former friend, Peter Quint: 'I want my own sort' (TOTS, 192). Longing for her dead mother, Flora draws the woman's ghost from – in the words of the Governess – 'from where they come from' (TOTS, 156). And Miss Jessel, in search of her dead child, longs to 'mother' Flora.

The class-worshipping Mrs Grose cannot bring herself to believe that her master could do wrong and so does not *discourage* the Governess in her belief that it was Quint who had the affair with Miss Jessel that led to the pregnancy. Here, it might amuse the reader to ponder upon why she tells the Governess that Quint liked to wear his master's clothes (TOTS, 147). The Governess is correct in her assertion that the ghosts have come for the children, but without reckoning *why* they have come (TOTS, 153). And she never questions why, if Miss Jessel and Quint were lovers, are their 'ghosts' never together? My interpretation is incomplete but it does illustrate how easy it could be for the Governess – or for anyone else - to act on assumptions without complete knowledge. The final scene points towards what the Governess sensed earlier in the narrative, that something unexpected was about to 'spring' in the Bly environment (TOTS, 135). In her own words, she has 'justified' her own beliefs (TOTS, 221). The Governess (literally) presses upon the dying Miles to know for whom is he looking, and he shouts 'Peter Quint – you devil' (TOTS, 236). In addressing the Governess as a 'devil', the cycle is complete. Over the dead body of Miles: 'his little heart stopped beating' the Governess has found 'evil' and succeeded in completing her mission to find evil in the house, which is arguably her masquerade (TOTS, 236).

I stress again that Henry James's text is arguably the apotheosis of literary psychological manipulation, i.e. deception in all of its possibilities. But here, I refer to deception by the author of the readers, not the machinations or manipulations of any character. Just as the Victorians derived endless amusement from table-top puzzles such as mahjong, no doubt the 'meaning' of James's text occupied many a fireside discussion, in the era before the dawn of TV and movies. However, the psychological age had been born and has never departed since.

Overall, self-deception is the expression of a person filled with emotion but with no-one to expend it upon and Dale Bailey is correct in asserting that the melodrama of the late eighteenth-century literature foreshadows the intensely psychological novels of the twentieth century. At the outset of meeting Maxim, the soon-to-be Mrs de Winter, imagines him as a medieval troubadour (R, 20). Eleanor Vance refuses to leave Hill House because of her belief that it 'wants' her, when no-one else does, because she can hear music play that no-one else responds to (HH, 226). In today's less transparent world, where the edges of the black and white squares on Frye's notional checker board blend into grey, the ability to deceive others is often presented as a form of self-preservation. In Philip Pullman's trilogy, Lyra Belacqua is perfectly capable of fibbing in order to preserve herself. This pragmatism is shown as a 'good' quality. And this change in literature was accompanied by another device. In Chapter Four of *Northern Lights*, the first book of the trilogy, following her concealing the altehiometer from Mrs Coulter, Lyra contemeplates her own image in a glamorous looking-glass in which she is 'softly illuminated', the author's way of indicating that Lyra's life will never be the same again (HDM, 70). But long before Pullman was writing, the *doppleganger* and *duality* burgeoned in literature.

Comedy and fantasy

As in deception, the comedy doppelganger enters into the realm of Shakespearean. William de Stancy appearing at the moment that Paula Power contemplates his ancestor's portrait (AL, 207-9) parallels the scene in *The Winter's Tale*, where the 'statue' of Hermione comes to life. But later in Hardy's text, the doppelganger theme takes on a darker twist as William Dare uses a subverted photo to defame the character of George Somerset. As the nineteenth century progressed, other selves and other worlds featured increasingly in literature. Lewis Carroll's second most famous book, *Alice Through the Looking Glass*, tells of how the heroine/protagonist steps into a mirror – and into a world that is actually a mirror image of this one. In addition, the alternative world is laid out like a chess board. This treatment of a parallel world is all the more curious when we consider that Carroll – the pen-name of Charles Lutwidge Dodgson, a lecturer in mathematics at Christ Church College, Oxford – published the book in 1871, more than eighty years before scientist Hugh Everett put forward the theory of parallel universes.

Perception of reality

At the opening of his article 'American Gothic Images' Irving Malin explains how 'the double' in literature is a way of suggesting the emphemerality, the brittleness of reality (Malin, 145). I have already shown how the doppelganger may be a form of deception: throughout the history of literature, writers have played with notions of reality and illusion by placing the device of the doppelganger into their narratives. At the most simplistic level, a doppelganger is simply an image or replica of a significant character, often the protagonist of the narrative. And it is a device frequently placed to enable the reader to question his or her own reality.

Very few people, men or women, can imagine getting through a normal day without looking at least once in a mirror. Modern self-consciousness means that we must see ourselves as others see us. *A mirror is a polished surface, usually of amalgam-coated glass, or metal, which reflects an image,* reads the Oxford English Dictionary. A mirror need not be the familiar object of silvered glass that we are all used to, but any surface that reflects an image. We can only imagine that our forbears looked at their images in pools of still water before the existence of manufactured mirrors. Judging by the number of fables and stories that involve reflections and mirrors, people believed that there was something magical surrounding this doppelganger world. Higher mammals all share a capacity for fascination with imagery; just picture a dog gazing at his reflection in a pond or a mirror. The question is, of course, one that the dog will never answer: does the dog know that it is his own reflection or does he think it is another dog? Man does not have this dilemma. Aeons ago, our opposing thumbs enabled us to create avatars and images of ourselves and other animals, witness the stencilled hands, mammoths and bison on the walls of the Lascaux and other prehistoric caves. In classical times, mythology embraced the avatar and the doppelganger, the themes running in counterpoint for centuries. In Ovid's *Metamorphosis*, Narcissus was a handsome youth who saw the reflection of his face in the waters of the Styx River. He became so captivated by his own reflection that he sat looking at himself until he died and a small flower grew in his place. Pygmalion fell in love with the statue of a beautiful woman and he brought her to life. The story of how the artist, Xeuxis, painted grapes that looked so real that crows flew down and tried to pick them off of his murals is, although unauthenticated, quite possibly true. As literature assumed sophistication, writers began to find an increasing number of devices for the role of the doppelganger.

Across William Shakespeare's spectrum of plays, the use of doubling is used to much comic effect, most notably in the *Comedy of Errors*, where nurses confuse the identities of two pairs of twin brothers at birth. In typical Shakespearean fashion, the grown-up brothers' paths cross so that each man gazes at a pair of brothers identical to his own sibling pair – and one of them is identical to himself. In *The Winter's Tale*, the statue of Hermione comes to life as admirers gaze upon it.

But Shakespeare is at his most profound when demonstrating the theme of the doppelganger as an effect of growing self-awareness. The indulged boy-king Richard II, grew into a very entitled young man, unable to deal with the crisis that he and his rulership, faced. In his play about the monarch, the Bard externalises the monarch's inner turmoil by having him perform a long and eloquent speech in front of a glass mirror, which he then shatters: *Hath Sorrow struck/So many blows upon this face of mine/And made no deeper wounds?* (Act 4, Scene 1) Like many characters who follow him, Richard is questioning reality, asking: who am I? Is he the all-powerful monarch that his subjects bowed to when he was a boy and young man, or is he the suffering and powerless person that he sees in the glass? Shakespeare's text is suggesting to the reader that the protagonist may not always be the person that he believes he is, that he may regard himself differently from what other people do and indeed, disparate parties may have differing views on who he really is. Sandra Gilbert and Susan Gubar might have been writing about a feminine version of Richard when they wrote of 'conscious acceptance of powerlessness' (G&G, 161-2). Throughout the gothic sub-genre, protagonists are often in a struggle for survival, physically and psychologically, and need to grow, and the device of the doppelganger is quite often the means through which this happens. This often has an unsettling effect on the reader.

Mirroring, projecting likeness and changing places

Verisimilitude has ever unsettled and intrigued man. Six thousand years ago, people looked into surfaces of polished obsidian, a volcanic rock and later in history, mirrors were made of highly polished bronze and copper.

In the ancient world, only aristocracy and the priestly classes had access to mirrors, rendering them objects of awe. In the developed world, mirrors were associated with wealth. The spread of mercantile wealth made mirrors more ubiquitous but even by the 1500s, few people still had access to one. Leonardo da Vinci famously wrote his notebooks in mirror writing, making his work more arcane.

In the century following Shakespeare's death, a plethora of optical devices were invented, and then perfected by scientists like Galileo Galilei. The age of *looking* had arrived. The universe had opened up and the world would never be the same again. By the later decades of the eighteenth century, the theme of doubling and the doppelganger had become a feature of the gothic novel and also, narrative poetry. In 1832, Alfred Lord Tennyson published his famous narrative poem, *The Lady of Shallot*. I quote: 'And moving thro' a mirror clear/That hangs before her all the year,/Shadows of the world appear./There she sees the highway near/Winding down to Camelot:' The world that she sees in the mirror is a representation of the one with which she longs to interact.

In Hans Andersen's tale, *The Snow Queen*, the mirror serves as the instrument to enslave the new 'enlightened' Kay and the Snow Queen possesses the Mirror of Understanding: 'the only one and best thing in the world'. In 1848, Andersen's friend, Charles Dickens, published a short story, *The Haunted Man and the Ghost's Bargain*, one of his so-called Christmas stories. The subject of the narrative is the chemistry teacher, Redlaw, who has had an unhappy past. He broods and broods until a phantom: 'an awful likeness of himself' appears and makes a proposal to Redlaw to allow him to: 'forget the sorrow, wrong, and trouble you have known.' In short, the phantom will help him to forget all of his memories. Redlaw agrees to this strange proposal, but without memories, he has trouble explaining all of the emotion he feels. Eventually, Redlaw reverts to his normal, emotional self. The subject has learned his lesson: without memories, even bad ones, we cannot be the complex people that we are. Here, the memories that a person entertains are so profound, that they take on the substance of another person. The link between *The Haunted Man* and Dickens's other Christmas story, *A Christmas Carol*, is apparent.

For the majority of writers and for Dickens himself, the instance of the essence of a person taking on a life of its own was veering close to the supernatural. As the nineteenth century progressed, the doppelganger became a much-used authorial device in realist literature. In his 'Introduction' to *Bleak House*, J. Hillis Miller explains how each character seems to refer, in an emblematic way, to one another (BH, 15). Certainly, unlikely instances of characters recognising similar traits in one another also take place. When, following an absence of many years, Sir Leicester Dedlock and George Rouncewell meet again, the chastened and ailing baronet says to the younger, former soldier: 'Thank you, George. You are another self to me' (BH, 849). The lonely young Esther Summerson converses continually with her doll. When Esther's guardian dies, she buries her doll, the 'childhood' part of herself, before she goes on to school. In her new environment, Esther encounters the interchangeable twin sisters, the Miss Donnys. This is Dickens' pointer to Esther's own future, in which her resemblance to Lady Dedlock will sew confusion and attract attention, wherever she goes. Mr Guppy is mesmerised when he first sees a picture of Lady Dedlock: 'I do assure you that the more I think of that picture the better I know it without knowing how I know it' (BH, 139). Not long afterwards, his hapless pursuit of Esther begins. The first event to disturb Esther's peace takes place when she catches her first glimpse of Lady Dedlock in church: 'But why her face should be, in a confused way, like a broken glass to me, in which I saw scraps of old remembrances; and why I should be so fluttered and troubled (for I was still) by having casually met her eyes; I could not think' (BH, 304). This twinning of characters extends to Ada Clare, Esther's foil and almost exact opposite in terms of background and fortune. When the narrative opens, Esther's murky past is in stark contrast to the trust-funded, sunny-natured blonde Ada. But the good looks attract the attention of the capricious Richard Carstone and as the narrative progresses, Ada and Esther seem to switch places. The veil lifts slowly on Esther's past and, although the author sees fit to blight her looks with smallpox, she emerges from the darkness. At the end, the reader sees her happily married to lover Allan Woodcourt. Meanwhile, the dead Richard has ruined Ada and we see her, penniless and with a child to bring up. Of course, she has – as Esther did at the beginning of the novel – the philanthropy of the good John Jarndyce to save her from penury. And Jarndyce has rather disquietingly provided Esther and her spouse with a replica of Bleak House, bringing the novel and its doppelganger theme to a close.

Pip of *Great Expectations* occupies the pivot in the class system upon which the narrative rotates. Pip is Dolge Orlick's *alter ego* and, as John Bowen puts it, Orlick is Pip's 'dark double' (GE, xiv), and whom Pip describes as 'my own warning ghost', the person that Pip might have been if he, Pip, hadn't had a supportive (if harsh) sister, and a loving foster father (GE, 361). Pip's lack of self-awareness (the *deception*) may be the cause of his overlooking these social advantages. And it is doubtlessly awareness on the part of Orlick of Pip's advantages that causes the journeyman to chastise the young boy, with tales of a 'Devil' living in the forge (GE, 95). Orlick is an orphan in the sense that he is disconnected from his family throughout the narrative, and he is obliged to lodge in a sluice house (GE, 95). His existence is miserable: 'on Sundays he mostly lay all day on the sluice-gates' in contrast to Pip's comfortable life in the forge (GE, 95). It is a tribute to Dickens' comic mastery that Orlick carries out the bashing of Pip's sister and the humiliation of Uncle Pumblechook: '(Orlick) stuffed his mouth full of flowering annuals', incidences that Pip feels 'guilty' about, without drawing attention to the reader's notion that Pip may have relished the opportunity to carry out these deeds himself, yet innate propriety forbade him from doing so (GE, 396). And it is to Pip's shame that *he* stalks Orlick, just as Orlick has stalked Biddy, ensuring that the journeyman is perpetually unemployed. And of course, a fair part of the narrative describes Pip's stalking of Estella: 'Oh, the many, many nights and days through which the unquiet spirit in me haunted that house when Estella lived there' (GE, 256). And Pip has yet another *alter ego*, that is, Abel Magwitch. In his discourse about his origins, Magwitch points out a number of facts about himself to Pip and Herbert. They – and the reader – discover that like Pip, Magwitch is an orphan. Magwitch is aware of this interchangeability: 'I have lived rough, that you should live smooth' (GE, 273). This harmless banter begins to fill Pip with terror when Magwitch declares, quite candidly to Pip: 'Where will you put me?' (GE, 273). While Pip's relatives have constantly reminded him that he was brought up 'by hand', Magwitch informs us that he, Magwitch, was 'took up' (GE, 293). While Orlick had threatened the boy Pip with tales of a devil in the forge, a nameless 'they' constantly threaten Magwitch with a similar phenomenon (GE, 293). Like Pip, Magwitch finds 'expectations' and a tutor, but one such as Compeyson, except that: 'C's business was swindling, handwriting forging, stolen banknote passing, and such-like' (GE, 294).

Dickens uses the doppelganger to comic effect in other areas of the novel, not least the episode where Pip and Bentley Drummle enter into a notional battle for a place in front of the fire when they encounter each other in a wayside inn (GE, 301). Wemmick's Aged Parent is a comic comment on Clara Barley's father, who: 'lies a-bed in a bow window where he can see the ships sail up and down the river' (GE, 314). Grown-up children take care of both of these older men who mark time as their days approach their end, Mr Wemmick senior by listening for the firing of the guns and Mr Barley, by following the tides of the river. Wemmick's listing of his skills: 'I am my own engineer, and my own carpenter, and my own plumber, and my own gardener, and my own Jack of all Trades' is a comic presaging of the activities that Abel Magwitch had to resort to, in order to survive: 'a bit of a poacher, a bit of a labourer, a bit of a waggoner, a bit of a haymaker, a bit of a hawker, a bit of most things that don't pay and lead to trouble' (GE, 126, 294). Dialogue like this, and the naming of Jagger's office 'little Britain' is the author's way of indicating that social condition – poor or middleclass or well-to-do – is one of social context. The salaried Wemmick, with his portable property, does not have to worry about getting into trouble; the poor and hunted Magwitch does. Lovely Estella is both socially nurtured and mentally poisoned by the twisted Miss Havisham, who has brought her up to take revenge upon all mankind. Even before she succumbs to the conflagration that kills her, Miss Havisham is repenting of what Estella has become 'I stole her heart away and put ice in its place' and apologises to Pip: 'Until you spoke to her the other day, and until I saw in you a looking-glass that showed me what I once felt myself, I did not know what I had done. What have I done! What have I done!' (GE, 338). Pip and Miss Havisham may seem an unlikely pairing but they are both matched in passion: 'that showed me what I once felt myself', Miss Havisham in her romantic devastation and Pip in his desire for Estella.

Charlotte Brontë's novel, *Jane Eyre*, has given rise to the famous moniker: *the madwoman in the attic*. The presence of the woman who is married to the man whom Jane loves, haunts the novel. Yet, the reader gains very few glimpses of this woman who stands in the way of all of Jane's hopes and dreams. We certainly hear *her* though, her manic laughter unsettling Jane in the earlier part of her sojourn at Edward Rochester's home, Thornfield Hall. When we finally meet Berthe face to face, the effect on the reader borders on the shocking: 'In the deep shade, at the further end of the room, a figure ran backwards and forwards. What it was, whether beast or human being, one could not, at first sight, tell: it grovelled, seemingly, on all fours; it snatched and growled like some strange wild animal: but it was covered with clothing; and a quantity of dark, grizzled hair, wild as a mane, hid its head and face' (JE, 293).

I say 'shocking' because of the constant use of the pronoun 'it', and the entire depersonalisation of the person whom the author is describing. Jane is as unsettled as the reader, of course, not least because at the outset of the novel, Jane was living with relatives who had degraded her to the same status of object as Berthe Rochester has now become. Because of her poverty and her status as an orphan, Jane's cruel relatives, the Reeds – legally obliged to care for her but hating her all the while – regarded her as wicked and uncontrollable. They punished her for the slightest childish misdemeanour – most often imagined rather than actual, and locked her away whenever circumstances provided an opportunity. In one instance, they lock her in the so-called Red Room and when the dark falls, Jane – believing that she is in the presence of the supernatural, takes fright: 'I was oppressed, suffocated: endurance broke down – I uttered a wild, involuntary cry – I rushed to the door and shook the lock in desperate effort' (JE, 17). Jane's cries summon her Aunt, servants and other members of the household. With one exception, they are less than sympathetic. Aunt Reed is never going to pander to Jane's terrors. She not only does not release Jane from her imprisonment, she increases the punishment: 'Silence! This violence is most repulsive ... I was a precocious actress in her eyes: she sincerely looked on me as a compound of virulent passions, mean spirit, and dangerous duplicity' (JE, 18). 'Violence' and 'dangerous duplicity' in a girl of eight? Jane experiences a breakdown following these events and on the advice of a physician, she is removed from her cousins' house, Gateshead, and is sent to school where, although she is not always happy, she is touched by the civilising experience of learning. Eventually, she becomes a teacher and a governess. The reader must wonder what would have happened to Jane had not she had the learning opportunity? Would she have ended up in some fearful institution, such as the Victorians were famed for? But how does the doppelganger relate to Byronism?

In relation to Eleanor Vance, Dale Bailey cites Narcissus, the character of Greek myth, who became so enchanted by his own beauty that he could not cease from staring at this reflection in a pool (Bailey, 34). He became the flower of the same name, rooted to the spot and condemned to gaze at himself for eternity. I remind the reader once again of that other edict of Bailey that the way in which we behave is often a simple reflection of the culture that produces us (Bailey, 34). Bailey is writing with relation to Eleanor Vance, suggesting qualities in her personality that may be in tandem with the self-absorption of Narcissus (Bailey, 38). When Eleanor arrives at Hill House, she sees her reflection in the polished floor of the hall, a suggestion by the author that Eleanor is about to become enmeshed into the fabric of the house, its 'personality' suggested by the anthromorphism of an earlier scene where Eleanor likened the facade of Hill House to the face of a person watching her (HH, 37, 34). Instantly, Eleanor feels a sensation of dislike, one that she projects onto the house, suggesting that events in the house are going to show Eleanor a side of herself that she might not like (HH, 37). In her room, Eleanor's uneasiness continues, imagining herself transported to Hill House and Dr Montague watching her with his 'unerring eye' (HH, 40).

Now, she is transposing the anthropomorphism of the house exterior onto the imagined person of Dr Montague, imagined because she has yet to meet him. Eleanor continues to perceive threat in the actual fabric of the house, which fills her with discomfort because of its 'wrong' dimensions (HH, 40). But this unruliness could be the architectural parallel of Eleanor's rampage towards the end of the narrative. If it can be unruly so can she. Before that happens, however, Eleanor becomes involved with another *alter ego*.

According to Bailey, 'Eleanor and Theodora mirror one another' (Bailey, 34). The author indicates this connection in the reflective language' used by the women during their bonding process upon meeting: "I won't if you won't.' 'I won't if *you* won't" (HH, 46). This suggests that in certain respects, the women are interchangeable. Out of doors, the women engage in another bonding session, one that demonstrates their common upbringing and adolescent uncertainties. Both women have a deal of nervous energy to expend; in Eleanor this shows in her reaction upon first seeing Hill House, when she struggles to light a cigarette (HH, 34). On the second evening in the house Eleanor feels increasingly unsettled, even in the company of others, her cherished new friends (HH, 123). Immediately, she admits to Dr Montague that she is 'nervous' (HH, 124). Yet, a little later, Eleanor senses that Theodora is also nervous and alert, sensing something in the air (HH, 125). This demonstrates that Theodora is as easily agitated as Eleanor. Yet, the author indicates that the women, though connected by these traits, are not twins but opposites (Bailey, 39). At the opening of the narrative, the author describes Eleanor's devotion to her invalid mother, and then points out how much Theodora disdains duty (HH, 8). These opposing qualities are represented metaphorically by the women's appearance, Eleanor thinking that Theodora is lovely and in the same instant wishing *she* were lovely, indicating to the reader that she is *not* lovely (HH, 47). Both Eleanor and Theodora fantasise, but Theodora fantasises in an ironic and mocking way. When she invites the statue of Hugh Crain to dance with her, she is merely joking (HH, 109). Later in the novel, when Eleanor breaks down and goes on a personal rampage, she believes that she *is* dancing with the founder of the house (HH, 231). According to Dale Bailey, Theodora is everything Eleanor wants to be, but is not (Bailey, 39). The major difference in the personalities of Eleanor and Theodora is shown through the incident in Eleanor's past, a past that causes Dr Montague to invite her to Hill House. A psychical magazine records how a shower of stones fell for three days upon the house that Eleanor and her family lived in when she was twelve years old, a mystery that was never solved (HH, 7). In incidental juxtaposition, Theodora admits to having thrown a brick through the roof of *her* family greenhouse and despite being punished, she enjoyed it so much that she went out and did it again (HH, 73). Eleanor and her family return to living in the house of the unexplained incident. Neither she nor her family take any action over it but assumed that neighbours must be to blame (HH, 7). This lack of action demonstrates the passivity of Eleanor's family profile, which has filtered into her own personality. Whereas the women have similar levels of nervous energy and hail from similar backgrounds, Theodora *acts*, Eleanor is *acted upon*.

Dichotomies and duality

Shakespeare's plays are filled with characters that switch identities, males who masquerade as females and vice versa, the disguises assumed in order to escape a death sentence – as Rosalind in *As You Like It* – or gain access without being recognised, as Viola in *Twelfth Night*. Yet, even this playwright, who brought comedy to his plays, could venture into the moralistic. Dorothy McMillan, in her Introduction to *Measure for Measure*, writes of the motivations of Vincencio going into disguise, which is to find out what people really are like beneath their facades of sociability. Of course, the Duke's plan is to observe the lives of 'lesser' mortals. By contrast, later writers use the doppelganger theme to unmask the truth about main characters, including the protagonist, to reflect what he or she might be in reality, a working of *anagorsis*.

In *Romance of the Forest*, the wicked Marquis proves to be Adeline's uncle, her late father's younger brother. Throughout the remainder of the narrative, Adeline never questions the connection between the two men, assuming that where her uncle is 'bad', her father was bound to have been 'good': 'The contrast of (Philipe and Henry) prevented that cordial regard between them which their near relationship seemed to demand. Henry was benevolent, mild, and contemplative. In his heart reigned the love of virtue; in his manners the strictness of justness was tempered, not weakened, by mercy; his mind was enlarged by science, and adorned by elegant literature. The character of Philipe has been already delineated in his actions; its nicer shades were blended with some shining tints; but these served only to render more striking by contrast the general darkness of the portrait' (ROTF, 343).

In outlining the plot that murdered Henry, the author more than hints that the surviving Marquis wasn't *thoroughly* wicked: 'why (the Marquis) did not employ the same means to secure the (death of) the child, seems somewhat surprising' (ROTF, 343). It is tempting to dismiss Ann Radcliffe's incomplete explanation as a mere plot mechanism; if Adeline had died as an infant, then no narrative would have ensued. But it is just as tempting to believe that the 'wicked' Marquis nursed a secret regard for this infant who was his closest surviving family, flesh of his brother's flesh. And the reader must wonder: could the roles have been reversed? If Adeline's father had been the younger brother, would the desire for wealth have corrupted him or would he still have been the more responsible sibling, imbued with the 'strictness of justness'?

In *A Laodicean*, this situation is repeated in a most sinister way. Paula Power is under the subtle coercion of her uncle Abner – an eerie reincarnation of her father – who is scheming unwittingly in collusion with William de Stancy and William Dare to bring about marriage between Paula and de Stancy: 'It is so dreadfully reasonable that we should marry. I wish it wasn't!' (AL, 353). By making Abner Power a fugitive from a European secret and political society, Hardy produces a lumbering and improbable situation to invest him as the 'bad' living uncle in contrast to the 'good' dead father. But the reader must wonder what would have happened if Paula's father had been alive at the time of the staged wooing? Would the uber-wealthy engineer have really been truly indifferent as to whether his daughter married an 'ordinary' man –

or one who could imbue his hard-won wealth with a dash of aristocratic nous?

It stands to reason that if sibling pairs can embody 'good' and 'bad' in the objective sense, then a single subject must be able to embody the two qualities. Today, very few people are unaware of the story of *Dr Jekyll and Mr Hyde*, which makes it difficult for readers to understand how his friend, Dr Lanyon, died of shock soon after witnessing Mr Hyde transforming back in Dr Jekyll, following his consumption of the potion (DJMH, 40-41). Even today, an entire raft of psychologists, criminologists and psychotherapists grapple with the reality that the world is more than amply supplied with persons who live double lives, respected professionals and steady-going family types at home and in society, only to emerge as perpetrators of the worst types of crimes. In the late nineteenth century, that good and evil could sit side by side in the same person was a new act to follow, and the world was about to embark on the age of psychology.

Uncovering the truth

As in the masquerade, mirroring and duality are used to reveal the truth of the character of the person *seeing*, rather than what or who is seen. In *Measure for Measure*, the Duke goes about Vienna in disguise, uncovering the truth of what other people think of *him*. In more recent literature, various characters mirror traits – and thus the truth – in each other. In the matter of Henry James's text, *The Turn of the Screw*, once again I cite Shoshana Felman, that the novel is about the 'act of seeing' (Felman, 132). The Governess seeing herself in a full-length mirror for the first time is an externalisation of what T.J. Lustig describes as her 'fractured' self (TOTS, 124, xx). Before going to Bly, the Governess meets the master in his Harley Street office, of which, the frame narrator informs us, gives her the impression: 'She figured him as rich but fearfully extravagant – saw him all in a glow of high fashion, of good looks, of expensive habits, of charming ways with women (TOTS, 120). This addiction to good living is not so admirable, it seems, in her employer's *alter ego*, Peter Quint, his valet, of which the Governess learns: 'there had been matters in his life, strange passages and perils, secret disorders, vices more than suspected, that would have accounted for a good deal more' (TOTS, 152). The reason that the Governess has taken time to look into the life of Quint is because she has learned that he died by slipping on a patch of ice, following a night of imbibing on liquor, in a local inn. To the reader, these 'vices' run in parallel to the life of the master, also addicted to good living, that is, 'fearfully extravagant', but less likely to come to a bad end because he would presumably have had the use of a carriage to take him back to his comfortable town house at night. And his wealth entitled him to 'charming ways with women.' And Quint has another *alter ego.*

When the Governess sees familiarity in the face of Peter Quint as he looks in the window: 'it was as if I had been looking at him for years and had known him always' (TOTS, 142). Later, she places him – a man she has never known – in the social order of things: 'Quint was only a base menial' (TOTS, 163). It is likely that the Governess is seeing her own humble origin, educated though she is, in the person of the valet, whose ghost she dismisses as 'a living detestable dangerous presence' (TOTS, 170). Here, I repeat my earlier statement: 'It is one matter to be aware of oneself or at least, know what posture one is trying to convey to others; what is most strange about the Governess is that she claims to know the hearts and minds of other people, even those whom she has never met'. I question where the 'good' Governess – in the words of meta-narrator Douglas 'the most agreeable woman I have ever known in her position' draws her knowledge from? (TOTS, 117). Her own beliefs, combined with odds of information from Mrs Grose, lead her, the Governess, to believe that 'ghosts' are stalking the children, with the intent of corrupting them. In consequence, the Governess embarks on a mission to 'save' the children: 'I was there to protect and defend the little creatures'; from what, she never defines (TOTS, 153). She embarks on her mission, following the children wherever possible, to the point of stalking them (Felman, 191). In doing so, her behaviour parallels the Narcissus that Bailey refers to with relation to Eleanor Vance, projecting the reflection of her own dark ideas onto other subjects (Bailey, 34).

Modernity, surreality and the doppelganger today

According to Dale Bailey, the twinning of Eleanor and Theodora demonstrates how the gothic tale plays with 'doubles and split personalities' (Bailey, 38). In *His Dark Materials* trilogy, twentieth and twenty-first century author Philip Pullman uses the theme of the double to sublime effect when he assigns every character in Lyra's fantasy world a 'daemon' or animal familiar to accompany him or her through life, an entity with which to share thoughts and adventures. The daemon is a spirit in animal form that represents the soul of the character, an animal with a personality that the connected subject can converse with, a guardian angel and familiar, a person to look out for the subject all the days of his or her life. The extent of the success of this device is arguable, but what is evident are the ways in which the limitations of the daemon – can interact with other daemons, vanishes upon the death of its human twin, no human can touch another human's daemon – add structure to what might otherwise be a rather vapid fantasy saga.

Charles Dickens borders on surrealism when he places twin sisters, two Miss Donnys, in *Bleak House* (BH, 72-73). Today, the theme of twinning, dark-doubling and duality runs through films, plays and books. In the twentieth-century novel, *The Stepford Wives*, by Ira Levin, married men replace their wives by high-functioning avatars, lovely robots that carry out housewifely duties to perfection. A generation later, Kazuo Ishiguro reworked the theme in *Never Let Me Go*, a novel in which young people are cloned to provide organs for their 'original' selves. Both novels reflect the technology of their times, that is, advancing microtechnology and later on, genetic engineering. Both novels voice contemporary fears, fears that humanity may be replaced by machines that function better than the human person, and that our individuality is ever open to being subsumed into a system that is not of our own making. And both raise many more profound questions about the avatar.

One hundred years ago, film-maker Fritz Lang made *Metropolis*, the tale of citizens living in a fabulous, technically advanced city furnished with lit-up skyscrapers and – to us – futuristic modes of travel. But underneath this stunning veneer lies a dark secret; the city is actually run by a beaten-down population of workers, who labour day and night to keep the city functioning. But they have no control over their own lives. Revolution is never far away and a young woman named Maria seeks to control the growing unrest of the workers by preaching to them, declaring that both classes can live peacefully together so long as there is communication between them. Frederson, the ruler of the City, spies her preaching and is not pleased. He needs misrule in order to rule, else he will not be able to control the workers. So he hires a magician named Rotwang to create a robot, a replica of Maria, to sew discord amongst the workers. Andreas Huyssen writes that the 'real' Maria must be tamed, so that the robot Maria, over which the male has authority, can by proxy rule the Metropolis.⁵² For a while, the workers are fooled – and seduced – when the robotic Maria does an erotic, oriental dance for the men before running amok. But Frederson's plan fails; the workers riot in any case, and almost succeed in destroying the city. Freder, the son of Frederson, has already seen and fallen in love with the original Maria. He intervenes improbably – and order and peace are restored. The fairy-tale motifs are obvious here: the hero (Freder), the lovely princess (Maria), the corrupt ruler (Frederson), and the wicked magician (Rotwang). The spell is cast and broken and good prevails.

The message of *Metropolis* is ambivalent in that it shows workers slaving to uphold the smooth running of the city for the benefit of a comfortable elite. Yet, it casts Rotwang as the 'bad' magician-cum-technologist whose creation promises to uphold this unsettling (to the modern viewer) social equilibrium. Today, debates on whether technology is 'good' or 'bad' still rage. But Fritz Lang's movie has one, unambivalent message: between workers and their bosses there must be a *heart*, the *heart* being metonymic of effective communication and good will on either side. Neither labour leaders nor the owner class could fail to agree with this edict; at least, not in principle. In *Metropolis*, Freder agrees to step into the role of this *heart*, the smooth runner between the classes whose interests, if not principles, often appear to be in conflict. Throughout literature, these 'runners', under various guises, have always been in existence.

The nebulous Dis

Today, readers are so used to encountering narrator servants, detectives and their side-kicks, e.g., Sherlock Holmes and Dr Watson, that we do not blink when we encounter yet another literary or screen detective. However, even this class of protagonist has its literary genesis. Once again, I refer to Northrop Frye's framing of the development of literature, in which the protagonist has shifted from the hero of old with special powers and the ability to communicate with supernatural entities, to being the 'ordinary' man or woman, boy or girl. Unless the author is possessed of extraordinary powers of narration, this mono-vision can render a tale flat and

---

⁵²Andreas Huyssen, 'The Vamp and the Machine' in *After the Great Divide; Modernism, Mass Culture, Postmodernism (Theories of Representation and Difference)*, (Indiana: Indiana University Press, 1987), p71. Subsequent references will be to this edition and will be inserted parenthetically into the text, for example '(Huyssen, 71)'

uninteresting. Even Charles Dickens writes *Bleak House* through two points of view: the omnipresent, impersonal narrative and the voice of Esther Summerson.

In a narrative, this movement between points of view adds the dimension of drama and suspense for readers of the *low mimetic*, tales of everyday life about ordinary people. But this shifting point of view does not suit every narrative, for example, a first-person narrative such as *Jane Eyre*, or narratives in which the author writes the story solely from the point of view of the protagonist. In classical times and indeed, in later ages, when society was still polarised by the very wealthy and powerful in contrast to the illiterate masses, movement was literal and often through the use of the Dis. In his 'Introduction' to *Paradise Lost,* John Leonard refers to Claudian's classical poem, *The Rape of Prosperine*, the god of the underworld, Pluto, lured Prosperine to Hades by promising to make her his Queen (PL, xxxvi). Leonard then points out the stanza in *Paradise Lost* in which Milton references the same incident: 'that fair field/Of Enna, where Prosperine gath'ring flow'rs/Herself a fairer flow'r by gloomy Dis/Was gathered (PL, iv, 268-71)'.

Leonard likens the role of Satan in Milton's epic to the part that Pluto plays in Claudian's poem. Whatever influences writers draw upon for their characters and action, it is clear that the 'gloomy Dis' plays a vital role in literature. Without the activity of Pluto or Satan, wherever they come from or wherever they go to, the dark Dis is the catalyst in both Milton, Claudian and the works of countless other authors. If the 'rape', actually an abduction, in Claudian's narrative had never taken place, if the temptation of Eve had not taken place in Genesis, the narratives would not exist.

In classical times, the Dis was often Mercury, or his Greek counterpart, Hermes, the deity who had the power to transcend boundaries of time and place and was endowed with a raft of talents. On the day that he was born, he managed to steal a herd of cattle and on the same day, he constructed the first lyre. Later on, he invented the syrinx or Pan pipe. His roles included ascending to the gods, interpreting divine will, telling the future, protecting heroes, facilitating flight and commerce, guiding travellers and accompanying the spirits of the dead to Hades. Because of this variegated array of roles and talents, we describe a person with the ability to constantly shift in moods and adapt easily to many situations as *mercurial.* In the sixteenth century, Mercury was reborn as Puck in Shakespeare's play, *A*

Midsummer Night's Dream, an entity who travels between the world of men and that of the supernatural, and influences the lives of all whom he encounters.

In the chapter, **The Journey**, I stressed that the progress in a gothic novel depends upon the tension between movement and stasis. In addition to the protagonist, the narrative quite often includes a figure that has the capability of flitting between worlds, by which I mean social class rather than actual physical places – although this is relevant also – a movement that is vital to the workings of the plot. By the eighteenth century, with the supernatural in literature becoming notional rather than actual, authors needed other devices to facilitate movement between disparate groups of people and classes, and the secular servant was right at hand. In literature, the first notable servant was undoubtedly Sancho Panza, the companion of the eponymous Don Quixote, the novel by Don Miguel de Cervantes, published in 1605. In creating Panza, Cervantes established that literary staple, the sidekick. The sidekick provides the main character with an audience through which to express his feelings, opinions and plans of action. The sidekick has the privilege to answer back to the main character, to agree or disagree with him, and he has the hidden but real power of anchoring the more high-flown plans of the protagonist in reality. More than two centuries later, the sidekick was reborn as Sam Weller in Dickens's *Pickwick Papers*.

The servant/housekeeper

The changing attitude towards the status of the servant can be observed across the range of primary texts. In Walpole's text, a scene between Manfred and two servants, Jacques and Diego, illustrates the less progressive attitude, prevalent in the eighteenth century. Manfred, who has already witnessed and been petrified by the ghost of his grandfather, dismisses as 'blockheads' the two servants when they admit that they are frightened by events in the castle. His statement: 'it is only a ghost, then, that thou hast seen?' (Walpole, Horace, *The Castle of Otranto*, ed. Michael Gamer [London: Penguin Classics, 2001], p171) illustrates the scorn of the nobleman for emotion demonstrated by those of a lower class. This mode of thinking continued for another generation. In *Romance of the Forest*, when the La Mottes flee Paris, the entourage includes Peter and Annette, and the author refers to them as 'the family' (ROTF, 3). Initially, Peter is not shown in a good light, being portrayed as oafish and stupid when he unwittingly betrays the whereabouts of La Motte to a stranger (to him) in the local town and botches Adeline's first attempt to flee the abbey. In addition, La Motte is unremittingly rude to him: 'Your opinion was not asked,' said La Motte, 'learn to be silent' (ROTF, 69). Yet, before the narrative is out, the same man has escorted Adeline on a hazardous and extensive journey across land and water to *his* native town. The mystery is: how does Peter come to be the servant of the Paris-based La Motte, to begin with? In a narrative carefully constructed with the back-stories of other characters, the author never reveals this information. Presumably, Peter is not socially significant enough to effuse about, though his presence truly is essential to the plot.

The servant as a character does not feature in the narratives of Jane Austen, aside from occasional and impersonal references to maids, cooks and butlers. But the Dis is still an essential element in her tales. In *Northanger Abbey*, middle-class John Thorpe takes on the role of a dark Dis, travelling between high society and the middle classes, and causing mischief to all about him, not least for the young heroine, Catherine. But the *idea* of the servant as Dis is notionally present. In his teasing of Catherine on the journey to the Abbey, Henry Tilney refers to a trope common to the gothic literature of the day that foreshadows the growing importance of a rank of servant in the wider body of literature. In his comic denouement of the sub-genre, Henry says to Catherine: 'While (the family) snugly repair to their own end of the house, she (the heroine) is formally conducted by Dorothy the ancient housekeeper up a different staircase, and along many gloomy passages, into an apartment never used since some cousin or kin died in it about twenty years before' (NA, 150).

Later in the century, the occurrence of the Dis imbues *Bleak House*, from the all-pervading fog in the opening chapter, from the Mercuries in Sir Leicester's town house, to the extraordinary number of characters that behave – however unwittingly – as messengers as they flit between town and country, between lowly office and elevated stately home: Mr Guppy, Mr Tulkinghorn, Inspector Bucket, the unfortunate young Jo who is obliged to keep 'moving on' and even, Esther herself. Therefore, the reader is not likely to blink at one of the characters being named 'Miss Flite'. In this narrative, Esther occupies an odd and liminal situation. On arrival at Bleak House, she has a bunch of keys thrust into her hands and understands that *she* is to be the housekeeper, a task in which she complies diligently. However, unlike the majority of Victorian servants, Esther eats at table with Jarndyce and the other young people, Richard and Ada, who are slightly socially elevated because of their private means. Esther travels to London and to the countryside with Jarndyce, Richard and Ada, and sees life at all different levels, spanning the wealth of the Dedlock family and the bitter poverty of the brick makers. In every aspect, Esther is a true Dis.

Before the nineteenth century was out, the housekeeper had become a fixed point in a wide number of novels, from Mrs Fairfax in *Jane Eyre* to Mrs Grose of *The Turn of the Screw*. It is not difficult to understand why: the housekeeper was in a position of privilege, the conduit between the above-stairs family and the below-stairs servants. Usually female, she was of impeccable character and was omnipresent, acting as confidant and even friend to the protagonist just arrived in unfamiliar environment. In *Bleak House*, Mrs Rouncewell is the true, hereditary housekeeper, the old retainer, as she was often called, in contrast to Esther's more chequered role. Mrs Rouncewell's loyalty and Esther's diligence throw the oddity of the twentieth-century housekeepers into relief. The very name 'Dorothy', used by Henry Tilney, comically presages the housekeeping Mrs Dudley of Shirley Jackson's novel, written about 150 years later. Henry continues teasing Catherine: 'To raise your spirits, moreover, (Dorothy) gives you reason to suppose that the part of the abbey you inhabit is undoubtedly haunted, and informs you that you will not have a single domestic within call' (NA, 150). In Jackson's narrative, Mrs Dudley informs Eleanor Vance that she and her husband live six miles away and that no-one is any nearer if they need help, a broad hint of the unnatural happening within the house (HH, 39). To push the joke even further, General Tilney's obsession with timekeeping is cleverly transposed onto Mrs Dudley (HH, 38).

Although the Dudley pair are never about when the haunting episodes occur – we never encounter Dudley the caretaker again following Eleanor's meeting with him – they are evidently aware of the strangeness of the house. The house does not belong to them and since they both desert it after dark, they are not the 'old retainers' of popular nineteenth-century literature. Dudley the caretaker is the guardian of *place*, not unlike the Charon of Greek mythology, the ferryman of the dead, who transported spirits to the Underworld and demanded a fee. Dudley quibbles with Eleanor as she seeks to gain entrance to Hill House and later, both Theodora and Doctor Montague hint at a similar experience. Mrs Dudley is the guardian of *time*, and she sets out a strict chronology for the consumption of all meals. General Tilney controls time because he is lord of his manor but Mrs Dudley's obsession stems from her lowly social status, time being the one factor that she *can* control. She pushes this control to the point where she won't even serve a pot of coffee out of hours. Yet, this mean-ness is countered by the sheer sumptuous-ness of the food that *does* arrive, the endless procession of fancy sauces and desserts. Indeed, the lush fruits that Eleanor and the others consume seem descended from the industrialized fruit production of Northanger Abbey. From this point of view, Mrs Dudley seems to parallel the witch in *The Snow Queen*, keeping Gerda (and Eleanor) at bay with the delicious food and drink that they serve. And it may place another housekeeping temptress in the mind of the reader. In *Rebecca*, the monochrome Mrs Danvers tries to tempt Mrs de Winter into stroking Rebecca's clothing (R, 191). This imagery resonates more strongly when the reader remembers that Mrs de Winter has already described Rebecca's nightdress as 'apricot in colour' since apricot is a fruit as well as a colour (R, 187). It is as if Mrs Danvers is 'tempting' Mrs de Winter to taste forbidden fruit. During the nineteenth century, another Dis had established itself in literature.

The governess

Delia Da Sousa Correa cites the governess as being in the problematic position of belonging neither to the (usually) upper class of her employer, nor that of the servants (DDSC, 101).

A 'difficult' position maybe, but certainly a very powerful one. In *Jane Eyre*, the eponymous heroine takes on the role of agent, surmising the motives and weaknesses of the characters that she encounters. Every character in the book is affected by her, their actions coloured by what she does – or does not allow – to happen. Like a centre of gravity, she moves through the narrative, taking on the roles ascribed to her; a despised poor relative, an eager school pupil, an ardent young governess, the lover of the saturnine Mr Rochester, an object of desire by the evangelising John Rivers and finally, a happy young wife. She behaves with humility at all times, befriending Thornfield housekeeper Mrs Fairfax. She is given access to Berthe Mason (eventually) and Grace Poole, and yet she is polished enough to sit with the socially elevated friends of Mr Rochester.

This section would not be complete without referring at least once to Henry James's Governess, and much has been written on these pages of her less than salubrious qualities: her impulsiveness and tendency to exaggerate, her self-glorification and likely indulgence in fantasies. To expound all these issues again would be less than helpful to the reader. Suffice it is to say that times were changing (Bannerjee, 543). With the arrival of mass compulsory education, the need for the governess and indeed, the male tutor, was on the wane. However, in the twentieth century the governess/nanny as Dis had one last wheeze in the form of P.L. Travers's *Mary Poppins*. But a new Dis was needed for the changing times and the nineteenth century had brought a foreshadowing of this.

In his narrative, *The Murders in the Rue Morgue*, Edgar Allan Poe writes: '(the analyst) derives pleasure from even the most trivial occupations bringing his talent into play. He is fond of enigmas, of conundrums, of hieroglyphics; exhibiting in his solutions of each a degree of acumen which appears to the ordinary apprehension preternatural. His results, brought about by the very soul and essence of method, have, in truth, the whole air of intuition' (Poe, 61). Throughout this text, the importance of the burgeoning education of the masses upon the type of literature produced and consumed, has been stressed. By the middle decades of the nineteenth century, Poe's narrative having been published in 1841, the reader would have admired and appreciated the sharp and agile intellect of fictional detective C. Auguste Dupin. What is more, his presence would have opened the way for a new respect from the reader for a central character whose effectiveness did not depend upon an aristocratic heritage nor the possession of preternatural powers, even though, as Poe points out, such talent may have *seemed* preternatural. And in yet another of his narratives featuring Dupin, Poe may have touched upon one more evolving strand of human consciousness. From *The Mystery of Marie Roget*, Poe's narrator states: 'Prone, at all times, to abstraction, I readily fell in with (Dupin's) humour ... we gave the Future to the winds, and slumbered tranquilly in the Present, weaving the dull world around us into dreams' (Poe, 92). Auguste Dupin is one of the earliest detectives in fiction, possibly *the* earliest, a man scrupulously mechanical in his perception of a crime scene, yet aware of the power of imagination and ever ready to foray into the world of dreams in search of solutions to the atrocities that the constabulary seem unable to solve. In certain instances of the text, Dupin's narrating companion describes him as wearing 'green glasses', possibly to dull his, Dupin's waking consciousness, in order that he may draw upon the deeper levels of consciousness available to those engaged in sleep and dreaming. Indeed, it is no surprise that Sigmund Freud and his *Interpretation of Dreams* were but a generation away from Poe. In the **Introduction**, I explained how the gothic protagonist is ever prone to dreaming because she or he is *becoming*, that is, moving from the margins of society to material appreciation and success, thus occupying the liminal ground between yearning and realisation. Readers aware of the physiology and psychology of dreaming will know that the dream-time enables the subject to become a type of Dis, psychologically accessing areas and places inaccessible to the conscious subject on the physical plane. In fact, Adeline, Esther, Mrs de Winter and other protagonists all descend occasionally into the REM state.

It was these evolutions in the intellect of the reader that opened the way for a new breed of Dis. But Jane Austen may have referred to it, however unwittingly, half a century before Poe. In her 'Introduction' to *Northanger Abbey*, Marilyn Butler provides a brilliant denouement of the events in the novel, explaining how the apparently chance meeting of Catherine and Mrs Allen with the Thorpe family was no accident but a stunningly-manoeuvred event managed in no small measure by socially ambitious Isabella Thorpe. And this spins the argument around to the opening assertion of this chapter, that Isabella Thorpe is *the* deceiver of *Northanger Abbey*, her agenda being to forge a marital alliance between at least one member of her family and that of the Morland family. In addition, Marilyn Butler asserts that the plot of the modern novel all but requires the reader to become a detective in tandem with the narrative's detective, whether actual or notional.(NA, xl). Indeed, following Poe's fiction, the fictional detective was just around the corner. But before the days of Arthur Conan Doyle, another type of Dis gained one, short wheeze.

The lawyer and the detective

Initially, it seemed like the literary lawyer was going to usurp the place of the governess as the Dis. *Bleak House* is imbued with the legal system, from the intricacies of the wards in Chancery to the raft of lawyers and their clerks that populate the narrative, a motif that is repeated in *Great Expectations*. And with the triumph of R.L. Stevenson's *Dr Jekyll and Mr Hyde*, the trend looked set to continue. Gabriel Utterson is the proactive protagonist, seemingly able, like his celestial namesake, to travel between worlds, unravelling the mystery that surrounds his friend, Dr Jekyll.

But over two decades earlier, Charles Dickens had introduced another contender for the Dis.

Mid-way through *Bleak House*, the author creates the character of Inspector Bucket, possibly descended from Poe's Auguste Dupin, the genesis of every detective in fiction ever since – Sherlock Holmes and Dr Watson, Miss Marple and Inspector Poirot.

Suffice it is to say that the detective, whether former policeman or private citizen, is the ultimate democrat – and Dis. Unlike the servant, he or she is – theoretically, at least – unimpressed or obfuscated by class or rank, financial advantage or social status. Unlike the lawyer, he or she is not hidebound by a raft of regulations and requisite qualifications. He or she can be anyone from any walk of life. The detective can walk easily with presidents and kings, traders and actors, the professional and the labouring classes. In fiction, the detective is at ease with people of all ages, from the person in his dotage to the very young child, indeed, anyone who has the ability to communicate the memory of a sequence of events, however imperfectly, to this omnipresent interpreter of circumstance. All the detective needs to know of a subject is: *who has done wrong?* And the majority of detective stories and crime thrillers end with the wrong-doer (president, pauper, king?) transferred to the agents of the law, in prep for standing before the agents of justice. It is a glorious bargain for the modern reader, the event of learning the story from all points of view (of the characters) in advance of seeing good vindicated and evil punished. So many are today's fictional detectives that to list them here would be futile.

But I will refer briefly to one twentieth-century detective that shows a direct descent from Dickens. At the end of *An Inspector Calls*, by J.B. Priestly, the Birling family discovers that the so-called Inspector Goole who provided its disaffected members with a run-down of their shortcomings, was not a 'real' inspector at all, but a mysterious caller. In *Bleak House*, Inspector Bucket bears similar, preternatural qualities: 'Mr Snagsby is dismayed to see, standing with an attentive face between himself and (Mr Tulkinghorn), at a little distance from the table, a person with a hat and a stick in his hand, who was not there when he himself came in, and has not since entered by the door or by either of the windows ... there is nothing remarkable about him at first sight but his ghostly manner of appearing' (BH, 361). Esther Summerson describes 'him': 'a very respectable old gentleman, with grey hair, wearing spectacles, and dressed in a black spencer and gaiters and a broad-brimmed hat, and carrying a large gold-headed cane' (BH, 403). The hat could be a substitute for the winged helmet of Mercury and the stick, the distaff that the deity was reputed to carry. Dickens strengthens Inspector Bucket's association with the Dis when, in a later scene, the character seems to morph from one outward appearance into another.

In this scene, the Inspector is posing as a doctor, to gain entry to a building where the character, Gridley, is avoiding him. But once indoors, the 'doctor' changes character: 'When we had all arrived here, the physician stopped, and taking off his hat, appeared to vanish by magic, and to leave another and quite different man in his place' (BH, 404). For further emphasis, Dickens invests the Inspector with what, even today, may be seen by the reader as a super-power. Says Inspector Bucket: 'I know where my man is because I was on the roof last night and saw him through the skylight' (BH, 404). Here, I pose the question: what manner of citizen just happens to be upon a roof and looking through a skylight, at such an opportune moment?

I rest my case: it is already almost a century since George Orwell published *1984*, a novel that foresaw the surveillance culture. A long time ago, the reader may think. But I have just enunciated on how long it took for the modern Dis to come into his or her own. At this point in the history of literature, we are faced with two certainties: that the Dis will be needed in future narratives and that the type of Dis present will continue to evolve. How?

I explore these questions briefly in the chapter, **The Future**. In advance of this finale, the gothic sub-genre has one more tenet that requires exploration.

The Power of Nature

The origins of the landscape, the pastoral and the Romantic ♦ The female paradigm ♦ Healing and perverted nature ♦ The Landscape as metaphor: patethic fallacy, turbulence and calm ♦ Chiaroscuro

The origins of the landscape in literature, the pastoral and the Romantic

At a pivotal point in Charlotte Brontë's narrative, Jane Eyre observes: 'Nature seemed to me benign and good: I thought she loved me, outcast as I was; and I, who from man could anticipate only mistrust, rejection, insult, clung to her with filial fondness' (JE, 323). Jane has just left the damaging male world, epitomised by John Reed, Mr Brocklehurst and Edward Rochester, and is in the wilderness of Whitcross Moor. In describing her surroundings 'it was dry, and yet warm with the heat of the summer day', and 'it was pure, a kindly star twinkled just above the chasm ridge' and 'The dew fell, but with propitious softness; no breeze whispered', she is using the language of Romantic poetry (JE, 323). According to Delia da Sousa Correa, Brontë's language is comparable with that of the Romantic poets, including William Wordsworth (DDSC, 92). In fact, Brontë's language is comparable with that of Wordsworth: In his poem, *Tintern Abbey, on revisiting the banks of the Wye during a tour July 13, 1798*, he wrote 'Therefore am I still a lover of the meadows and the woods/And mountains; and of all that we behold from – This green earth'. (Wright, 109) Poet and author perceive nature as benign and initially, Jane finds it so.

It is no coincidence that Romanticism arose just following the Industrial Revolution, that time in history when the needs of the individual stood in danger of being swept aside in favour of the darker consequences of economic and technological progress. Together with this new consciousness arose an awareness of the significance of nature, not least because of the danger to the natural environment, although this awareness was to reach its zenith centuries later. More profound was the way that the later eighteenth and nineteenth-century mind observed nature. It is around this time that landscape artists such as John Constable and J.M.W. Turner began to produce their collections of work. Constable (1776-1837) and Turner (1775-1851) present a dichotomy in landscape painting. Constable came from a middle-class county family, while Turner was the son of a London barber. Turner's downbeat background did not deter him from a career in art. Quite the contrary, he used his urban connections to build his fame and considerable fortune, not least of which was placing his paintings in his father's shop window. Such tactics assured his success before he attained the age of twenty. Constable, meanwhile, was obliged to reluctantly play the country gentleman, and his financial independence only arrived when he received a legacy when he was past forty.

The cessation of the Napoleonic wars in 1812 made way for freedom of movement in Europe, and Turner travelled widely, making thousands of watercolour sketches, from Alpine scenery to the buildings of cities such as Venice. Aside from sojourns in Hampstead and Salisbury, Constable's collection of paintings and sketches are mainly of his native Norfolk, scenes of people at work in the countryside, reaping harvests and driving ploughs. Unlike Turner, Constable did not espouse the grandeur of Ehrenbreitstein, or evoke scenes from Greek mythology. But Constable's works are not cold, utilitarian sketches, rather, warm evocations of nature tamed by man, often with a church spire in the background. 'Painting is another word for feeling,' the artist famously said, his works evoking the stirrings of Romanticism.[53]

This recurrence of the landscape is universal in the gothic narrative; the action almost always taking place in a 'far away' setting, almost as in a fairy tale. In the *typical* gothic narrative, the landscape has a healing presence. The heroine encounters a series of crises, which she must survive to solve her personal dilemma. At intervals, she is or has been in such peril that she is often on the verge of collapse. Indeed, she sometimes does *actually* collapse and most often, the presence of the landscape helps her to recover. How did

---

[53]Michael Rosenthal, *Constable* (London: Thames and Hudson Ltd, 1987), p122. Subsequent references will be to this edition and will be inserted parenthetically into the text, for example "(Rosenthal, 122)"

this notion of the healing landscape originate?

From the earliest writings, poets have evoked the natural world in their epics, for instance, an apple tree features prominently in the Heraclean myth, the garden of the Hesperides: 'the apples so closely watched by the sleepless dragon'.[54] This writing echoes one of the most well-known narratives involving the natural world, the book of *Genesis*, with Adam and Eve in the Garden of Paradise. This text from the Old Testament of the Bible was translated from Hebrew to Greek, around 250 BC.[55] When the erring Adam and Eve are expelled for committing an offence against their Creator, the offence is defined as clandestinely eating a piece of fruit from the Tree of Knowledge. What is significant here is the symbolism. The couple have affected an offence against *nature*; they have not coveted gold, jewels or other mineral treasures. In *Paradise Lost*, John Milton describes Eden and the attachment of the pair to it, in organic terms: 'I saw/Hill, dale and shady woods and sunny plains, And liquid lapse of murmuring streams' (PL, Book 7: 261-263). On the other hand, Heaven 'The roof was fretted gold', and its darker foil, Hell, are places of mineral abundance (PL, Book 1: 717). Tellingly, Eden is an organic paradise, the expulsion from which is a dreadful catastrophe: 'Oh unexpected stroke. Worse than of Death!/Must I thus leave thee of Paradise? Thus leave/Thee native soil, these happy walks and shades,/Fit haunt of gods where I had hope to spend,/Quiet thought sad, the respite of day/That must be mortal to us both' (PL, Book 11: 268-273).

The reader should not suppose that *Paradise Lost* was simply a grander re-rendering of *Genesis*. It is a major literary work of the seventeenth century, one that has influenced literature ever since. If we take the major themes of *Paradise Lost* – the significance of nature, the disobedience by younger people of a parent or parent figure, the expulsion of these younger people from a paradise or fixed way of life – it will not be difficult for the reader to see how these strands tie in with the gothic sub-genre. In *Romance of the Forest*, almost every action takes place against a backdrop of nature, and the theme runs through other literary genres. According to Bruno Bettelheim, getting lost in a forest, in a fairy tale, is often an instance of opportunity for self-discovery (Bettelheim, 220). This ties in with the *bildungsroman* element

---

[54]Ovid, translated by David Raeburn, *Metamorphosis* (London: Penguin Books, 2004), Book 9, 190.

[55]J. David Pawson, *Unlocking the Bible* (London: William Collins, 2003), p20.

of the gothic narrative. Early in the narrative, heroine Adeline falls into a fever immediately following her rescue from the brigand's house by the La Motte family, where her supposed father has sequestered her. Much later in the narrative, Adeline falls ill again following her long and perilous journey from France to Switzerland. In both instances, Adeline recovers her faculties by rapt gazing at vistas of natural beauty, for example, on the morning following her rescue from the brigands: 'The fresh breeze of the morning animated the spirits of Adeline, whose mind was delicately sensible to the beauties of nature. As she viewed the flowery luxuriance of the turf, and the tender green of the trees, or caught, between the opening banks, a glimpse of the varied landscape, rich with wood, and fading into blue and distant mountains, her heart expanded in momentary joy' (ROTF, 9).

Since the early Renaissance, poets and artists had been reviving a mode formed in ancient Greece, that is, the pastoral. In the world of art and literature, the pastoral is a mode or setting that uses the beauty of the *natural* world as a metaphor of innocence and loveliness, a rarefied atmosphere that stresses the corruption and ugliness of the political and metropolitan worlds. For the centuries between the ancient, classical world and the dawning of the Renaissance, artists in the west had focussed upon depicting the *supernatural* world, placing images of saints against backdrops of gold leaf, often in the company of angels, which was their way of imagining the afterlife. However, the fifteenth century saw wealthy patrons suddenly wanting portraits of themselves, their spouses and their courtiers, in more naturalistic surroundings.

As the centuries progressed, it was inevitable that the landscape was going to provide a backdrop for drama. In 1599, William Shakespeare wrote *As You Like It*. The plot involves a group of people who seek refuge in a forest, the Forest of Arden, from the political forces that threaten them. Throughout the action, characters respond in various ways to the power of nature. According to the Duke Senior, exiled to the Forest: 'And this our life, exempt from public haunt, finds tongues in trees, books in the running brooks,/ Sermons in stones, and good in everything. I would not change it.' (Act 2, Scene 1). Later on, the Duke Senior sings: 'Blow, blow, thou bitter wind/ Thou art not so unkind/As man's ingratitude;/Thy tooth is not so keen/Because thou are not seen/' (Act 3, Scene 1).

In other words, the unkindness of nature is not a jot on that of the inhumanity of man to man, and in this instance, he is commenting on his brother Frederick who has sent him into exile. But attitude to nature in the sixteenth century was imbued with a dash of realism. Awareness of the material benefits that accrue to the time-wary town-dweller in contrast to the peasant whose time is his own eventually results in a bitter outburst from the similarly-exiled Orlando: 'in this desert inaccessible/Under the shade of melancholy boughs/Lose and neglect the creeping hours of time ... Let gentleness my strong enforcement be/In which hope I blush and lose my sword' (Act 2, Scene 7).

Overall, in eighteenth-century literature, nature was perceived as a force for good - by 'good' characters. In Radcliffe's narrative, M. Verneuil, Clara's lover, declares: 'To think well of his nature ... is necessary to the dignity and the happiness of man. There is a decent pride which becomes every mind, and is congenial to virtue' (ROTF, 270). Jane Austen, in *Northanger Abbey*, takes pains to burlesque this strand of the gothic sub-genre. '(Catherine) was fond of all boys plays, and greatly preferred cricket not merely to dolls, but to the more heroic enjoyments of infancy, nursing a dormouse, feeding a canary bird, or watering a rose-bush. Indeed she had no taste for a garden; and if she gathered flowers at all, it was chiefly for the pleasure of mischief – at least so it was conjectured from her always preferring those which she was forbidden to take' (NA, 15). But eventually, the author's awareness of the significance of nature in literature, as well as in life, breaks through. At the beginning of Chapter 14, the reader perceives Catherine, *enjoying* nature when she and Henry and Eleanor Tilney go on a walk to Beechen Cliff: 'I never look at it ... without thinking of the south of France' (NA, 102). Her words mislead Henry, who assumes that she has spent time abroad. But Catherine reveals that she has only ever read about Europe in novels. However, she goes on to protest that her erstwhile enjoyment of the outdoors is as positive experience as that of her companions and as Gilbert and Gubar point out also, she states to Henry: 'Mamma says I am never within' (G&G, 142).

Here, the reader must wonder: at what point did Jane Austen realise that enjoyment of nature was not solely a literary foible, but an experience that encompassed a much wider range of human responses? In effect, the opening paragraphs of *Northanger Abbey* only set up debates surrounding these responses, Austen's final published work, *Persuasion*, culminates with the marriage of heroine Anne Elliot to a sea captain thus obliging the heroine to engage practically with the natural world. By the end of the eighteenth century, writers had begun portraying nature in a new and darker and more subjective mode. Romantic poets and painters strove to achieve a depiction of what is *felt* rather than seen and made use of natural imagery when doing so. Rather than providing us with descriptions of pretty sunsets and waterfalls, nineteenth-century writers made use of natural imagery to express feelings of fear, and the perception that danger may not be far away. Perhaps the work of Ann Radcliffe had already foreshadowed this change?

In Chapter 21 of *Romance of the Forest*, Adeline's attempt to escape the Marquis's chateau lands her in 'an extensive garden, resembling more an English pleasure ground than a series of French parterres' (ROTF, 164). Chloe Chard explains that the less-cultivated English garden was more in keeping with the irregular, picturesque aesthetic than the formal French style (ROTF, 380-381). Here, the incident serves as a metaphor of Adeline's free spirit, which refuses to be corralled and contained by the designs of the Marquis. Nineteenth-century writers continued to develop this mode of writing. In *Jane Eyre,* a narrative that the reader may discern as occupying a position between realist novel and romance, the author enunciates this metaphorical position by her use of nature in the text. The changing dichotomy of the protagonist's attitude towards indoors and outdoors stresses this point. *Jane Eyre* opens with Jane dreading an afternoon out of doors: 'I had never liked long walks, especially on chilly afternoons: dreadful to me was coming home in the raw twilight, with nipped fingers and toes' (JE, 7).

Delia da Sousa Correa puts this dislike of the outdoors down to Jane's awareness of herself as an outsider metamorphised by her dislike of being pushed to the margins of the family she lives with, unable to sit by the fire and barely protected from the cold and rain by her place at the windowpane (DDSC, 87). Jane's attitude towards nature changes gradually but definitely. Later on, when she is settled at Lowood school, she feels the outdoors as a healing vibe against the horrors of the typhus fever epidemic that is ravaging the school. In describing the school garden, she writes: 'these fragrant treasures were all useless for most of the inmates of Lowood: except to furnish now and then a handful of herbs and blossoms to put in a coffin. But I, and the rest who continued well, enjoyed fully the beauties of the scene and the season: they let us ramble in the wood like gipsies, from morning till night, we did what we liked, went where we liked' (JE, 77). Here, the author contrasts the cultivated garden with the wilderness of the wood, the discipline of indoors and the freedom of outdoors, and the latter is juxtaposed favourably against the macabre image of the 'herbs and blossoms' that the young women have cultivated to place on their own coffins.

Later in the narrative, Jane's lover Edward Rochester stresses the toxicity of indoors in contrast to outdoors: 'you cannot discern that gilding is slime and the silk draperies cobwebs; that marble is sordid slate, and the polished woods mere refuse chips and scaly bark. Now *here* (he pointed to the leafy enclosure we had entered) all is real, sweet, and pure' (JE, 217). But this almost worship of nature puts Jane in a very dangerous position. When she flees Thornfield (society) and arrives at a crossroads in the moor, she describes her surroundings 'there are great moors behind and on each side of me; there are waves of mountains far beyond that deep valley at my feet' (JE, 322). The phrase 'at my feet' creates the impression that Jane believes she has nature at her command, and that she can control it as dictators are reputed to have commanded seas to roll back. She continues 'Not a tie holds me to human society at this moment' (JE, 322). In addition to being alone, she disavows all human relations: 'I have no relative but the universal mother, Nature: I will seek her breast and ask repose' (JE, 323). As Jane observes the surrounding wilderness, she enters into a fantasy that nature will provide for her physical needs: 'Nature seemed to me benign and good: I thought she loved me, outcast as I was; and I, who from man could anticipate only mistrust, rejection, insult, clung to her with filial fondness' (JE, 323).

I have already mentioned how critic Delia da Sousa Correa refers to Brontë's treatment of landscape as having been associated with the romantic poets that were widely read at the time (DDSC, 92). But presently, Jane learns that the bucolic paradise of Whitcross is as unremitting as the glittering artifice of Thornfield. As with society, nature owes her nothing. Though not impassive, nature is impersonal and Jane will be subject to starvation or exposure as much as anyone else. Indeed, at this juncture, Jane's view of nature runs parallel to that of the insouciant Harold Skimpole when he delivers admiring words to the pretty Ada Clare: 'She is a child of the universe' (BH, 122). A little later in the narrative, Esther's guardian, John Jarndyce, delivers a stern warning to Skimpole: 'The universe,' (Jarndyce) observed 'makes rather an indifferent parent' (BH, 122). Jane Eyre does eventually learn the lesson: that nature is benign only when man works in conjunction with it, rather than depending entirely upon it. Her journey to this knowledge is not unlike that with which Roman poet Virgil takes the reader through his poetry book, *Georgics*. In **Book 1,** he writes 'O universal lights', with regard to the stars, when eulogising nature. On her first night following her flight from Thornfield, Jane looks up at the sky and thinks: 'I, saw with tear-dimmed eyes, the mighty milky-way' (JE, 324). In **Book 2** of *Georgics*, the poet declares: 'Soothly on all must toil be spent', and he continues, explaining how man must cultivate the earth before he can hope to derive any benefit from it. His text is a development on *Genesis* in which Adam and Eve receive earth's bounty without enduring any of its toil. Before hunger overcomes her entirely, Jane begins the struggle back to the hamlet. While doing so, she has another vision of nature, a more pastoral and cultivated perception than earlier: 'All the valley at my right hand was full of pasture-fields and corn-fields and wood; and a glittering stream ran zig-zag through the varied shades of green, the mellowing grain, the sombre woodland, the clear and sunny lea' (JE, 325). Jane's perception of agricultural labourers at work has renewed her hopes of finding a place in this 'natural' society. In accordance with Virgil, she concludes: 'I must struggle on: strive to live and bend to toil like the rest' (JE, 325).

The female paradigm

Jay Griffiths equates women with nature and men with the forces of regulation and commerce. Not alone does Griffiths present these forces as opposite, she explains how they are in opposition, nature warm and vibrant and fertile, regulation and commerce, cold and sterile and threatening to stifle the forces of 'female' quality (JG, 238).

Today, we see this association of woman and nature in the constant barrage of advertisements that seek to equate the 'fair sex' with floral-print clothing and house furnishings, flower-scented toiletries and bathroom products. The joke is that men use these things too, but the masculine outfit (furniture, aftershave, etc) is perennially devoid of floral scent or ornament. A thorough exploration of why the *woman* came to be associated with nature is outside the scope of this text – although fertility does offer one explanation. The chapter, **Maid in the Mirror** lays out John Berger's argument, that the female creates her own subjective version of herself to present to other people. And she creates this version with visual and auditory contrivances, including her immediate surroundings. In fairy tales, the girl or young woman most likely to survive whatever predicament is she who is closest to nature. When Snow

White goes into her long sleep, the birds cover her with leaves. In certain versions of Cinderella, she is helped to the ball by a conglomeration of reptiles and rodents. The eighteenth-century heroine blossomed, quite literally, in natural surroundings. And Theodore falls in love with Adeline when sees her in the forest. Nineteenth-century literature twinned woman with nature in a darker and more profound way.

In Hans Andersen's narrative, *The Snow Queen*, when Gerda finds out that Kay is missing, her first appeal is to the natural world. She offers her shoes in sacrifice to the river to help find him. When the shoes float back to her, she gets into a boat – in an almost self-sacrificial way – and her travels into the world have begun. From there onwards, most of Gerda's encounters are with the plants and animals. When a witch – Gerda's first encounter with the demonic world – interrupts her search, a picture of a rose on the witch's hat jogs the memory of the former flower-filled innocent youth, and Gerda resumes her journey. Andersen shows nature, both in its 'natural' state and as a channel for magic, as benign. The exception is the snow, which acts as a vehicle for the enchantment and evil intent of the Snow Queen. And although the story is pre-Freudian, there is no escaping the allegory on innocence, growing up and maturity. Snow, in the story, acts as a metaphor for adolescent uncertainty and emotional obfuscation. When the flowers are in bloom, Kay and Gerda have no trouble rendezvous-ing across the rooftops of their homes. But when it snows, Kay is bound to take the trouble of descending through the building and climbing to the apartment where Gerda lives, so that the snow encumbers the relationship between the boy and girl.

Gerda's grandmother warns Kay about the snow: 'It is the white bees swarming', a strong suggestion of the role that snowy weather will play in the story. When she tells him of the Snow Queen, he expresses a wish to 'put her on the stove, and she'd melt', in other words, a childish desire to destroy the sexual danger that she represents. But following his infection with chips from the broken mirror into his eye (the channel of knowledge) and into his heart (the channel of feeling), Kay changes. He suddenly finds the natural world ugly, and scorns Gerda and her grandmother. When the winter comes round again, he finds snowflakes more interesting than real flowers, and when the terrifying, icy Snow Queen travels through the town, Kay no longer wishes to destroy her. Instead, he finds her glittering artifice so alluring that he absconds with her. In the sleigh, her wrapping her cloak about him has obvious adult connotations.

Gerda's journey to maturation is rather different. She waits until the snow has melted, that is, she has a more clear-eyed view of the world, to begin her search for Kay. The tossing of her red shoes on to the river may indicate the onset of biological maturation, while her delight in roses indicates that she is not yet ready to cast off her innocence. The stories that Gerda hears from the flowers in the witch's garden are all tales of women, young and old, in various stages of life. These stories indicate to Gerda that her own life is passing. When she leaves the garden, it is autumn and winter – the winter of her own adolescence. But not having been infected with the slivers of broken mirror, Gerda approaches the challenge with wisdom and judgement. She rejects a life of luxury in the Princess's palace, though she does accept the gift of a golden coach to facilitate her journey, an act that nearly costs her her life. But she continues to trust in nature, allowing the Raven, the pigeons and Bac the reindeer, to guide her towards the North Pole. When Gerda and Kay emerge from the Snow Queen's palace, the snow is gone and the world is in bloom. The boy and girl have now grown up and they return home. With the obfuscation of adolescence vanquished it is, in the words of Andersen 'summer, glorious summer!' Overall, it is the woman who is twinned with nature, the evil Snow Queen and good Gerda, while it is the male imp who creates and smashes the mirror that enchants the world.

And, as I have already pointed out, although Jane Austen takes pains to burlesque this woman-as-nature strand of the gothic sub-genre: '(Catherine) ... greatly preferred cricket not merely to dolls, but to ... watering a rose-bush.' Austen also tells us that Catherine greatly enjoyed rolling down the grass hill at the back of her parents' house (NA, 15). Unlike Gerda, Catherine is not enamoured of roses, but she revels in her own nature. In fact, this endeavour of Catherine is analogous to the mud-pelting games that Lyra Belacqua enjoys with her friends (HDM, 36). This childhood exuberance is in contrast to the natural paradise that the reader finds Lyra in, at the end of the narrative, in a garden somewhere in 'her' Oxford, with the nightingale singing, bells in the background ringing and her longing for her lover/friend (HDM, 1087). This twinning of woman with nature could be because, as explained in the chapter **Maid in the Mirror**, the woman is seen as untramelled emotion just as nature is often beyond control.

In his play, *As You Like It*, William Shakespeare makes use of this device of behaviour and association in his characterisation of Rosalind/Ganymede to deflect attention away from her true identity. When Jacques, attendant of the banished Duke Senior, meets his master following his wandering in the forest, he tells a rather strange tale, and describes a 'fool' that he has just met. Quoth Jacques: 'And then he drew a dial from his poke/And looking on it with lack-lustre eye,/Says very wisely 'It is ten o'clock;'/Thus we may see, quoth he, 'how the world wags;'/'Tis but an hour ago since it was nine;/And after one hour more 'twill be eleven'. (Act 2, Scene 7) Here, the reader can assume that the 'fool' that Jacques has encountered is actually Rosalind in her guise as Ganymede.

In assuming a male identity, Rosalind becomes 'Father Time' in contrast to 'Mother Nature'. It is she who takes on the notionally male role of buying land and of reminding characters constantly of the time: 'How say you now: It is not past two o'clock' (Act 4, Scene 3). Although in the late 1500s, the Industrial Revolution had yet to begin, Shakespeare was a native of Stratford-upon-Avon, a country boy who had come to London and was obliged to dwell there just to make a living. This was why he was well able to chart the different attitudes to time and the contrasting lifestyles between the fugitives in the forest of Arden, and the more regulated lives of the courtiers from the Duke's palace and other urban dwellers. But the play is not just a eulogy to nature; rather, it points out nature's shortcomings. Bred in the fashionable time-keeping world, a matter that Shakespeare would identify with, there is no hint that the courtiers are going to stay there; As Philip Hobsbaum puts it, 'once the self is discovered, they all troop back to town' (CWS, 276).

But the twinning of woman with nature leads to another phenomenon. In the chapter, **Maid in the Mirror**, I explain how in literature, a man rarely sees a woman outside of her context. William de Stancy conceives his passion for Paula when he sees her exercising in her gym: 'the clouds, till that time thick in the sky, broke away from the upper heaven, and allowed the noonday sun pour down through the lantern upon her' (AL, 197). Although this setting is naturalistic rather than natural – he sees Paula as her natural self – the reader may have not failed to notice how many males conceive their amour at the sight of a pretty face surrounded by flowers, grass and trees. Think of Theodore glimpsing Adeline in the forest, or the prince spying Snow White: no wonder Henry James's Governess hadn't a chance when her master interviewed her in his Harley Street office? And perhaps, awareness of his fatal penchant for young and pretty women in bucolic surroundings was the reason for his avoiding Bly, entirely?

Healing and perverted nature

'Insupportable – unnatural – out of the question' (*Jane Eyre*, 416)

The above words from *Jane Eyre* are those of Diana Rivers, her reaction to the news that her brother wishes to marry the eponymous protagonist of the novel, her cousin and adopted sister. But this is no reaction against the Victorian penchant for first cousins marrying first cousins. It is Diana's outrage against her brother wanting to take Jane as wife with him abroad, to qualify him to work as a missionary in India, a marriage that Jane knows (and Diana knows) will be devoid of the love, tenderness and physical intimacy that a union stemming from true love should be. In fact, St John River's violations of this natural course of things may put the reader in mind of the other male cousin, John Reed, who ravages nature from the narrative's beginning, destroying young chicks in their nests, and other atrocities. These instances are among the many in Brontë's narrative in which 'nature', whether human nature or the natural environment, are subverted for the personal and political motives of the less self-aware and downright perverted characters in the novel.

From its outset, Shakespeare's play *Macbeth* presents a troubled landscape, opening with a scene that the author describes as 'the heath: thunder' (Scene 3). From the beginning of the scene to the end, the words of the witches evoke the natural world: 'When shall we three meet again/In thunder, lightning, or in rain?' (Act 1, Scene 1). In the scene, the witches discuss how they have the power to actually manipulate the weather, and they boast of doing it so successfully, that they force a ship to endure a tempest that lasts for eighty one 'nine times nine' weary days (Act 1, Scene 3). Here, the supernatural element seeks to subvert nature.

In Ann Radcliffe's novel, it is the weak, ineffective and downright wicked characters who spout rhetoric *against* nature. In Chapter 12, when desperately trying to help the severely wounded Theodore, Adeline is appalled by the words of the inept surgeon who is supposedly treating his wounds: 'Nature, Madam!' pursued he, 'Nature is the most improper guide in the world. I always adopt a method directly contrary to what she would suggest; for what can be the use of Art, if she is only to follow Nature? This was my first opinion on setting out in life, and I have ever since strictly adhered to it' (ROTF, 185-6). Later on, when laying out his rationale for what proves to be the notional execution of Adeline, the Marquis de Montalt presents the reader with yet another, subverted vision: 'Nature, uncontaminated by false refinement,' 'resumed the Marquis, everywhere acts alike in the great occurrences of life' (ROTF, 222). Through his parody on what he calls 'Nature', the Marquis actually shows his contempt for the *other*, culturally speaking: 'the Turk, when ambition fires, or revenge provokes, gratifies his passion at the expence of life, and does not call it murder'. And the Marquis uses his perverted visions of nature and culture as the justification for wanting to rid himself of his unwanted niece.

This chilling disdain by the surgeon and subversion, indeed, almost perversion, by the Marquis, seem almost to presage the words of Mr Brocklehurst in Jane Eyre, when expressing his disgust at the female pupils of Lowood School at trying to wear their hair naturally: 'we are not here to conform to nature: I wish these girls to be the children of Grace: and why that abundance?' (JE, 64). Presently, nature, red in tooth and claw, bites back by visiting a typhoid epidemic upon the pupils of Lowood, which no railing against by Brocklehurst or any other character, can quell. And Brocklehurst's disdain is reflected by the behaviour of Jane's later nemesis, St John Rivers, when she says of him:'I think, moreover, that Nature was not to him that treasury of delight that it was to his sisters' (JE, 351). William de Stancy in *A Laodicean* shows a similar disdain of nature: 'The air was charged with a lurid exhalation that blurred the extensive view ... had something in it that was more than melancholy, and not much less tragic, but for de Stancy, such evening effects had little meaning. He was engaged in an enterprise that taxed all his resources and had no sentiments to spare for air, earth or skies' (AL, 350). De Stancy is, of course, plotting to ensnare Paula Power into marriage to secure his own material comfort.

From all of these varying views on nature, it is evident that nature in literature acts as an impersonal force, one that is only subverted by the attitudes and activities of mammon. In *Bleak House*, Esther says of Mr Turveydrop, on their first encounter: 'false complexion, false teeth, false whiskers, and a wig ... pinched in, and swelled out, and got up, and stepped down, as much as he could possibly bear ... he had everything but any touch of nature' (BH, 244). Esther goes on to describe the account of Turveydrop's 'absorbing selfishness', his condescension towards his son, and other instances of his personal indulgence and entitlement (BH, 245).

It was inevitable then that following the pastoralism of the eighteenth century, writers of the nineteenth century were going to use subverted nature itself as a metaphor of blighted lives and emotion. Here, the reader should remember that it was a serpent invading paradise, not paradise itself, that blighted the lives of Adam and Eve. Delia Da Sousa Correa likens Thornfield to a type of Eden from which Jane 'fell', presaged by the splitting of the chestnut tree (JE, 257). The implication is that Jane is beguiled by a false paradise from which a fall will be imminent (DDSC, 114). And, as in the Bible, the despoilation of the natural world is the result of human activity and misbehaviour. Charles Dickens writes in *Hard Times*: 'All closely imprisoned forces rend and destroy. The air that would be healthful to the earth, the water that would enrich it, the heat that would ripen it, tear it up when caged' (HT, 247).

The moon, that nearby satellite to Earth, which has so often been the backdrop for much romance in literature, is indicative of perversion in two, later nineteenth-century narratives. In R.L. Stevenson's *Dr Jekyll and Mr Hyde*, a maid servant gazing from her window is entranced by the sight of the moon (DJMH, 15). Within the same sight, she witnesses the murder of Danvers Carew. This uneasiness associated with the lunar body had already been touched upon by Thomas Hardy in his narrative, *A Laodicean*: 'Finding there was a moon shining, Paula (Power) leaned out of her window. The tall rock of Ehrenbreitstein on the opposite shore was flooded with light' (AL, 356). The remainder of the scene is indicative of the poisonous relationship with William de Stancy that Paula is about to forge.

In his article, *Knowledge and the Inadequacy of Eden: The Turn of the Screw*, Joseph Firebaugh likens the children's uncle to God, a deity who retreats to a worldly heaven where he pursues his own pleasures. He appoints the Governess as his 'priestess', presenting her with the task of looking after the children (Firebaugh, 59). In addition is the uncle's curious proviso as to why they live in the remote house: 'the proper place for them being of course the country' (TOTS, 120). Firebaugh asserts that this is because he perceives 'the country' as a type of Eden in which the children (and by implication, the Governess) may maintain a type of prelapsarian innocence. To the reader, this may seem a misjudgement on the part of the uncle; the 'pure' environment of Bly not only does not calm the restless mind of the Governess, she begins seeing the angelic Flora through a jaundiced lens: 'she'll say she isn't – she'll lie' (TOTS, 157). And so the narrative progresses towards its devastating end. Firebaugh claims that it does not matter whether the Governess was neurotic or merely experiencing visions, that her chief failing is her incompetence and her determination to prevent the children from gaining knowledge that *she* has not endorsed (Firebaugh, 58).

Firebaugh explains also, citing 'Professor (Robert) Heilman, that it is the arrival of the Governess that is the cause of the events, that she is the force that disturbs the erstwhile Eden that is Bly. Heilman claims that the Governess detects a sort of primal glory in Miles and Flora, and her uneasiness with their youthful innocence and intelligence in their 'natural' environment is at least as much to blame for the arrival of Peter Quint and Miss Jessel, as any intention to decieve on their, the children's, part (Firebaugh, 58). In the text, the author more than hints at this blight in the mind of the Governess in the scene by the lake where Flora wields 'a big ugly spray of withered fern' (TOTS, 210). From this point of view, it does not matter whether the ghosts are 'real' or whether Peter Quint is 'real' or merely a fabrication of housekeeper Mrs Grose, as discussed in the chapter, **Deceptions, the Doppelganger and the Dark Dis**; it is what the Governess believes and how she acts upon it, that drives the plot. Indeed, her abhorrence of the 'knowledge' that Firebaugh claims is good and liberating, is akin to the shock of Maxim de Winter, when he witnesses a certain attitude upon the face of his new wife, and he claims that she is in possession of the wrong set of knowledge (R, 226). Mrs de Winter has actually been in a fantasy that she is Rebecca, and that Rebecca's personality is taking over her, but she does not tell Maxim this.

The theme of blighted nature runs through Du Maurier's narrative in other ways. On first encountering Mrs Danvers the new Mrs de Winter perceives her as a skeleton with a white, skull-type face (R, 74). This use of 'dead' imagery reminds us that though Rebecca is no more, her former servant lingers about Manderley like the avenging heap of bones that she eventually proves to be. But despite this connection with the dead, a jarring sensuality surrounds Mrs Danvers. This is evident when she tries to tempt Mrs de Winter into stroking Rebecca's clothing: 'Put it against your face. It's soft, isn't it? You can feel it, can't you? The scent is still fresh, isn't it?' (R, 191). This action of Mrs Danvers evokes the serpent in paradise theme, once again. The imagery resonates more strongly when the reader remembers that Mrs de Winter has already described Rebecca's nightdress as 'apricot in colour' since apricot is a fruit as well as a colour (R, 187). It is as if Mrs Danvers is 'tempting' Mrs de Winter to taste forbidden fruit.

An expulsion from paradise

The tradition of the expulsion from paradise is one that refers to Genesis and to Milton's work. Almost from the beginning of the epic poem, Milton uses metaphors to indicate to the reader that Paradise, as described by him, has many sinister undercurrents, quite literally. In Book 4, Milton writes: 'Of porous Earth with kindly thirst up drawn,/Rose a fresh fountain, and with many a rill/

Watered the garden; thence united fell/Down the steep glade, and met the nether flood,/Which from his darksome passage now appears,/And now divided into four main streams,/Runs diverse, wand'ring many a famous realm' (PL, Book 4, 227-234). Here, with the rivers crossing and dividing into 'four main streams' Milton's paradise seems to parallel Northrop Frye's 'sinister cross', within a 'sinister circle', the sinister circle being analogous to the serpent swallowing its tail (symbol, ouroboros) in the animal world, which belongs to the demonic imagery of literary archetypes (Frye, 150). And indeed, a serpent does enter Milton's paradise. In *The Turn of the Screw*, the serpentine pond that encircles Bly has parallel connotations. Milton's prose continues: 'if Art could tell,/How from that sapphire fount the crisped rooks,/Rolling on orient pearl and sands of gold,/With mazy error under pendant shades/Ran nectar' (Book 4, 237-240). Milton may be using words like 'sapphire' metaphorically to refer to colour rather than the actual mineral. But his paralleling *rock* and *sand* with *pearl* and *gold* more than suggests that his Eden is not the naturalistic paradise that is superficially appears to be but rather, one that is tainted with the drive of acquisition.

And many protagonists of the gothic sub-genre discover that paradise comes with a price. Following the consummation of their marriage, Mrs de Winter and Maxim are expelled from the 'paradise' of Manderley. Catherine Moreland is expelled from the dubious Eden of General Tilney's hothouses, only to find her home in his son's more orthodox paradise. Esther Summerson – the name indicative of a pastoral environment – is presented with a number of paradises, from the garden at Bleak House, to Boythorn's lush garden and the formal gardens of Chesney Wold. She finds her home in the rather eerie parallel paradise, created for her and Allan Woodcourt by John Jarndyce. Jane Eyre flees the paradise of Thornfield for a natural wilderness in which she almost loses her life. She finds a kind of paradise for a while, among cousins, but this too proves to harbour a serpent, in the form of St John Rivers, and she leaves it. Finally, she finds her home in leafy Ferndean. In Shirley Jackson's text, Eleanor Vance succumbs to disaster by refusing to leave the paradise that is poisoning her.

In certain texts, persons or violated places are restored to paradise. The biblical imagery in Stevenson's book is indicative of a poisoned paradise, the battle between good and evil. Early in the text, Stevenson describes Mr Hyde's reaction to lawyer Utterson's approaching him: 'Mr Hyde shrank back with a hissing intake of the breath' (Stevenson, 11). This sound is evocative of a serpent, and the reader of Stevenson's time would construe this word as a reference to the Bible, suggesting that Mr Hyde might be evil. The author stresses the theme of evil later on, when he writes of how Hyde moves 'with extraordinary quickness' (Stevenson, 11). This quickness of motion evokes the movement of a serpent, which is a continuation of the earlier notion. This serpentine imagery in the text links with other areas of the narrative that suggests the invasion of evil into good. When Utterson and the servant Poole find Edward Hyde dead in Jekyll's laboratory, they find a letter from Jekyll – addressing him as 'Gabriel John Utterson'. The name 'Gabriel' is evocative of the archangel of the Bible, a reference to the metaphorical paradise that the serpent has invaded. This theme of paradise is further strengthened by the view that Poole and Utterson see in the cheval mirror, which is angled so that it reflects 'the rosy glow' playing on the roof. This upward view suggests that with Hyde dead, evil has left the environment and 'heaven' or paradise, has been restored.

By the twentieth century, many writers had begun incorporating growing eco-awareness and other realist elements into their novels, to create a darker strand of literature. Ira Levin published *The Stepford Wives* in 1972, a narrative concerning a young wife and mother, Joanna Eberhart, who moves with her family to live in the small town of Stepford because her husband has been offered a good job. At first, everything seems idyllic; Joanna rapidly makes friends, her children settle down at school and her husband seems to love his new position. But slowly, Joanna – who is a semi-professional photographer – begins to feel uneasy, chiefly because of the apparent perfection of the other wives in the town, their flawless grooming, their obsession with housework and their utter devotion to the needs of their spouses and children. Furthermore, female friends who had been normally *im*perfect and had interests outside of the domestic sphere transform, one by one, overnight into one of these obsessed creatures. Joanna's 'normal' friend, Bobbie Markowe, puts the phenomenon down to a poisoned environment: in the tale, Stepford is the location of much heavy industry – and Bobbie will only drink bottled water. Eventually, Joanna's crystal-clear photographer's vision springs into action, and she soon realises that Bobbie's fears about the natural environment were unfounded. But Bobbie was right to be concerned: danger is stemming not from the landscape but from a male population with a warped view of womanhood.

The landscape as metaphor: pathetic fallacy, turbulence and calm

The ending of Philip Pullman's text sees Lyra returned to her sylvan environment, 'a nightingale was singing' (HDM, 1087-1088). Throughout the text, Lyra has arrived at and shrugged off many paradises – her mother's ritzy London apartment, the fecund land where she and Will are reunited. To heighten the biblical imagery, she even spends three days underground . But she renounces all of this to make her home in the place where she began her story. At Jordan College, she is going to 'cultivate' herself as a scholar, and the above description acts as a metaphor of this.

In literature, pathetic fallacy is a subjective mode of describing the natural world, usually as an externalisation of feelings or situations. In its ponderous opening, a paragraph of *Bleak House* runs thus: 'The raw afternoon is rawest, and the dense fog is densest, and the muddy streets are muddiest, near that leaden-headed old obstruction, appropriate ornament for the threshold of a leaden-headed old corporation: Temple Bar. And hard by Temple Bar is Lincoln's Inn Hall, at the very heart of the fog, sits the Lord High Chancellor in his High Court of Chancery (BH, 50). Adjectives such as 'densest', 'muddiest' and 'leaden-headed' are metaphorical of the obfuscation and the bewilderment of many characters in the text. Most obviously, this blighted natural environment is the appropriate setting for the High Court of Chancery. This corporation, in turn, blights everyone and everything that it touches. *Bleak House* is filled with allusions to circularity, so many that the reader wonders eventually: who or what is blighting whom?

Dickens uses this device when, just before she falls prey to smallpox, Esther Summerson takes note of a particular type of sky: 'In the north and north-west, where the sun had set three hours before, there was a pale dead light both beautiful and awful; and into it long *sullen* lines of cloud waved up, like a sea *stricken* immovable as it was heaving. Towards London, a lurid glare overhung the whole *dark waste*; and the contrast between these two lights, and the fancy which the redder light engendered of unearthly fire, gleaming on all the unseen buildings of the city, and on all the faces of its many thousands of wondering inhabitants, was as *solemn* as might be. I had no thought, that night – none, I am quite sure – of what was soon to happen to me' (BH, 484). The words I have italicised expresses the author's foreshadowing of Esther's ordeal.

In *Great Expectations*, Dickens's use of prose, just following Pip's first encounter with the convict, seems to parallel Esther's externalisation: 'The marshes were just a long, black, horizontal line then, as I stopped to look after him; and the river was just another horizontal line, not nearly so broad nor yet so black; and the sky was just a row of long, angry, red lines and dense black lines intermixed' (GE, 7). The use of red contrasted with black (colours of danger) does indeed prove a portent of events to come. Throughout the narrative, Dickens's descriptions of nature are used to intensify the negative experiences of the protagonist. On arrival at Satis House, Pip discovers that its owner, Miss Havisham, has had all of the clocks inside stopped. In fact, she has called a halt to all industry in the house, site of a former brewery, at the time of the day she discovered her lover had jilted her. This subversion of a natural progression of events is expressed in the mutated vegetation that grows in the 'rank garden' surrounding Satis House: 'It was quite a wilderness, and there were old melon-frames and cucumber-frames in it, which seemed in their decline to have produced a spontaneous growth of weak attempts at pieces of old hats and boots, with now and then a weedy offshoot into the likeness of a battered saucepan' (GE, 76).

When feeling down about Estella's disdainful treatment of him, Pip muses as he wanders about: 'It opened to the ground and looked into the most miserable corner of the neglected garden, upon a rank ruin of cabbage stalks, and one box-tree that had been clipped round long ago, like a pudding, and had a new growth at the top of it, out of shape and of a different colour, as if that part of the pudding had stuck to the saucepan and got burnt. This was my homely thought, as I contemplated the box-tree. There had been some light snow, overnight, and it lay nowhere else to my knowledge; but it had not quite melted from the cold shadow of this bit of garden, and wind caught it up in little eddies and threw it at the window, as if it pelted me for coming there' (GE, 68). Here, Pip's language suggests that he sees the garden of Satis House as a rather nasty kitchen. He talks about cabbage stalks, that is, cabbages run to seed, as distinct from lush and green and edible vegetables. In the same way, he likens the box-tree to a pudding that 'had stuck to the saucepan and got burnt'. The effect upon the reader is such as to evoke the smell of burnt food, a horrible smell for anyone. But this reference to burning and by implication, fire, evokes no warmth. In addition, the references to the wind that had blown the snow evokes Pip's miserable home life. The snow gives him the same, unwanted feeling that his sister gives him. All in all, it is a chill and uncomfortable experience for him and the reader. Later in the narrative, Pip rejects the world of nature, and moves into the world of business, letters and legalities. Throughout, he is never slow to equate his passion for the lovely and cold-hearted Estella with subverted nature, her presence whenever he walks with her making him feel as if, as Dickens puts it, 'the green and yellow growth of weed in the chinks of the old wall had been the most precious flowers that ever blew' (GE, 203).

In a few instances, Pip does experience the healing power of nature, one of these being when Biddy and he go for a walk: 'When we came to the river-side and sat down on the bank, with the water rippling at our feet, making it all more quiet than it would have been without that sound, I resolved that it was a good time and place for the admission of Biddy into my inner confidence' (GE, 107).

But presently, Pip's inner agitation reveals itself by his violation of nature by plucking strands of grass that grew where he was seated and tossing them into the river (GE, 108). In Chapter 57, on his recovery from his illness, Pip goes on a drive with Joe: 'I looked on the loveliness around me, and thought how it had grown and changed ... while poor I lay burning and tossing on my bed' (GE, 397). Here, two of the malign forces have gone from Pip's life, that is, the warping of Pip's life represented by Miss Havisham and Abel Magwitch. I do stress, however, that neither character is evil in himself or herself; it is the damage that Pip suffers in his life that is evil. And nature only manifests as good and beautiful when both characters are deceased.

The 'loveliness' that Pip experiences is a projection of Joe's benevolent nature. Later in the narrative, Pip senses the same peace and beauty when Joe and Biddy experience that happiest of days, their wedding day: 'The sky was blue, the larks were soaring high over the green corn' (GE, 405). It is the author's way of indicating to the reader that something wonderful is in the offing – but not, alas, to Pip. Later in the narrative, the emotionally bruised and battered Pip does recover in the same, rural environment, but it is by gentle treatment from Joe, his foster father, as much as by contemplating pretty scenery.

Overall, Pip does not enter into eulogies about nature; he is ever aware of the dangers to the unwary: 'And then I looked up at the stars and considered how awful it would be for a man to turn his face up to them as he froze to death and see no help or pity in all the glittering multitude' (GE, 42). This awareness of the harshness and physical hardness of nature is in contrast to Jane Eyre's metaphysical and religious framing of cosmic forces: 'Looking up, I, with tear-dimmed eyes, saw the might milky-way. Remembering what it was – what countless systems swept there like a soft trace of light – I felt the might and strength of God' (JE, 324). Jane is apparently unaware of what Pip already knows, the harshness and impersonality of nature, a truth she soon learns. Indeed, Pip's indifference to nature parallels that of Phil Squod in *Bleak House*, when Phil tries to describe incidences from his earlier life to George Rouncewell. Phil knows that he has lived in the country but is not sure where. He knows he has been in the country because the large growth of grass and the swans that he remembers. When George asks Phil what the swans had been doing, Phil laconically replies (concerning the grass): 'They was a-eating of it, I expect' (BH, 420).

Another way of expressing inner turmoil is through the event of the *storm*. The storm is a disruption of nature that punctuates the fictional narrative, not least the gothic sub-genre. In the majority of texts, tension is built up gradually in the manner described in **The Lexicon of Haunting**. One purpose of the event of a storm is to build in a frisson of Dionysian variation to punctuate Apollonian harmony. Writers have often used storms and other weather events as a backdrop as a type of pathetic fallacy, whenever the heroine or hero is undergoing intense emotion.

Dickens orchestrates this theme to perfection in *Bleak House*, when Eleanor first speaks with Lady Dedlock. This event takes place when Esther and her companions are besieged by a thunderstorm as they walk in the woods and take shelter in a keeper's lodge. Unknown to them, Lady Dedlock is also sheltering in the darkened place, and presently, the parties speak. But before then, they witness the storm, furious and analogous to the emotions that Esther eventually undergoes: 'The lattice windows were all thrown open, and we sat, just within the doorway, watching the storm. It was grand to see how the wind awoke, and bent the trees, and drove the rain before it like a cloud of smoke, and to hear the solemn thunder, and to see the lightening; and while thinking with awe of the tremendous powers by which our little lives are encompassed, to consider how beneficent they are, and how upon the smallest flower and leaf there was already a freshness poured from all this seeming rage, which seemed to make creation new again' (BH, 308-309). Later in the narrative, Lady Dedlock knowing that her secret, that she once had a child out of wedlock, is about to be exposed, she flees her husband's house, and all of society. The detective, Inspector Bucket, goes in search of her and aware that protagonist Esther Summerson is Lady Dedlock's secret child, he takes her – Esther – on a journey to find her mother: 'The sleet fell all that day unceasingly, a thick mist came on early, and it never rose or lightened for a moment. Such roads I had never seen. I sometimes feared we had missed the way and got into the ploughed grounds and the marshes' (BH, 838). Esther survives the storm; her mother does not.

The storm in which Jane Eyre almost dies plays a similar role to the snowstorm in externalising Esther's inner turmoil. The *ignis fatuus* that Jane imagines she sees on the marsh is, in reality, the by-product of organic decomposition and her interest in it signifies that she is prepared to die. She will mingle with nature as a dead organism, not a living force. With this acceptance of reality, her fortunes change and she survives the storm. Sandra Gilbert and Susan Gubar draw parallels between Milton's frozen hell and all of the romantic narratives that feature snow and ice, including *Frankenstein*: 'It recalls too the 'deep snow and ice' of Milton's hell' (G&G, 262). It is quite likely that much nineteenth-century writing involving ice and storms stemmed from metamorphising inclement weather as a challenging or transitory period in the protagonist's life, one that they do not always survive. Lady Dedlock in the snow, Gerda battling through the Arctic landscape in order to rescue Kay, not to mention the wintry setting of *A Christmas Carol*, following which the protagonist discovers his better personality. This vein continued into twentieth century nomenclature, that is, Maxim de Winter and even, the snowy wastes of *His Dark Materials*.

In her 'Introduction' to *A Laodicean*, Barbara Hardy writes of the summer storm 'as co-relative of strong feeling' during which George and Paula admit to there being more than friendship between them (AL, 26). In *The Woman in Black*, author Susan Hill subverts this theme and uses the nature good/nature bad dichotomy in more complex and ambivalent ways. In the opening chapter, Arthur Kipps is celebrating Christmas with his second wife and her grown-up children. The jollity of the occasion darkens when they begin to tell ghost stories. This activity unsettles Arthur, obliging him seek refuge out of doors. Outside, Arthur keeps walking until he reaches 'the scrubland beyond the orchard' (Hill, 18). Here, removed from all man-made organisation and cultivation, even that of the orchard, Arthur reflects on his past life and achieves a kind of solace. Later, Arthur shows the darker side of nature in his narrative, when he recounts the episode from his visit to Eel Marsh house where the little dog Spider almost loses her life in the quicksand. Thanks to Arthur's bravery, she does not. Here, Hill's narrative emphasises that nature is an unstoppable force, which no man-made situations or legalities can hold back. When Arthur first encounters the woman in black, he receives an impression from the natural world: 'I saw a blackbird on the hollybush a few feet away' (Hill, 59). The blackbird opens his mouth and sings what Arthur describes as 'a sparkling fountain of song'. This benign image, in conjunction with the word 'hollybush' evokes the opening chapter, *Christmas Eve*, and memories of the family Christmas he has earlier described. Earlier in the church, Arthur had seen a woman: 'pathetically wasted, so pale and gaunt with disease, that it would not have been a kindness to gaze upon her' (Hill, 58). Seeing the woman is, of course, Arthur's first encounter with the supernatural. And his enthusing about the pretty scene in the graveyard is in direct juxtaposition to the profound and horrible effect that meeting the woman will have upon his person and his life. Nature is now in collusion with the supernatural, or un-natural world, against Arthur.

In *Rebecca*, nature is omnipresent, not just as an extension of Manderley, but as a vehicle for the narrative. It is nature – both the betrayal by her own body and the enfolding sea – that destroys the character Rebecca. And nature, in the form of a storm, delivers her back to humanity again. The gruff Maxim is obsessed by flowers, having had them grown specially for the house (R, 33). The reader cannot but wonder if his sojourn on the Mediterranean coast isn't because it echoes that sea that surrounds his home turf? And it is nature, both fire and rampant vegetation, that eventually destroys Manderley.

Chiaroscuro

One quality that writers often add to their narratives is *chiaroscuro*, that is, the contrast of light and dark. In certain cases, juxtaposing opposite conditions can add irony to a narrative. On the night of Catherine Morland's arrival at Northanger Abbey, a storm breaks out: 'The storm still raged, and various were the noises, more terrific even than the wind, which struck at intervals on her startled ear. The very curtains of her bed seemed at one moment in motion, and at another the lock of her door was agitated, as if by the attempt of somebody to enter. Hollow murmurs seemed to creep along the gallery and more than once her blood was chilled by the sound of distant moans' (NA, 162). In the context of the narrative, Jane Austen's account is funny, not because it is funny to see a young woman frightened, but because the storm – and Catherine's agitation – serves no purpose in the narrative, except to highlight what is *not* taking place. Unlike the typical gothic heroine, Catherine is not an agitated soul; her life is not in peril, and she is not in moral danger. Indeed, her only reason for agitation is the unfamiliarity, familiar to all readers, at having to spend the first night in a new environment.

The majority of gothic novels include dichotomies of light and shade, either condition highlighting what the other condition is not. Greek mythology is filled with this *chiaroscuro* or dark/light pairings. Hecate is the darker twin of Artemis. She is the goddess of magic and night-time while sturdy Artemis goes hunting by day. The world was plunged into winter when Demeter lost her daughter Persephone to Pluto, king of the shades or Underworld. Through a number of clever manoeuvres, Demeter won Persephone back but only for six months of the year, which is why – according to myth - we have bright, hot summer and cold, dark winter.

Esther Summerson's earlier life is all shadow. Never having known who her natural parents are, a foster mother brings her up. All Miss Barbary will tell her is that: 'Your mother, Esther, is your disgrace and you were hers'(BH, 65). This pronouncement leaves the reader in no doubt as to Esther's social status. She grows into womanhood, docile and servile, occupying herself with needlework and housework. In Esther's own words 'to do some good to someone and win some love if I could' (BH, 73). In Hablot Knight Browne's original illustrations, Esther is dark and Ada is blonde – the word 'Clare' meaning light. Like Esther, Ada is orphaned and sunny-natured, but she is in possession of a financial 'independence' left to her by her mother. She beams with the self-confidence of someone who expects to do well in life. However, almost from the start of the story, the positions of the two women begin to subtly and perceptibly change. Though not proactive heroines in the modern sense, but enmeshed in the mores that surround them, the women make active use of the choices that they do have. Ada falls in love with wastrel cousin, Richard Carstone. All her efforts to disengage him from interest in the lawsuit that has ruined most of their relatives are in vain. Richard spends all of Ada's money. He sinks into ill-health and dies, leaving a penniless Ada to bring up their child. Esther, meanwhile, conducts herself with intelligence and single-mindedness through every situation. She waives aside the greed and petty-mindedness of other characters and fends off one very pernicious proposal of marriage. Even her near-fatal bout of smallpox fails to quell her spirit. When circumstance brings her face to face with her natural mother, she behaves with courage, love and compassion. Though she loses her mother again, Esther's prize is the love of and hand in marriage to young doctor, Allan Woodcourt. The novel closes with the pair surrounded by their children.

Meanwhile, Ada is left in the same position as Esther was at the opening of the book, dependent on the (considerable) good will of those around her. This reversal of fortunes is perhaps the most complete and plausible metamorphosis in all of literature. In the hands of a lesser author, *Bleak House* could have been a crude 'good girl rewarded, bad girl punished' fairytale. But Dickens's writing is too subtle for that. Throughout, Dickens uses *chiaroscuro* to foreshadow events in the story: 'So young, so beautiful, so full of hope and promise, (Richard and Ada) went on lightly through the sunlight, as their own happy thoughts might then be traversing the years to come and making them all years of brightness. So they passed away into the shadow, and were gone' (BH, 233).

In literature, the workings of nature provide a kind of *chiaroscuro*, for example, intervals of storm interspersed with vistas of natural beauty. J. Hillis-Miller states that the 'meaning' of the novel lies in the irresolution of Esther's happy ending and the mud and fog soaked opening of the narrative (BH, 33). Indeed, 'the muddy streets are muddiest' is much in contrast to Esther's response to the beauty that she encounters on arrival in Lincolnshire: 'O, the solemn woods over which the light and shadow travelled swiftly, as if Heavenly wings were sweeping on benignant errands through the summer air; the smooth green slopes, the glittering water, the garden where the flowers were so symmetrically arranged in clusters of richest colours, how beautiful they looked' (BH, 300). On the morning following her arrival at Bleak House, Esther looks out of the window to see her candles: 'reflected in the black panes like two beacons, and, finding all beyond still enshrouded in the indistinctness of last night, to watch out how it turned out when the day came on' (BH, 142). This subtle metaphor, a pointer towards Esther gradual discovery of the truth about her own life, is balanced by the author's imagery of later on, when a dangerously-ill Esther is plunged back into darkness, actual this time: 'Dare I hint at a worse time when, strung together somewhere in great black space, there was a flaming necklace, or ring, or starry circle of some kind, of which I was one of the beads' (BH, 544).

In *Great Expectations,* Dickens uses darkness and light as metaphors of the conditions that Pip tries to leave behind. Pip lives in the shadow of gloomy Satis House, home of the mysterious Miss Havisham and even when he 'escapes' to London to be educated and to pursue the lovely Estella (whose name means 'star') Pip finds shadows in every corner: 'A new fear had been engendered in my mind by (Magwich) his narrative; or rather, his narrative had given form and purpose of the fear that was already there' (GE, 299). The constant instances of fire in the novel, two fires at Joe Gargery's house, the kitchen and in the forge, the fire that Miss Havisham sits at and the fire that the patrons of the Jolly Bargemen are seated around, the fire in Bernards Inn and at the Temple, the fires in Little Britain and in Wemmick's house, and the fire of Orlick that almost destroys Pip, render the text of the narrative almost like an ember, by turns glowing hotly in shades of orange and red, and cooling in greys.

In *Rebecca*, the idea of 'light good and dark evil' is reversed; it is good-girl Mrs de Winter who spends her life in the shade, deferring to her betters – in the context of the narrative – eating cold food and wearing old clothes. Meanwhile, it is the deceased Rebecca who continues to stand in the light. Early in the narrative, Mrs de Winter describes feeling obliged to hide her worn and patched underwear from her assigned personal maid, Alice, who had known Rebecca. It is to Mrs de Winter's relief when Clarise, who had never been a lady's maid before and is unlikely to judge her, replaces Alice (R, 152).

This almost-cliche is repeated by Shirley Jackson. In *The Haunting of Hill House,* the glamorous, non-conforming Theodora stands in contrast to the 'drab, timid' Eleanor, a metaphor of the social success of the former subject and the ossified-debutante mentality of the latter (HH, 147).

Conclusion

In conclusion, I point out once more that the landscape began to play a prominent role in literature, just as it became a significant genre in visual art. It has progressed from the Picturesque, through to an outer expression of inner turmoil, a passive force to being a poisoned entity in its own right. But where will literature turn next?

Gothic Literature: The Future

A very popular novel of the past generation has been, since its publication in 1993, *The Secret History* by US author, Donna Tartt. This late twentieth-century narrative is written in first person, and its protagonist is Richard Papen, a youth in a disaffected family (*family troubles*) who desires to escape his parents' fate of running a gas station, discount shopping and attending product parties. In pursuit of an academic career, Richard leaves the dusty Californian hinterland where he has grown up and travels to Hampden College (*the journey*) in lush Vermont. The college building (*allegorical castle*) proves to be a sprawl of dormitories, libraries, lecture halls and the dominating Commons. Accustomed to homogeneity, Richard responds with enthusiasm to the variety of eccentrics, both students and academics, that he encounters.[56] In addition, he falls under the spell of his physical environment (*healing in nature*), the trees laden with ripe apples, redolent of the changing seasons that is a welcome foil to his parents' arid, motorway-defined environment (SH, 13).

Richard bears the same awareness of the insignificance of his person and life as many gothic heroes and heroines have done, being quiet and freckled and bookish and longing to break out of the school and home again routine that he had grown up in (SH, 6). It is all present and correct: Adeline's angst at her lack of family background, Jane Eyre's longing for freedom,

---

[56]Donna Tartt, *The Secret History* (London: Penguin Books, 1992), p18. Subsequent references will be to this edition and will be inserted parenthetically into the text, for example '(SH, 18)'.

Pip wishing to escape his humble home for a grander life, and Eleanor Vance's trepidation on arriving at Hill House. And like Eleanor, Richard finds himself with a group of people more socially advanced than he is. But unlike Eleanor, it is Richard who survives both physically and psychically in the longer term. He is to learn that social ease and wealth do not guarantee a life free from personal troubles, the *bildungsroman* element of the narrative. In his early state, Richard envies (in the manner of Caddy Jellyby) the orphaned twin brother and sister, Charles and Camilla (SH, 19). Incidentally, the twin pair is a *doppelganger* element of the narrative, the other being the likeness between Henry and Bunny, wearing similar spectacles, and, as Richard soon discovers, a very superficial connection between two very different young men (SH, 18).

The glasses are as metaphorical as they are actual; Bunny desperately tries to ape Henry, in both his person and his lifestyle, a situation that has tragic consequences for both of them, in fact, for all the characters. With his damaged early life and obscure motives, the Byronic role is assigned to Henry Marchbanks Winter. Tutor Julian Morrow is undoubtedly the alchemist of the narrative, the author taking pains to render him arcane: 'the gatekeeper in a fairy story' his suite of rooms apart from the wider college and his selection of students exclusive to the point of discriminatory (SH, 28). Julian is the academic who brings the student group together and behaves as the unwitting catalyst of subsequent events. And it is he who fields the printed item (*the document*) that reveals the truth of the situation, his only error being Richard's unfortunate implication. But the reader must wonder: did Richard really have no inkling of what was going on; the increasing tension between Bunny and the others; the snatches of overheard conversations; the series of seeming coincidences that provided clues to the truth? In summary, did Richard really not know that he was being used or was he so desperate to maintain his friendship with this group of elites that he adjusted his radar so that his association with them would not be a source of agitation? (*the deception*) Or maybe Richard really was just curious, in which case his adolescence is even more closely aligned with that of the inquisitive young woman of the early gothic writers' imagination, for example, Adeline or Catherine Moreland. Indeed, so disingenuous is Richard that the reader may wonder if the author hasn't assigned Henry with the surname 'Winter' in a nod to Maxim de Winter, who just as readily pulls the naive young bride into his foul conspiracy? The supernatural, when it is introduced, is subtle rather than *outre*. Henry claims that he had seen Dionysus at the bacchanal, Camilla imagining that she had been transformed into a deer, and the remaining party imagining that they had chased a deer through the forest. And the question remains: who in the narrative takes on the role of Dis? The narrative is peppered with a myriad college drop-outs, substance abusers and those not-quite-recovered from mental illness, the majority of which could qualify. But following an extensive consideration, I have decided to cast Richard in the role of Dis.

This protagonist hails from the darker recesses of the Sunshine State, with a parent whose occupation is pumping the dark, oily stuff that originates in the bowels of the earth, requisitioning it for the use of mankind and his motor vehicles. From there, Richard ascends to a rarefied college in verdant surroundings, and seeks to gain mastery in the exclusive discipline of the Classics. In this endeavour, he encounters Julian Morrow. This academic appears almost as a figure out of a tale of enchantment as Richard, even at the end of the narrative, when he, Richard, has been grossly misrepresented to Julian, longs to reconcile with the person whom he perceived to have the power 'to make all my dreams come true' (SH, 604). I have already described Julian as the *alchemist* of the narrative. Richard bears witness to his – perceptibly, at least – elite companions in their exalted academic endeavours and, by contrast, sees their darker moods and learns of their nefarious deed, the *chiaroscuro* of the text. He eventually emerges from the mix of celestial light and smoky gloom, an academic prize in tow and anticipating the possibility of a better life. But he is a sadder and wiser person, not indeed unlike many a gothic hero or heroine before him. Assuming more than one role, in Richard's case, the ingenue and the Dis is a tenet of the contemporary gothic narrative. In the earliest narratives, such roles – ingenue, romantic/Byronic hero, alchemist, authoritarian figure, Dis – were almost always assumed by individual characters. Overall, *The Secret History* is a gothic tale for the modern era, devoid of fantasy or moralising. And Richard is a viable gothic protagonist, proof that the literary sub-genre is alive and well, two and a half centuries following its instigation.

Many centuries more have gone by since poets and bards sang only of warriors, kings and deities. But today, narratives are centred around characters that readers can identify with. Richard is a mixture of identifiable character strands: sensitive, intelligent, anxious to please, ambitious, proactive personally yet bearing a definite helplessness when faced with a situation that he cannot deal with. At times, Richard seems almost catatonic, rationalising his situation, yet unable to act rationally. Here, I stop short of moralising and ask: at what point will the reader lose sympathy with very human characters such as Richard, both in the context of whatever narrative and in the progression of literature itself? Because it is a universal law that when an art form is at its highest, that its popularity begins to fall, and the reader cannot assume that this state will continue. In the **Introduction**, I charted

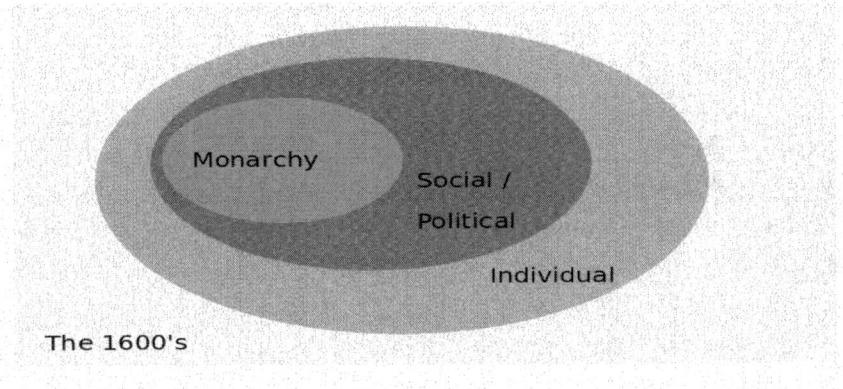

the seismic changes in publishing, just when the original gothic writers were at their zenith.

The first diagram demonstrates the type of society outlined in the **Introduction**. In what the reader could loosely consider the old world,

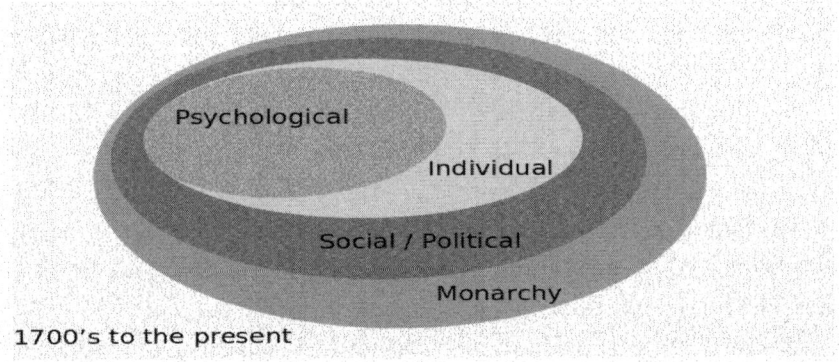

the monarch sat at the centre of the system, the nexus about which the wider society rotated, while the individual hovered uncertainly about the edges.

In the following two and a half centuries, this pattern has flipped so that the individual and his psychology sit at the centre, while the increasingly insignificant monarchy is but a decorative fringe at its edges. And society continues to evolve. The days when the confined, post-Enlightenment young person sought to fulfil his or her vision of domestic happiness by escaping *physical* peril have been replaced by narratives in which the same individuals seek to escape the mores that claim their psychology and neurology. Where are we headed next?

In the modern world, we have become used to parallel actions and situations. We have access to technology that allows us to capture exact images on a hitherto unimagined scale. The reader would imagine that the doppelganger world would have lost its magic, but there we are, creating virtual worlds with film and computer technology. Richard Papen may have fallen foul of 'a morbid longing for the picturesque' but the Richards of the future will be engaged in a battle for the psyche (SH, 5).

The modern reader is seeing a shift in publishing that parallels the Industrial Revolution, that is, the advent of electronic publishing. It would be ludicrous to imagine that this evolving technology is not going to effect a shift in literature, a shift that is more profound than that of merely changing fashion: it is one of a shift in the perceived importance of certain groups in the universe. This shift is taking place just as the world is transitioning from one in which the individual shares in the ideas and the benefits of the nation state to one defined by economic status and boundaries in which individuals are either appreciated or negated according to a raft of qualities that may include personal wealth, social connection and that mysterious quality known as 'talent'. And that shift may have started already.

Neuromancer by William Gibson, published in 1984, is described as 'one of the earliest and best-known works in the cyberpunk genre'.[57]

The plot involves Henry Case, whose central nervous system is crippled by his employer as punishment for stealing. The employer eventually restores Case's nervous system but with the threat of crippling it again unless Case completes a computer hacking mission. The adventures that follow, a

---

[57]https://en.wikipedia.org/wiki/Neuromancer

combination of Cold War conspiracy and space odyssey, drives the remaining plot, one that won Gibson three major literary awards. But what I find awesome and terrifying is the notion of an *employer* with the power to neurologically cripple an erring employee.

Certainly, Gibson's narrative is a dystopian fantasy, born of Cold War paranoia and the economic and political power that corporations had amassed by the late twentieth century. But bear in mind that Walpole's narrative was also a fantasy, albeit one set in a projected past rather than an imagined future. And ever since, much literary fantasy has paralleled the 'real' world. As I write this, forty years have elapsed since the publication

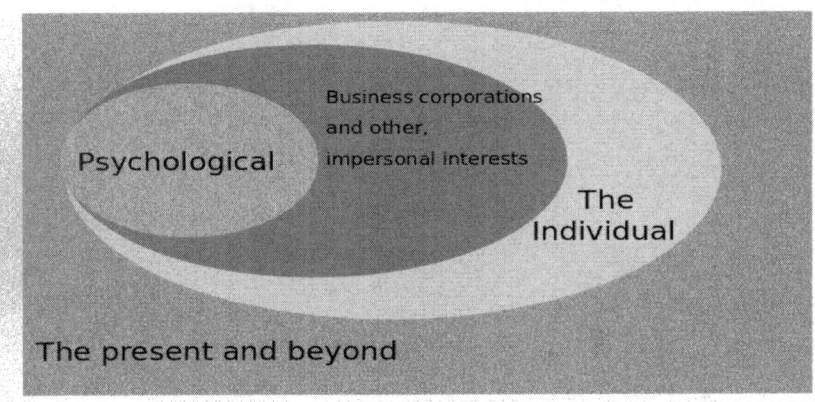

of Gibson's book. Ever since, debates have raged over the nature of freedom, political, personal and economic. In tandem, a technology has emerged so intrusive and influential and so reaching into our everyday lives that Gibson's vision seems all but to have taken place.

The future of society (and publishing) might look like the diagram above, with the individual riven from his own psychology, which has been corralled for use by big business and other, impersonal interests. Today, so many conspiracy theories abound, from the barely believable abductions to plausible phone tapping and internet interception, that it is not difficult to conjure a body of literature in which outside and impersonal interests harvest the psychology of the individual for political and commercial interests. More recently published titles include *Followers* by Megan Angelo, about a world where social media has taken over normal human interaction. Another title is *Sanctuary*, by Abby Sher, about a brother and sister trying to escape a world where citizens are chipped and tracked in everything they do. In tandem with fiction, this fear by the individual of alienation from his own psyche has given rise to a crop of so-called self-help manuals, embracing everything from ancient esoteric practices, such as prayer and meditation, to modern developments such as psychology and cognitive exercises.

What is interesting is that the eschewing of the family and partisan politics in favour of individual survival, which has lain at the heart of literature since Walpole penned *The Castle of Otranto*, has not, in the realm of literature at least, endowed the individual with profound and perceptible freedoms. The new debate then, is whether this psychologically-alienated individual seeks survival outside the strictures of society, as with the Byronic hero, or continues the fight to enter it, as with the gothic heroine. This debate looks set to go on.

BIBLIOGRAPHY

Primary Texts

Andersen, Hans Christian, The Snow Queen, http://www.online-literature.com/hans_christian_andersen/972/"

Austen, Jane, *Northanger Abbey*, ed. Marilyn Butler (London: Penguin Classics, 1818)

Brontë, Charlotte, *Jane Eyre*, ed. Margaret Smith (Oxford: Oxford University Press, 1980)

Dickens, Charles, *Bleak House*, ed. Norman Page (London: Penguin Classics, 1971)

Dickens, Charles, *Great Expectations*, ed. John Bowen (London: Wordsworth Editions, 1992)

Dickens, Charles, *Hard Times*, ed. David Craig (London: The Penguin English Library, 1969)

Du Maurier, Daphne, *Rebecca* (London: Virago Press, 2003)

Hardy, Thomas, *A Laodicean*, ed. Barbara Hardy (London, Macmillan London Ltd, 1979)

Hill, Susan, *The Woman in Black* (London: Profile Books, 1983)

Jackson, Shirley, *The Haunting of Hill House* (London: Penguin Classics, 2009)

James, Henry, *The Turn of the Screw and Other Stories* (New York: Oxford University Press, 1992)

Pullman, Philip, *His Dark Materials* (London: Everyman's Library, 2011)

Radcliffe, Ann, ed. Chloe Chard, *The Romance of the Forest* (Oxford: Oxford University Press, 1986)

Stevenson, Robert Louis, *Dr Jekyll and Mr Hyde*, ed. Tim Middleton (Hertfordshire: Wordsworth Editions, 1999)

Walpole, Horace, *The Castle of Otranto*. ed. Michael Gamer (London: Penguin Classics, 2001)

Other Texts

Ackroyd, Peter ed. *The Alexander Text of The Complete Works of William Shakespeare* (London, Harper Collins, 2006).

Bettelheim, Bruno, *The Uses of Enchantment: The Meaning and Importance of Fairy Tales* (London: Penguin, 1991)

Berger, John, *Ways of Seeing* (London: Penguin Books, 1972)

Brownmiller, Susan, *Femininity* (London: Paladin Books, 1986)

Burgess, Anthony, *English Literature* (Harlow: Longman Group UK Ltd, 1958)

Burke, Edmund, ed. Paul Guyer, *A Philosophical Enquiry into the Origin of Our Ideas of the Sublime and Beautiful,* (Oxford: Oxford University Press, 2008)

Butler, Marilyn, *Romantics, Rebels & Reactionaries* (Oxford: Oxford University Press, 1981)

Campbell, Gordon and Thomas N. Corns, *John Milton: Life, Work and Thought* (Oxford: Oxford University Press, 2008)

Da Sousa Correa, Delia, 'Jane Eyre and Genre' in *The Nineteenth-Century Novel: Realisms, Volume 1* (London, Routledge, 2000)

Defoe, Daniel, *Robinson Crusoe*, ed. Thomas Keymer (Oxford: Oxford World's Classics, 1983)

Dickens, Charles, *A Christmas Carol* (Hertfordshire: Wordsworth Editions Limited, 1993)

Eliot, Simon, and Jonathan Rose, *A Companion to the History of the Book* (West Sussex: Blackwell Publishing Ltd, 2007)

Finkel, Irving, *The First Ghosts: Most Ancient of Legacies* (London: Hodder and Stoughton, 2021)

Frye, Northrop, *Anatomy of Criticism: Four Essays* (Princeton: Princeton University Press, 1971)

Gilbert, Sandra M. and Susan Gubar, *The Madwoman in the Attic* (US: Yale University Press, 1984)

Golden, Catherine J., (editor), *Charlotte Perkins Gilman's The Yellow Wall-Paper (A Sourcebook and Critical Edition* (New York: Routledge Taylor Francis Group, 2004)

Gombrich, E.H., *Art & Illusion: A study in the psychology of pictorial representation* (London, Phaidon Press Limited, 1960)

Griffiths, Jay, *Pip Pip: a Sideways Look at Time* (London: Harper Collins, 1999)

Milton, John, *Paradise Lost*, ed. John Leonard (London: Penguin Classics, 2000)

Olsen, Donald J., *The City as a Work of Art: London, Paris, Vienna* (Yale: Yale University, 1986)

Poe, Edgar Allan, *Tales of Mystery and Imagination*, ed. John S. Whitely

(Hertfordshire, Wordsworth Editions, 1993)

Pawson, J. David, *Unlocking the Bible* (London: William Collins, 2003)

Rosenthal, Michael, *Constable* (London: Thames and Hudson Ltd, 1987)

Sophocles, *Antigone*, ed. John Harrison and Judith Affleck (Cambridge: Cambridge University Press, 2003)

Stoker, Bram, *Dracula*, (London, Orion Books Ltd, 1992)

Summerson, John, *The Classical Language of Architecture* (London: Thames and Hudson Ltd, 1963)

Tartt, Donna, *The Secret History* (London: Penguin Books, 1992)

Wright, David, *English Romantic Verse,* ed. by David Wright (London: Penguin Books, Penguin Classics, 1968)

Zimmer Bradley, Marian 'World Building in Horror, Occult and Fantasy Writing' by in How to Write Tales of Horror, Fantasy & Science Fiction, ed. by Williamson, J. N. (London: Robinson Publishing, 1987)

Critics cited

Bailey, Dale. 'June Cleaver In The House Of Horrors: Shirley Jackson's The Haunting Of Hill House' in *American Nightmares: The Haunted House Formula in American Popular Fiction*, University of Wisconsin Press, 1999.

Bannerjee, Jacqueline, 'The Legacy of Anne Brontë' in Henry James's *The Turn of the Screw* Published online: 13 Aug 2008, 532-544.

Bennett, Andrew and Nicholas Royle, *An Introduction to Literature, Criticism and Theory* (London: Pearson Education M.U.A, 2004) https://www-dawsonera-com.libezproxy.open.ac.uk/abstract/9781408211762

Cargill, Oscar, '*The Turn of the Screw* and Alice James' in *PMLA* (June 1963), 238-249

Da Sousa Correa, Delia, 'Jane Eyre and Genre' in *The Nineteenth-Century Novel: Realisms, Volume 1* (London, Routledge, 2000)

Felman, Shoshana, 'Turning The Screw of Interpretation' in *Yale French Studies,* (1 January 1977), 94-207

Firebaugh, Joseph, 'Inadequacy in Eden: Knowledge and '*The Turn of the Screw*'' in *Modern Fiction Studies*, (Spring 1957), 57-63.

Heilman, Robert B., 'The Freudian Reading of *The Turn of the Screw*' in *Modern Language Notes,* 7(Nov., 1947) 433-445

Huyssen, Andreas, 'The Vamp and the Machine' in *After the Great Divide; Modernism, Mass Culture, Postmodernism (Theories of Representation and Difference)*, (Indiana: Indiana University Press, 1987)

Janes, Dominic, (2014) *Gothic visions of classical architecture in Hablot Knight Browne's dark illustrations for the novels of Charles Dickens,* Gothic Studies 16 (2), pp33-51. ISSN 2050-456X.

Mazella, Anthony, *Henry James Goes to the Movies,* ed. Susan M. Griffin, University Press of Kentucky, 2015. http://ebookcentral.proquest.com/lib/open/detail.action?docID=1915197

Malin, Irving, 'American Gothic Images' in *Mosaic,* 6 (Spring 1973), 145

Pascal, Richard, 'Walking Alone Together: family monsters in *The Haunting of Hill House*' in *Studies in the Novel,* 46.4 (Winter 2014), 464-85

Russell Deborah, *Domestic Gothic: Genre and Nation in Charlotte Smith's The Old Manor House* (Correspondence: School of English, Queen's University Belfast, John Wiley & Sons Ltd, 2013), pp771-782.

Szollosy, Michael, 'Freud, Frankenstein and our fear of robots: projection in our cultural perception of technology' in *AI & Society,* 3 (2017), 433-439

Waldock A. J. A., 'Mr Edmund Wilson and the Turn of the Screw Author(s)'in The Johns Hopkins University Press: Modern Language Notes, Vol. 62, No. 5 (May, 1947), pp331-334.

Wilson, Michael T., ''Absolute Reality' and the Role of the Ineffable in Shirley Jackson's *The Haunting of Hill House,*' Journal of Popular Culture.

Other References

Chambers, Paul, *The Cock Lane Ghost: Murder, Sex and Hauntings in Dr Johnson's London* (Gloucestershire: Sutton Publishing, 2006)

This list includes works mentioned in the text, and that are not listed in the bibliography:

Poems: *The Odyssey* (Homer), *Georgics* (Virgil), *Metamorphosis (Ovid), The Rape of Prosperine* (Claudian), *Beowulf, The Canterbury Tales* (Geoffrey Chaucer), *Morte D'Arthur* (Sir Thomas Malory), *Lyrical Ballads, Tintern Abbey, on revisiting the banks of the Wye during a tour July 13, 1798* (William Wordsworth), *Don Juan* (Lord Byron), *The Lady of Shalott* (Alfred Lord Tennyson), *The Buried Life* (Matthew Arnold), *Goblin Market* (Christina Rossetti), *The Angel in the House* (Coventry Patmore).

Plays of William Shakespeare: *Romeo and Juliet, Anthony and Cleopatra, Hamlet, Macbeth, Richard II, Julius Caesar, Coriolanus, The Tempest, As You Like It, King Lear, A Midsummer Night's Dream, Twelfth Night, The Winter's Tale, Comedy of*

Errors, Measure for Measure.

Works of prose and plays: *Book of Genesis, Don Quixote* (Cervantes), *The Pilgrims' Progress* (John Bunyan), *Gulliver's Travels* (Jonathan Swift), *Advice to a Young Tradesman,* (Benjamin Franklin), *Analysis of Beauty* (William Hogarth), *Emile, or an Education* (Jean-Jacques Rousseau), *Tom Jones* (Henry Fielding), *Humphrey Clinker* (Tobias Smollet), *Pamela, or, Virtue Rewarded, Clarissa, or the History of a Young Lady* (Samuel Richardson), *The Mysterious Mother* (Horace Walpole), *The Monk* (Matthew Lewis), *The Old Manor House* (Charlotte Smith), *Sense and Sensibility, Pride and Prejudice, Mansfield Park, Persuasion* (Jane Austen), *Frankenstein* (Mary Shelley), *The Pickwick Papers, David Copperfield, Oliver Twist, Nicholas Nickleby, Dombey and Son, A Christmas Carol, The Haunted Man and the Ghost's Bargain,* (Charles Dickens), *Wuthering Heights* (Emily Brontë), *The Tenant of Wildfell Hall* (Anne Brontë), *Shirley* (Charlotte Brontë), *Wives and Daughters* (Elizabeth Gaskell), *Adam Bede* (George Elliot), *Those Happy Golden Years* (Laura Ingalls Wilder), *Tess of the D'Urbervilles* (Thomas Hardy), *The Canterville Ghost* (Oscar Wilde), *Alice Through the Looking Glass* (Lewis Carroll), *Interpretation of Dreams* (Sigmund Freud), *Mary Poppins* (P.L.Travers), *An Inspector Calls* (J. B. Priestly), *1984* (George Orwell), *The Stepford Wives* (Ira Levin), *A Handmaid's Tale* (Margaret Atwood), *Neuromancer* (William Gibson), *Never Let Me Go* (Kazuo Ishiguro), *Atonement* (Ian McEwan), *Our House* (Louise Candlish), *The Paris Apartment* (Lucy Foley), *Followers* (Megan Angelo), *Sanctuary* (Abby Sher).

Films: *Metropolis* (Fritz Lang, 1927), *The Innocents* (Jack Clayton, 1961), *Night of the Living Dead* (George A. Romero, 1968), *The Firm* (Sydney Pollack, 1993), *The Sixth Sense* (M Night Shyamalan, 1999), *Frozen* (Chris Buck, Jennifer Lee, 2013).

QUICK REFERENCE GLOSSARY

A Laodicean: Thomas Hardy's ninth novel, published serially between 1880-81, in which a beautiful, young heiress uses her wealth and position to indulge her fantasy of creating a manorial past. Architect George Somerset subtly and gallantly struggles to stay within acceptable social boundaries as he steers Paula through her pitfalls and triumphs.

Alchemist (archetype): an older person, usually male, who holds out the promise of improving the life of a young person, by wealth or influence or other means.

Allegory: literary term; an abstract idea expressed in concrete form.

Anagnorsis: a moment of recognition or 'cognito' in usually, a comedy

Andersen, Hans Christian: author (1805-75), prolific author of novels, plays and fairy tales that have inspired numerous movies, musicals and ballets. Andersen's work epitomised the nineteenth-century cultural revival known as the Danish Golden Age.

Animism: a literary mode used in fantasy and folk tales where objects from the natural world, trees, animals, rocks and so forth, come to life and take a role in the narrative.

Anthropomorphism: the psychological tendency to ascribe human qualities to inanimate objects, for example, the arms of the chair, the legs of the table, the face of the clock.

Apollonian: a mode pertaining to all that is ordered and rational in human nature.

Archetypes: archetypes are those characters that appear again and again in various fictional situations, novels, plays and movies. They include the good guy, the baddie, the innocent woman, the harlot, and so forth.

Austen, Jane: author (1775-1817) whose realist novels raised the bar on the social comedy. Her world-renowned and timeless works include *Sense and Sensibility* (1811), *Pride and Prejudice* (1813), *Mansfield Park* (1814) and *Emma* (1815). *Northanger Abbey*, began in 1798, was published posthumously in 1817, together with her final novel, *Persuasion*.

Baroque: raw material twisted into shapes that it was not intended for. (Burgess, 111) In literature, it refers to an over-the-top or exaggerated sensibility in events and characters.

Bathos: a shift in mood following an event that renders a serious situation ludicrous.

Berger, John: art critic (1926-2017), essayist and author, whose book *Ways of Seeing* has become a recognised academic text, encompassing art history and feminism.

Bettelheim, Bruno: author (1903-1990), Viennese-born psychologist who was imprisoned in Dachau and Buchenwald. Post-war, Bettelheim moved to the US, where he became a professor at the University of Chicago, and wrote several books on child psychology.

Bildungsroman: a work of fiction in which the protagonist grows to maturity.

Bleak House: Charles Dickens's novel published serially between 1852 and 1853, featuring characters from every tier of Victorian society, from the aristocracy to destitute children. The reader sees the narrative through the first-person viewpoint of Esther Summerson, alternating with an omniscient voice. Several gothic tropes feature in the narrative, the young woman alienated from her family, the intertwining of the natural and supernatural worlds, and the pervading theme of the doppelganger.

Brontë, Charlotte: author (1816-1855), one of a trio of Yorkshire writing sisters who novels were a milestone in English fictional history. Charlotte spent the majority of her short life in her father's remote parsonage, and her novel *Jane Eyre* combines social realism with romance, mystery and elements of the uncanny.

Butler, Marilyn: literary critic (1937-2014), and curator of Exeter College, Cambridge, who published books on Jane Austen, Maria Edgeworth and Mary Wollstonecraft.

Burke, Edmund: political historian (1729-1797), Anglo-Irish statesman and Member of Parliament, whose most famous work is *A Philosophical Enquiry Into the Origin of Our Ideas of the Sublime and Beautiful*. Burke is still quoted today, particularly 'Bad men need nothing more to compass their ends, than good men should look on and do nothing.'

Byronic hero: a literary archetype that emerged towards the close of the eighteenth century, providing a saturnine foil for the contrasting sociability of the gothic heroine. He lives in the everyday world but for various reasons, seeks to escape it, often going into a wilderness

Byronism: a mode pertaining to all that is disordered and frenzied in human nature, closely linked with the **Dionysian.** The difference is that it is associated with an individual, usually male, rather than pertaining to a situation.

Carroll, Lewis: the pen-name of Charles Lutwidge Dodgson (1832-1898), an Oxford mathematician whose children's books *Alice in Wonderland* and *Alice Through The Looking Glass* are pivotal works in the development of the literary genre involving word play and bizarre imagery.

Castle: (symbol) the action of a large number of gothic novels centres about a large house, abbey or castle. The castle acts as a static point amid the events that unfold about it. In addition, castles are symbolical, acting as sites of family pride, centres of authority, personal metaphors and more.

Chard, Chloe: lecturer in English literature at Osijek University of Yugoslavia, and her writings concern seventeenth and eighteenth-century travel literature.

Chiaroscuro: a word that literally means 'light and shade', an effect created in literature and other arts to heighten dichotomies of good and evil, happiness and sadness, and so forth.

Cognito: a moment of recognition or 'anagnorsis' in usually, a comedy.

Comedy: a drama of society manners, where conflicts are resolved and truths are exposed in a harmless and humorous fashion.

Deception: in gothic literature, deception is often practised by the protagonist upon him or herself, for a significant part of the narrative. It is strongly linked with the **masque**.

Dickens, Charles: author (1812-70) the most eminent fiction writer of the nineteenth century. Initially famous for *The Pickwick Papers*, the novel derived from eighteenth-century picaresque fiction, Dickens's voice darkened into social realism and portraits of psychological damage, as the 1800s progressed.

Didactic: imposing a personal, highly subjective mode of behaviour or opinion upon others.

Dionysian: a mode pertaining to all that is disordered and frenzied in human nature.

Dis (dark): in mythology, the Dis is a person or entity that can travel between worlds, from 'gods' or heaven, right down through the human world to the underworld or 'hell'. Mercury, the winged messenger, and Lucifer, the fallen angel, take on the role of the Dis. In realist literature, servants, governesses, lawyers and the twentieth-century detective, behave as the Dis.

Document: in the gothic sub-genre, it is an item of text, usually written by the male that conveys an authoritative voice, a significant date and/or anchoring information, usually to a female.

Doppelganger: literally meaning 'double', writers use the doppelganger as a device for exploring possibilities of how similar characters emerge in different situations. In *Bleak House*, Esther Summerson and Lady Dedlock are doppelgangers, the one a fine lady, the other her illegitimate daughter working as a housekeeper. In the same narrative, author Charles Dickens creates a world where doppelgangers occur frequently, for example, the two Miss Donnys at the Reading school and the eerie doubling of Bleak House at the conclusion of the narrative.

Dr Jekyll and Mr Hyde: published in 1886, Robert Louis Stevenson's novella holds its rank as the most profound study of duality, ever. This tale of a hubristic scientist who explores the darker personal forces inherent in him has been adapted for stage, screen and television. Even today, it still inspires fiction.

Duality: a literary device that highlights different and often, conflicting traits in the same character, for example, Dr Jekyll and Mr Hyde. In certain instances, authors create characters to highlight duality, for example, the 'evil' Marquis Montalt in *Romance of the Forest*, and his 'good' deceased brother.

Du Maurier, Daphne: author (1907-89) who began writing in 1928. Ten years later, she produced *Rebecca*, an evocation of love and betrayal, secrets and lies, set in Du Maurier's beloved Cornwall. *Rebecca* has proved a milestone in twentieth-century romance writing. Her short story, *The Birds*, was the inspiration behind the Alfred Hitchcock movie of the same name and her other short narrative, *Don't Look Now* is one of the most dramatized fictions of our times.

Enlightenment: an era in history, broadly encompassing the seventeenth and eighteenth centuries, which saw an expansion of scientific thought and philosophical ideas wherein reason triumphed over religious belief and superstition.

Existentialism: a nineteenth-century secular philosophy stemming from the principles of Kierkgaard and Nietzsche, in which truth to oneself and authenticity to nature rather than working within the conventional framework of legal, social, political and religious norms, marks the way to freedom.

Fantasy: a mode of literature in which characters weave in and out of various worlds, talk to animals and encounter imaginary creatures like unicorns, goblins and so forth. Folk and **fairy tales** fall into the realm of fantasy.

Fairy tale: a folk tale in which a mortal male or female, quite often a child, is subject for a limited time to magic or magical powers that assist through a personal dilemma. At the conclusion, the magic ceases, life returns to normal, albeit a life in which the protagonist is usually happier and psychologically better off than at the outset.

Family (symbol): a group of people who are closely connected, usually related though not necessarily, and interact on an intimate and routine basis. The gothic heroine is often alienated from and/or ill-treated by her family.

Foil: in art and literature, a marked contrast, ie, dark and light, happy and sad, frivolous and serious and so forth, to create drama.

Free indirect style: a writing mode in which the author writes in the omnipresent or third-person voice but describes the world through the filter of the mind of the protagonist.

Freud, Sigmund: author (1856-1939), Austrian-born psychologist and psychoanalyst. His signature book, *The Interpretation of Dreams* (1901) is still in print and his psychoanalytic methods in use, though increasingly combined with more progressive clinical practices.

Frye, Northrop: author (1912-1991), Canadian-born literary critic and theorist, whose books include *Fearful Symmetry* (1947) and *Anatomy of Criticism* (1957), that still influence literary writing.

Genre: a kind, style or type, novel, romance, poem or play.

Gnosis: a moment of recognition in a narrative, for instance, when Catherine Moreland learns the truth about the late Mrs Tilney, and Henry learns of

Catherine's state of mind.

Gothic: a sub-genre that, although the ending for the protagonist was invariably satisfactory as in romance, the author presented the character with a number of moral ambivalences throughout the narrative, as in a novel.

Great Expectations: published 1861, *Great Expectations* is Charles Dickens's most profound comment of emerging modernity. Although completely devoid of the supernatural, characters whose less noble deeds and inherent personal weaknesses 'haunt' them, fill the narrative, most notably those of protagonist Pip.

Hamartia: Hamartia: a flaw in a character, usually the tragic hero, a weakness that brings about his downfall

Hard Times: published 1861, Charles Dickens's satire on the darker side of rigid learning systems and the pitfalls of uber-organised workplaces, is also a fine demonstration of what the gothic novel is not. Stephen Blackpool's fallen wife is a parody of the madwoman as much as Louisa Gradgrind is the antithesis of a gothic heroine.

Hardy, Thomas: novelist and poet (1840-1921), a realist writer whose work spanned the nineteenth and twentieth centuries. His most famous novels include *Far From the Madding Crowd* (1874), *Tess of the D'Urbervilles* (1891) and *Jude the Obscure* (1895).

Hill, Susan: author (b. 1942), writer of novels with a supernatural twist. *The Woman in Black* (1983), is a recognised school text while the stage version is London's second-longest running play.

His Dark Materials Trilogy: by Philip Pullman, published as *The Northern Lights* (1995), *The Subtle Knife* (1997) and *The Amber Spyglass* (2000), brims with timeless themes: family, friendship, love, betrayal and suspicion. The chief characters are the young Lyra Belacqua and Will Parry, who lead a host of older characters through parallel worlds: Mary Malone, Charles Latrom, Mrs Coulter, Lord Asriel, Lee Scoresby and the nomadic gyptians, who prove by turns to be good or evil, helpful or hindering. Dichotomies such as magic and science, dark and light, church and academia, in combination with the fantastical creatures that they encounter, witches, talking polar bears, ghostly skeletons and others, highlight the more human aspects of the protagonists.

Ineffable (the): an experience, usually mystical or religious, which cannot be named or rendered into language, like viewing the face of a deity or their messengers, because to do so is more than mortals can bear.

Irony: a type of rhetoric in which there is a deliberate and obvious disparity or incongruity between the statement and its intent, as when we say one thing, but mean the opposite of what we say.

Jackson, Shirley: author (1916-65), was born in San Francisco. As she brought up her children, she worked as a journalist and writer. Her own troubled childhood is reflected in much of her fiction, including in her best-known novel, *The*

Haunting of Hill House (1959). Her short story, *The Lottery*, is the inspiration for the *Hunger Games* movie franchise.

James, Henry: novelist and writer (1843-1916), was born in New York and in his youth, lived in Paris with other modernist writers. His realist writing was imbued with a hint of the supernatural and he published *The Turn of the Screw* in 1892.

Jane Eyre: published in 1847, author Charlotte Brontë presented her readers with a unique and original blend of events that still influences literature today: the young woman struggling for her life, albeit for social recognition rather than just survival, mysterious encounters and more than a hint of the supernatural. In addition, this novel contains the archetypal 'mad woman in the attic'.

Journey (symbol): an intrinsic part of the gothic narrative, the journey not only functions as a riposte of movement to the stasis of the castle, it is often an element of the bildungsroman of the gothic heroine.

Literature: an art that exploits words, providing a verbal record of the progression of humanity.

Liminal: relating to a transitional process, for example, life to death, and/or occupying a position at, on or both sides of a boundary or threshold.

Lewis, Matthew: novelist (1775-1818), whose book, *The Monk*, eschewed suspense and suggestion for full-on graphic horror and the supernatural.

Magical Realism: literature that depicts the real world as having an undercurrent of magic or fantasy.

Maiden (symbol): the protagonists of the earlier gothic genres were usually lovely young women. Today, the maiden has translated into the final girl of the horror movie genre. Later writers of gothic literature have continued to use the motif of the maiden in more inventive and original ways.

Malin, Irving: American literary critic (1934-2014), who wrote hundreds of book reviews in his life-time, plus numerous literary essays. His book, *New American Gothic*, was published in 1962.

Masque: an aloof form of entertainment in which participants hide their identities. (Burgess, 115)

Masquerade: a showing of an assumed self to others to hide the reality of a situation.

Metonym: the craft of using words and expressions that substitute persons and functions with one another, or vice versa, for example, stating I'm going to *the office* instead of I'm going to *the person in charge*.

Metaphor: describing one thing in terms of another, for example, referring to a failing business or state as *a sinking ship*.

Miles gloriosus: defined by Northrop Frye, a military braggart, a Falstaffian character boasting of notional military victories. In the gothic sub-genre, this trait extends to boasting over other physical feats and even, gloating over notionally superior technology.

Milton, John: English poet (1608-1674), political writer and pamphleteer. A graduate of Christ's College, Cambridge, he grew progressively blind and was totally so when he published his epic poem, *Paradise Lost*, in 1660.

Mimetic – high: a mode of literature set in the 'real' world, and in which the heroes are flesh-and-blood humans who create their own fates, but are often pitted against supernatural forces that surprise, scare and confound them.

Mimetic- low: a mode of literature that includes the gothic sub-genre, which can include unexplainable happenings, possibly supernatural entities, that express truths about the natural world and/or the mentality of the protagonist(s).

Mode: a conventional power of action assumed about the chief characters in fictional literature, or the corresponding attitude assumed by the poet towards his audience in thematic literature. Such modes tend to succeed one another in a historical sequence. Examples include the myth, the romance, the high mimetic mode, the low mimetic mode and the ironic modes. The ironic mode, is one in which the hero feels a constant sense of bondage and frustration, unable to escape his or her fate. As in the low mimetic mode, the protagonist of an ironic saga is not a god, hero nor person endowed with special powers.

Modern publishing: modernity in publishing dates from 1780 and onwards. This date coincides with the outset of the Industrial Revolution, the advent of mass literacy and the proliferation of the gothic sub-genre.

Mysticism: the belief that certain minds can establish contact with God. (Burgess, 109)

Mythology: a body of beliefs that touch the imagination of a race or of an age, inspire its literature and its behaviour, and provides glamour to colour the dullness of everyday life. (Burgess, 24)

Mythos: a pattern of beliefs expressing often symbolically the characteristic or prevalent attitudes in a group or culture). In literature, the mythos are expressed as one of the four archetypal narratives, classified as comic, romantic, ironic, tragic.

Natural world: During the eighteenth century, English artists like William Turner and John Constable made studies of the landscape, initially in imitation of seventeenth-century Dutch artists, most notably those of Jacob Von Ruisdael. Eventually, the English landscape became a genre in its own right, prompting authors to incorporate it into fiction. For many gothic heroines, the landscape has served as a refuge from peril, a place of healing and inspiration for flights of imagination and philosophical thought, before finding a place in society.

Northanger Abbey: Jane Austen's first novel, though not published until after her death in 1817, this two-hundred-plus year-old work is as readable, fresh and funny as the day the author put pen to paper. Through the story of naive young

Catherine Morland's trip to fashionable Bath in the company of the kindly but inadequate Allens, the author pokes sly fun at the late eighteenth-century craze for novels of the gothic sub-genre. However, as the narrative progresses, the heroine curiously morphs into the kind of protagonist that Austen disdains at the outset.

Novel (the): a mode of literature in which the writers create a simulacrum of society. The protagonist is usually a character trying to connect with and find status within this society, and the compromises that he or she works under make for ambivalence at the novel's conclusion.

Oxymoron: a verbal phrase or literacy construct that embodies a contradiction, e.g., bitter sweet.

Ouroboros: the symbol of the sinister circle or serpent swallowing its tail is defined by Northrop Frye as belonging to the demonic imagery of literary archetypes.

Pastoral (the): a mode of art and literature in which nature and the natural world are presented as benevolent, and every character has an unambivalent place within the pictorial or literary schema. The artist/author employs various techniques to place the complex life into a simple scheme, for example, sheep in a field, apples on a tree, and so on.

Pathetic Fallacy: a subjective mode of describing the natural world, usually an externalisation of feelings. For example, Gabriel Utterson, when he is obliged to lead the policeman to the place where he knows Mr Hyde to be living, observes the sky: 'A great-chocolate coloured pall lowered over heaven' indicative of his unsettled feelings.

Pathos: a mode devised to evince sympathy from the reader.

Personification: a mode of referring to inanimate objects as if they possessed personalities, e. g., 'now the moon walks the night in her silver shoon'. (Walter de la Mare)

Phase: one of several distinguishable phases of a mythos. For instance, the romantic mythos includes the quest, the pastoral and the comedy phase.

Picaresque (the): a literary mode in which a (usually) male character carries out a series of dubious escapades, with little of consequence for him.

Picturesque, (the): popularized by the Rev. William Gilpin, in his published *Tours* series of books, and originating in the Italian *pitteresco*, which means 'after the manner of painters', the picturesque is a visually attractive scene, usually a landscape, as seen through a window frame or within a framed painting. (Rosenthal, 20)

Pistis: a mode in literature whereby the subjects accept dogma without question, for example, the characters in *Hard Times*.

Pullman, Philip (Sir): English author (b. 1946) and Oxford graduate whose first book, *The Haunted Storm*, was published in 1972. John Milton's *Paradise Lost* influenced his fantasy trilogy, *His Dark Materials*, published 1995.

Radcliffe, Ann: nee Ward, author (1764-1823), was born in London, lived in Bath and married William Radcliffe in 1787. With her husband's encouragement, she began writing and published *Romance of the Forest* in 1791. Her other novels include *The Italian* (1797) and *The Mysteries of Udolpho* (1794), the success of which earned her the name 'the Great Enchanted'. She also authored travel books.

Rebecca: published 1938, Mrs de Winter, protagonist of Daphne du Maurier's novel finds herself trapped in the very way of life that she sought to escape from. The narrative explores the theme of duality, the two wives of Maxim de Winter bearing natures that highlight the contradictions in his own nature. Eventually, events at his ancestral home Manderley and his devotion to aristocracy crush and destroy his personality, as it does several other characters in the narrative.

Realism: in the arts and literature, realism refers to the nineteenth-century movement that was the precursor to modernism. It challenged the accepted view of what art should be, namely the pursuit of the beautiful, the moral and the improving. Instead, realism aimed to record what is.

Reeve, Clara: novelist (1729-1807), who spent much of her life in Ipswich. She published *The Old English Baron* in 1777, written in imitation of Walpole's book, *The Castle of Otranto*. Reeve was also a literary critic and published *The Progress of Romance* in 1785.

Renaissance, the: a period stretching from c. 1400 to c. 1600, in which advances in art and literature, science and philosophical thought led to the learning disciplines that define our modern world.

Romance: (genre) a form of fiction in which the protagonist pursues his or her love interest, free of the constraints of society.

Romance: (mode) a tale set in a world in which the known laws of nature are suspended, for example, folk tales and fairy tales. Because the majority of these tales have been handed down through the ages, few of them can be given a definite 'age' but even the earlier Egyptian civilizations bear evidence of folklore.

Romantic: (hero), a male that is (usually) handsome, and whose actions demonstrate bravery and selfless-ness. In the gothic sub-genre, he is pre-destined to become the lover of the heroine.

Romantic: (mythos) The romance was born of medieval poetry, the off-shoot of recognition that marriage alliances were forged for a combination of physical attraction and the deepest affection, rather than for dynastical, property ownership and the sheer necessity of breeding offspring.

Romanticism: a personal, partly spiritual apprehension of nature as environment and life-force, as envisioned by poets and painters, c. 1790 – 1830. (Yale Dictionary)

Rousseau, Jean-Jacques: philosopher (1712-78), and writer. Born in Geneva, Rousseau is associated with post-Enlightenment theories on teaching and learning, expressed in his novel, *Emile or On Education*. Rousseau was also a composer.

Rule of three: a motif present in many narratives, esp. fairy tales, where events, wishes, etc., recur in threesomes.

Satire: a narrative set in a world where exaggerated forms and behaviour and rules subvert everyday life.

Shakespeare, William: poet and playwright (1564-1616), whose work has defined Elizabethan and early Jacobean theatre. The exact extent of his output is unknown, but he is believed to have authored 37 plays, 154 sonnets and poems that include *Venus and Adonis*, *The Rape of Lucrece*, *A Lover's Complaint*, *The Passionate Pilgrim* and *The Phoenix and Turtle*.

Shelley, Mary: (nee Godwin) daughter of William Godwin and Mary Wollstonecraft, who died giving birth. Mary Godwin became the wife of Pierce Bysse Shelly and authored *Frankenstein*, supposedly following a dream in which she saw a pair of eyes gazing at her from the chest of a human torso.

Stevenson, Robert Louis: (1850-1894): the prolific Scottish author of *Dr Jekyll and Mr Hyde*, the seminal work in which a respectable doctor who loses his sanity and his life when he discovers a drug that enables him to morph into another person. Stevenson, who was an invalid, reputedly wrote the novel following a drug-induced dream

Sublime, (the): impressing the mind with a sense of power and producing the strongest emotion possible (Edmund Burke), because of elevated beauty and quality of excellence.

Supernatural (the): generally, the supernatural is any phenomenon, event or set of circumstances that cannot be explained by the scientific discoveries of the day. Logically, this should mean that the supernatural ought to play a smaller and smaller role in day to day life, that is, belief in ghosts, banshees, fairies and so forth. But since Enlightenment, belief in the supernatural seems to be expanding, partly due to electronic recordings of esoteric entities, for example, poltergeists. However, another explanation may be the human need to believe in the unknown.

Surrealism: In the wake of Andre Breton writing the *Surrealist Manifesto* in 1924, the surrealist artists and poets emerged, their dream imagery becoming part of popular culture.

Symbol: A symbol is an intuitive idea that words do not adequately express, tangible and visible emblems that articulate emotion and political ideas. For example, the symbol of hearth might signify security and comfort to one subject, while providing an expression of social entrapment to another.

Synecdoche: the craft of using words and expressions that refer to part of a situation or person to mean its entirety, for example, stating *the hands* instead of *the workers*.

Syzygy: a yoking together of opposites, for example, Jekyll and Hyde, night and day, sun and moon.

The Haunting of Hill House: published in 1959, Shirley Jackson's novel has received accolades from a range of luminaries and writers, including Stephen King. The plot sounds archetypal, a group of people convening to investigate an allegedly haunted house. But the interaction of the characters takes over and soon, it is clear that the underdeveloped personality of protagonist Eleanor Vance has a decided disadvantage when dealing with whatever troubles Hill House.

The Snow Queen: published in 1844, Hans Christian Andersen's fairy tale is the apotheosis of his fictional writing. Not only is it, in the words of Bruno Bettelheim 'a real fairy tale' in the traditional sense, the themes that converge in the narrative are contemporary to Andersen. These include the progress of adolescence, the potency of womanhood and nature, the value of formal learning, and it is a comment on the Danish golden age.

The Turn of the Screw: since its 1898 publication, Henry James's novella has rarely been free of controversy. The inspiration behind stage plays, movies and even an opera, numerous critics have sought to unravel the motivation of the Governess: sexual frustration, plain old-fashioned curiosity or genuine concern for the welfare of the children. Ultimately, the reader must make his own judgement on this multi-layered novella.

The Woman in Black: in spite of its horrible – and objective – spectre, Susan Hill's novel (published in 1982) is a postmodern comment on the gothic genre, a study of what might happen when the tale of the young and lovely woman does *not* have a happy ending. Its protagonist, Arthur Kipps is adept as a lawyer's clerk, but his under-developed personality renders him vulnerable to the supernatural happenings of his new environment, when he leaves home on business.

Tragedy: a narrative in which the main protagonist meets an unhappy end.

Uncanny, The: Delia Da Sousa Correa quotes Andrew Bennett and Nicholas Royle's definition: 'The uncanny has to do with a sense of strangeness, mystery or eerieness ... has to do more specifically with a disturbance of the familiar.' (DDSC, 109)

Verisimilitude: the attempt in art and literature to create realism by use of words, imagery, and so forth.

Virgil: Roman poet (70 BC-19 BC), whose works, the *Ecologue*, the *Aeneid* and the *Georgics* have had a profound influence upon Western literature and thought.

Walpole, Horace (1717-1797): landowner, writer and Member of Parliament, who published the 'first' gothic novel, *The Castle Of Otranto*, in 1765, thus establishing the sub-genre in Britain. Son of Robert Walpole, he redesigned an old farm building in Strawberry Hill, Twickenham, transforming it into the gothic-themed house that it is today, It was there, reportedly following a dream about a falling helmet, that he penned his seminal novel.

Wollstonecraft, Mary: author and journalist (1759-1797) she became a philosopher, feminist and writer. She travelled widely and published her most famous work, *A Vindication of the Rights of Women,* in 1792. The entire underpinning of her philosophy is that women are equal to men and deserve access to the same education, and that the social order should be based upon reason. Ironically, she died giving birth to her daughter Mary Godwin, author of *Frankenstein*

Index

A Christmas Carol 163, 164, 175, 206, 248

A Laodicean *A Laodicean* 24, 45, 51, 53, 56, 60, 61, 64, 76, 77, 78, 80, 85, 90, 92, 96, 97, 98, 99, 114, 115, 119, 121, 122, 128, 129, 136, 145, 147, 148, 149, 150, 151, 153, 154, 160, 193, 203, 213, 237, 239, 240, 248, 268

A Midsummer Night's Dream 164, 219

Angelo, Megan (Followers) 259

Andersen, Hans Christian 21, 22, 50, 97, 98, 268

Anthony and Cleopatra 33

Appignanesi, Lisa 124

Arnold, Matthew (*The Buried Life*) 66

As You Like It 99, 100, 192, 212, 230, 231, 236, 237

Atwood, Margaret (*A Handmaid's Tale*) 44

Bailey, Dale 91, 123, 126, 154, 159, 175, 176, 190, 194, 195, 196, 203, 210, 211, 212, 215

Bannerjee, Jacqueline 93, 223,

Beauman, Sally 126

Bennett, Andrew/ Nicholas Royle 45, 155

Beowulf 31, 32,

Berger, John (*Ways of Seeing*) 60, 63, 66, 71, 75, 234, 268

Bettelheim, Bruno 47, 48, 49, 56, 69, 74, 79, 100, 126, 127, 129, 135, 136, 138, 140, 183, 184, 186, 194, 229, 268, 269

bildungsroman 29, 51, 123, 157, 182, 183, 229, 269

Blake, William 85

Bleak House 23, 24, 29, 43, 49, 65, 66, 68, 70, 75, 79, 80, 81, 82, 85, 86, 88, 89, 93, 95, 95, 97, 102, 104, 105, 110, 111, 117, 118, 121, 124, 125, 126, 128, 129, 132, 133, 134, 137, 138, 139, 140, 142, 143, 146, 148, 151, 153, 159, 165, 179, 185, 186, 187, 188, 193, 197, 207, 216, 218, 220, 221, 224, 225, 226, 227, 233, 239, 242, 244, 245, 247, 248, 250, 251, 252, 255, 269

Book of Genesis 67, 218, 229, 234, 241

Bowen, John 207

Bradley, Marion Zimmer 114

Bronte, Anne (*The Tenant of Wildfell Hall*) 66, 67

Bronte, Emily (*Wuthering Heights*) 52, 53, 71, 91, 115, 159

Browne, Hablot Knight 110, 250

Brownmiller, Susan 60, 64, 68, 78

Burgess, Anthony 32, 33, 34, 39, 40, 55

Burke, Edmund 19, 68, 69, 70, 71, 110, 158, 269

Butler, Marilyn (*Romantics, Rebels and Reactionaries*) 26, 32, 59, 85, 120, 127, 181, 191, 194, 224, 269

Bunyan, John (*The Pilgrims' Progress*) 177

Byron, Lord (*Don Juan*) 55, 135

Byronic hero 19, 26, 32, 52, 53, 56, 70, 71, 74, 81, 106, 112, 113, 135, 148, 150, 152, 153, 154, 161, 174, 210, 255, 256, 260, 269

Candlish, Louise (*Our House*) 113, 114

Cargill, Oscar 90

Carroll, Lewis (*Alice in Wonderland, Alice Through the Looking Glass*) 203, 204, 269

Cervantes, Don Miguel de (*Don Quixote*) 15, 33, 150, 219

Chambers, Paul (*The Cocklane Ghost*) 35, 36, 164, 165

Chard, Chloe 27, 96, 232, 269

Chaucer, Geoffrey (*The Canterbury Tales*) 32, 177

Chiaroscuro 250, 251, 252, 269, 270

Claudian (*The Rape of Prosperine*) 218

Clayton, Jack (*The Innocents*, movie) 201

Coleridge, Samuel Taylor 55

comedy, mythos of 42, 43, 269

Comedy of Errors 205

Congreve, William 55

Constable, John 228

Coriolanus 46

Da Sousa Correa, Delia 41, 45, 117, 155, 222, 227, 232, 233, 240

David Copperfield 73, 96, 144, 177, 180

Da Vinci, Leonardo 206

De Hooch, Pieter 65

De Villeneuve, Madame (*Beauty and the Beast*) 56

Defoe, Daniel (*Robinson Crusoe*)15, 16, 17, 20, 33, 148, 150, 154

Dr Jekyll and Mr Hyde 24, 70, 85, 90, 105, 111, 112, 150, 154, 214, 224, 240, 243, 270

Dombey and Son 98, 180

dream, the 17, 120, 121, 186, 223, 224

Edwards, Betty (*Drawing on the Right Side of the Brain*) 111

Elliot, George (*Adam Bede*) 67

Enlightenment (post-Enlightenment) 28, 46, 155, 169, 170, 271

Felman, Shoshana 116, 172, 201, 214, 215

Fielding, Henry (*Tom Jones*) 15, 33, 177

Finkel, Dr Irving (*The First Ghosts, Most Ancient of Legacies*) 162

Firebaugh, Joseph 94, 139, 240, 241

Franklin, Benjamin 101

Freud, Sigmund 56, 116, 172, 224, 271

Frye, Northrop 28, 30, 31, 38, 39, 40, 41, 42, 43, 44, 45, 46, 66, 134, 155, 156, 178, 179, 196, 203, 217, 242, 271

Galilei, Galileo 206

Gaskell, Elizabeth (*Wives and Daughters*) 96

Gilbert, Sandra/Susan Gubar, 13, 23, 66, 67, 68, 70, 72, 73, 78, 87, 89, 91, 120, 124, 145, 154, 156, 180, 205, 231, 248

Gibson, William (*Neuromancer*) 258, 259

Gillray, James 170

Golden, Catherine 129

Gombrich, Ernst (*Art and Illusion*) 65

Goya, Francisco de (*The Caprichos*) 170, 171

Grisham, John (*The Firm*) 115

Great Expectations 24, 28, 41, 51, 62, 78, 80, 84, 89, 90, 93, 94, 95, 98, 100, 101, 102, 109, 125, 128, 129, 133, 135, 137, 138, 140, 143, 144, 147, 148, 149, 152, 166, 167, 168, 169, 177, 193, 197, 207, 208, 209, 245, 246, 247, 252, 255, 272

Griffiths, Jay 19, 74, 99, 101, 185, 234

Hamlet 34, 40, 46, 74, 76, 162, 163

Handel, George Friedrich (*The Harmonious Blacksmith*) 101, 102

Hard Times 23, 44, 73, 76, 85, 96, 98, 100, 133, 152, 194, 240, 272

Hardy, Barbara 114, 248

hamartia 46, 272

Heilman, Robert 76, 172, 241

high mimetic mode 40, 46

Hillis Miller, J. 125, 132, 142, 185, 207, 251

His Dark Materials 26, 51, 66, 68, 70, 72, 73, 82, 83, 85, 87, 88, 94, 107, 108, 109,

120, 123, 126, 127, 134, 137, 138, 140, 141, 142, 148, 154, 156, 203, 215, 216, 236, 244, 248, 272

Hobsbaum, Philip 237

Hogarth, William (*Analysis of Beauty*) 65

Holman Hunt, William 61

Homer, (*The Odyssey*) 29, 177

Huyssen, Andreas 216

Industrial Revolution 46, 56, 85, 98, 100, 101, 104, 149, 150, 155, 169, 227, 237

Ishiguro, Kazuo (*Never Let Me Go*) 44, 216

James, M.R. 25, 157

Jane Eyre 23, 29, 40, 41, 51, 53, 56, 63, 64, 70, 71, 73, 74, 76, 77, 78, 79, 80, 86, 89, 91, 92, 109, 122, 127, 129, 133, 134, 136, 143, 146, 147, 148, 149, 150, 151, 152, 153, 157, 159, 160, 161, 167, 177, 178, 180, 181, 182, 192, 193, 195, 209, 210, 218, 221, 222, 227, 232, 233, 234, 238, 239, 240, 242, 247, 248, 254, 273

Janes, Dominic 110, 111, 117

Johnson, Samuel 165

Julius Caesar 40, 46

Keats, John 55

Kenton, Edna 76

Keymer, Thomas 20

King Lear 122

King, Stephen 21

Kirkegaard, Soren 98

Koontz, Dean 21

Lang, Fritz (*Metropolis*, movie) 216, 217

Le Fanu, J Sheridan 166

Leonard, John 218

Levin, Ira (*The Stepford Wives*) 108, 216, 243, 244

Lewis, Matthew (*The Monk*) 26, 34, 273

Louis XIV 59, 91, 100

low mimetic mode, the 40, 47, 218, 274

Lustig, T. J. 90, 158, 201, 214

Macbeth 34, 156, 169, 171, 172, 180, 238

Malin, Irving 27, 100, 111, 117, 127, 178, 180, 193, 204, 273

Malory, Thomas (*Morte de Arthur*) 33

Mansfield Park 153, 192, 194, 196

Marvell, Andrew 55

Mazella, Anthony 200

Measure for Measure 212, 214

McEwan, Ian (*Atonement*) 46

McMillan, Dorothy (*Measure for Measure*) 212

Middleton, Tim 18

Millais, John Everett 61

Milton, John (*Paradise Lost*) 29, 54, 67, 218, 229, 242, 248, 274

Nicholas Nickleby 98

Northanger Abbey 13, 22, 26, 29, 41, 42, 43, 44, 47, 53, 54, 59, 60, 63, 66, 67, 68, 69, 70, 72, 75, 79, 80, 85, 86, 88, 92, 93, 95, 97, 102, 103, 104, 105, 108, 118, 121, 124, 127, 128, 133, 138, 141, 142, 146, 148, 149, 151, 157, 170, 178, 179, 191, 193, 194, 220, 222, 224, 231, 236, 242, 250, 255, 274, 275

Oliver Twist 138, 177

Olsen, Donald J. 132

Orwell, George (1984) 44, 45, 226

Ovid (*Metamorphosis*) 204

Palladio, Antonio 65

Pascal, Richard 77, 145, 150, 151, 152, 154

Patmore, Coventry (*The Angel in the House*) 180

Perkins Gilman, Charlotte 129

Perrault, Charles 100

Persuasion 231

picturesque, the 253, 275

Piranesi, Giovanni Battista 186

Poe, Edgar Allan (*Tales of Mystery and Imagination*) 21, 100, 223, 224, 225

pre-Raphaelite 61

Pride and Prejudice 43, 44, 52, 71, 92, 135, 153

Priestly, J.B. (*An Inspector Calls*) 38, 276

psychological 57, 196, 214

realism 38, 270

Rebecca 25, 56, 62, 63, 64, 70, 78, 79, 81, 82, 92, 95, 118, 119, 122, 123, 124, 126, 129, 133, 136, 137, 142, 144, 146, 148, 152, 157, 159, 174, 179, 180, 187, 194, 203, 222, 224, 241, 242, 248, 249, 252, 255, 276

Reeve, Clara (*The Old English Baron, The Progress of Romance*) 15, 34, 64, 276

Renaissance, the 64, 65, 74, 84, 230, 276

Richard II 40, 67, 205

Richardson, Samuel (*Pamela, Clarissa*) 15, 34

Romance of the Forest 16, 21, 22, 38, 41, 49, 50, 51, 59, 63, 67, 71, 72, 74, 78, 79, 80, 81, 86, 87, 92, 94, 96, 100, 101, 108, 110, 118, 123, 124, 125, 127, 134, 138, 140, 141, 144, 145, 146, 148, 149, 153, 158, 170, 182, 183, 193, 195, 196, 197, 213, 219, 220, 222, 229, 230, 231, 232, 235, 237, 238, 239, 254, 255

Romanticism 54, 55, 56, 102, 150, 151, 227, 228, 276

Romantic hero 52, 276

Romeo and Juliet 33, 46

Romero, George A. (*Night of the Living Dead*, movie) 176

Rossetti, Christina (*Goblin Market*) 78, 145

Rossetti, Dante Gabriel 61

Rousseau, Jean-Jacques (*Emile, or on Education*) 35, 53, 55, 96, 100, 101, 277

Russell, Deborah 107, 108

Said, Edward 117

Sense and Sensibility 38

Shelley, Mary (*Frankenstein*) 70, 150, 154, 248, 277

Shelley, Percy Bysshe 55

Sher, Abby (*Sanctuary*) 259, 260

Shuttleworth, Sally 157, 160, 167

Shyamalan, M Night (*The Sixth Sense*, movie) 166

Smollett, Tobias 15, 33

Smith, Charlotte (*The Old Manor House*) 107

Song of Roland 33

Steig, Michael 110

Stevenson, Robert Louis 21, 150, 277

Stoker, Bram (*Dracula*) 160, 161

Stone, Lawrence (*Companion to The History of the Book*) 20

Strawberry Hill Villa 60,

sublime – the 110, 277

Summerson, John 61, 65

Swift, Jonathan (*Gulliver's Travels*) 55

Szollosy, Michael 150, 172

Tartt, Donna (*The Secret History*) 255, 256, 257, 258

Tennyson, Alfred Lord (*The Lady of Shalott*) 61, 68 74, 206

The Castle of Otranto 15, 20, 31, 33, 34, 35, 36, 38, 46, 47, 52, 54, 55, 58, 59, 78, 84, 118, 121, 133, 135, 146, 148, 151, 153, 165, 219, 260

The Haunted Man and the Ghosts Bargain 166, 206

The Haunting of Hill House 18, 19, 25, 49, 50, 51, 56, 57, 58, 64, 68, 75, 76, 77, 78, 79, 80, 81, 86, 91, 105, 109, 112, 113, 115, 118, 119, 123, 126, 127, 129, 130, 131, 133, 134, 137, 138, 145, 146, 148, 151, 152, 153, 154, 158, 159, 160, 162, 165, 170, 171, 174, 175, 176, 178, 184, 185, 189, 190, 194, 195, 203, 210, 211, 212, 215, 221, 222, 242, 243, 252, 253, 255, 278

The Pickwick Papers 23, 177, 219

The Snow Queen 22, 23, 50, 51, 72, 73, 79, 82, 83, 97, 108, 109, 142, 144, 148, 183, 184, 206, 222, 235, 236, 248, 278

The Tempest 99, 105

The Turn of the Screw 18, 24, 25, 56, 67, 70, 76, 81, 86, 90, 93, 94, 115, 116, 118, 125, 126, 133, 139, 146, 148, 158, 165, 172, 173, 174, 175, 178, 187, 188, 189, 193, 195, 196, 197, 198, 199, 200, 201, 202, 214, 215, 221, 223, 237, 240, 241, 242, 278

The Winter's Tale 205

The Woman in Black 25, 44, 70, 88, 94, 95, 105, 109, 115, 116, 123, 134, 139, 140, 156, 159, 171, 172, 174, 175, 248, 249, 278

Tompion, Thomas 103

Twelfth Night 192, 212

Turner, J.M.W. 228

Virgil (*Georgics*) 233, 234, 278

Waldock, A.J.A. 197

Walpole, Horace 15, 20, 26, 31, 32, 34, 35, 36, 53, 55, 58, 59, 60, 64, 278, 279

Waterhouse, John 61

Whitely, John S. 21

Wilde, Oscar (*The Canterville Ghost*) 165

Wilder, Laura Ingalls (*Those Happy Golden Years*) 21

Wilson, Edmund 76, 172, 197

Wilson, Michael 75, 130, 131, 159, 189, 190

Wise, Robert (*The Haunting*, movie) 131

Wordsworth, William (*Lyrical Ballads, Tintern Abbey, on revisiting the banks of the Wye during a tour July 13, 1798*) 55, 227

Wright, David 33, 54, 56, 135, 150